DADDY LOVER GOD

A SACRED INTIMATE JOURNEY

DON SHEWEY

Also by **Don Shewey**

Sam Shepard

*Caught in the Act: New York Actors Face to Face
(with Susan Shacter)*

Out Front: Contemporary Gay and Lesbian Plays

*The Paradox of Porn:
Notes on Gay Male Sexual Culture*

DADDY LOVER GOD

A SACRED INTIMATE JOURNEY

DON SHEWEY

Joybody Books • New York

Daddy Lover God:
A Sacred Intimate Journey

 Joybody Books • New York

Copyright 2023 by Don Shewey
All rights reserved.
Printed in the United States of America.

No part of this book may be reproduced or transmitted in any form or by any means, electronic or mechanical, including photocopying, recording, or by any information storage and retrieval system, without permission in writing from the publisher. For information address: Joybody Books, 50 W. 56th Street, Suite 3A, New York, NY 10019-3856.

Cover design by Chip Kidd
Cover photo by Max rada dada
Book design by Todd Cooper, All-D
Joybody Books logo by Paul Pinkman

Library of Congress Cataloguing-in-Publication Data is available upon request.

ISBN: 978-1-7321344-3-0 (paperback)
ISBN: 978-1-7321344-4-7 (e-book)

*To everyone who has ever sought, received, or provided
healing through erotic pleasure*

Desire is a horse that wants to take you on a journey to spirit.

— Malidoma Some

Johnny's laying there
in his sperm coffin
Angel looks down at him
and says
Aw big boy
can't you show me nuthin
but surrender?

— Patti Smith

TABLE OF CONTENTS

PROLOGUE: Sexual Healing and Sacred Intimacy   1

PART ONE: THE DRAGONS AT THE DOOR *(1993-1995)*   19

1. Complete with Release   21
2. Sex Work as Spiritual Practice   31
3. The Clock   37
4. Al (Part 1)   41
5. Boners   47
6. Al (Part 2)   51
7. Looky-Loos   55
8. The Vampires   61
9. Full-Body Orgasm   57
10. The Feeling Is Mutual   75
11 Daddy Practice   79
12. Four Sessions with a Friend Who Has AIDS   87
13. Oral Hygiene   91
14. The Client-Husbands   97
15. Lester   105
16. Self-Service   114

PART TWO: THE DADDY VARIATIONS *(1964-1994)*   121

17. Alter Boy   123
18. Home Leaves   133

19. Library Hours	141
20. Steam Room	151
21. New York Jacks	157
22. Sexual Healing	167
23. Celebrating the Body Erotic	175
24. Midwife to the Dying	185
25. Wildwood	195
26. The Food of Love	203
27. Stations of Priapus	207
28. Scared Inmate	215
PART THREE: COURSE CORRECTION *(1996-2022)*	219
29. Eugene (Part 1)	221
30. Eugene (Part 2)	227
31. Eugene (Part 3)	231
32. The Nether Eye Opens	239
33. Second Thoughts	253
34. Mandatory Sex	259
35. Geisha in the Pigpen	269
36. Hitting Bottom	277
37. Where Is the Love?	285
38. The Higher Octave	289
APPENDIX: Joseph Kramer – Portrait of a Sexual Healer	311
ACKNOWLEDGEMENTS	377
ABOUT THE AUTHOR	381

DADDY LOVER GOD

A SACRED INTIMATE JOURNEY

PROLOGUE:
Sexual Healing and Sacred Intimacy

This is a book about sexual wounds and sexual healing.

Sexual healing has a long and distinguished tradition, up to and including being the name of Marvin Gaye's last great record. But the term "sacred intimate" has a specific and recent origin. It was coined by Joseph Kramer, who was the founder of the Body Electric School of Massage in Oakland, Calif. In 1987 Joe Kramer created a pioneering weekend workshop called "Celebrating the Body Erotic," teaching the basic principles of tantra, conscious breathing, and Taoist (non-ejaculatory) erotic massage to groups of gay men across the country, largely in response to the fear and sex-phobia that the AIDS epidemic generated. A charismatic teacher and erotic visionary, Kramer decided in 1990 to develop a week-long intensive retreat for graduates of the weekend workshop. When the first one was held at Wildwood, a gay retreat center near the Russian River in northern California, he half-jokingly called it the Sacred Prostitute Summer Camp.

He was inspired by what he'd heard and read about the tradition of the sacred prostitute or temple whore, which dates back to pre-Christian times. These were people — men and women, although historical references mostly refer to women — who were available for sexual encounters in ritual space as selfless service or spiritual practice. He found, though, that most people had negative reactions to the word "prostitute" and didn't want to be associated with it in any way. So he met with a corporate image consultant in the Bay Area, and they came up with the designation "sacred intimate," which first appeared in public in 1991, when Kramer offered the first Sacred Intimate training, an eight-day workshop specifically devoted to helping interested gay men develop their skills as sexual healers. At that time a big part of sacred intimate work, in the training and in real life, had to do with being midwives to the dying — tending to the body, mind, spirit, and erotic energy of friends who were preparing to leave their bodies. Since that time, the concept of sacred intimate work has slowly but steadily entered the culture as Body Electric graduates began to offer their services professionally as sacred intimates.

What does a sacred intimate do? I like to say that sacred intimates combine the roles of priest, prostitute, and psychotherapist. In other words, they approach sexuality with the understanding that it's related to soul work and to spirituality. They use mindfulness and integrity to help people identify, embrace, and practice desire as holy, sexual embodiment as an expression of the soul. They hold the body as sacred and view erotic energy as a crucial component of human life and spiritual health. Their primary intention is that of healing — and by healing I mean not just addressing the wounds to the spirit and the flesh caused by sexual abuse, addiction, or disease but also acknowledging that the fun and the pleasure, the vitality and the divine mystery of sex have nourishing properties in and of themselves. That's a message that easily gets lost in a culture that is as ambivalent or sex-negative as ours.

Sacred intimacy has a relationship to sex therapy as it developed in the second half of the 20th century with the work of Masters and Johnson and Helen Singer Kaplan, who performed a great service by bringing accurate information about sex to the American public and developed effective treatments for sexual disorders. Sexual surrogates are trained to interact with patients who have sexual dysfunctions, under the supervision of a clinical psychologist, and they often use the same skills and techniques that sacred intimates do: working with breath and presence and sensate focus. One major difference is that most sexual surrogates are women who work with heterosexual men, whereas Body Electric-trained sacred intimates are primarily men who work with men. Also, surrogates work specifically with sexual disorders within a medical model. Sacred intimates may or may not treat dysfunctions, and they generally work from a wellness perspective, not fixing problems but encouraging and expanding sexual joy.

Although psychotherapy would seem to be the field most appropriate for sexual healing, in practice many psychotherapists are terrified of dealing with sexuality, either because they have their own unresolved sexual conflicts or they are afraid of legal liabilities. How often do psychotherapists acknowledge that they themselves have sex lives? How often do they share information about erotic resources or facilitate detailed explorations of masturbation or sexual fantasies? Today psychotherapists are intensely focused on boundaries and shy away from sexuality lest they be perceived as provocative, seductive, or harassing. However, it's possible that deflecting or avoiding sexual issues reinforces shame and cultural repression.

A lot of people who are sex workers are sacred intimates, although certainly not all of them. Sex workers can be and often are the first-line providers of care to the sexual health of men who have sex with men, especially those who don't identify as gay. The services provided by whores, escorts, and erotic masseurs begin with something that is often underrated in our culture: healing through pleasure. Inside every gay man are traces of a kid who's been shamed, humiliated, silenced, or terrorized for being queer. For some people, going to a professional for sex is one way to gain permission to experience pleasure in our own bodies, which can be an amazingly powerful healing event. Sex workers can also serve as providers of information on health matters ranging from safer sex to sexual hygiene. They can be role models of healthy male sexuality, sexual self-acceptance, and/or gay identity. They can be shame busters and stress-reduction engineers, and more.

I started working as a massage therapist in New York City in 1993. For the next two decades, I did approximately 500 sessions a year with clients. I got my state certification training in California at the Body Electric School, which also offers extensive training in erotic massage as a healing practice. The vast majority of the sessions I do combine Swedish/Esalen-style massage with tantric massage, which incorporates erotic touch with the intention of raising and circulating erotic energy around the body. More often than not, the client has an ejaculation — or "release," in the parlance of the trade — but always in the context of a full-body experience.

Most of the time I keep my clothes on and discourage clients from interacting with me. However, in the course of my work as a professional masseur, I have engaged with clients in oral sex (active and receptive), anal sex (active and receptive), fisting, foot worship, water sports, power-and-surrender, verbal humiliation and other kinds of role-playing, body shaving, and various forms of intense body play, including spanking, flogging, bondage and discipline, blindfolding, hot wax, cock & ball torture, and experimenting with toys like titclamps, buttplugs, and vibrators. So I consider my professional employment as a masseur to fall within the realm of sex work. I don't especially relate to the term "prostitute" — I like the designation one client bestowed upon me, which is "pleasure activist." [Memo From the Future: many years later, in 2019, a black queer feminist named adrienne maree brown published a beautiful book on the subject, *Pleasure Activism*, but in the early 1990s no one I know had put the two words together.]

While I have incorporated many kinds of sexual interaction into my bodywork, I have also coached people on breathing and meditation. I have referred people to acupuncturists, chiropractors, medical doctors, dentists, psychotherapists, psychic healers, colonic hydrotherapists, nutritional counselors, and yoga studios. I have worked with men and women who have a history of being sexually abused and assisted them in their struggle to regain contact with their erotic bodies, to practice consent, and to honor their desires. I have shared what I know about using diet, vitamins, herbal supplements, and homeopathic remedies to treat specific ailments. I've given people reading lists, xeroxed articles, and brochures on tantric sex workshops. I've turned people on to some great music. And I've listened. I consider myself a holistic health practitioner, meaning that I don't treat bodies, I treat people, and I try to remember that every person who arrives at my massage table has numerous dimensions — physical, emotional, erotic, ethical, and spiritual.

I don't claim to represent or speak for sex workers as a class of people. I think my experience and practice is not typical of sex workers. I also think I am not alone in my attitudes toward sex work. I came into this line of work at the advanced age of 39 with an almost absurdly idealistic attitude about sexual healing. That's because I trained with Joseph Kramer, who founded the Body Electric School as part of a mission to heal the split between sexuality and spirituality in Western culture. How's that for ambitious?

Joe Kramer also introduced me to the ancient concept of the sacred prostitute — or "sacred intimate," as he translated it — who held the space for sex to be an experience about connection to spirit or communion with God, if you needed that in your life. Since we don't have temples that provide that kind of worship ceremony in the United States, Joe Kramer devised an elaborate training for sacred intimates, envisioning it as a contemporary occupation. I was perhaps foolish enough to take it seriously as something to undertake professionally. In any case, I got a lot out of that training. Among other things, the Body Electric School is scrupulous in its training programs about hygiene and protocol. So in addition to excellent instruction in skillful touch and breathwork, I got instilled with basic hygienic practices that are important in maintaining a bodywork practice.

The cardinal rule of medical ethics is "First, do no harm." That means to yourself as well as to anybody else. A lot of the basic concepts of hygiene have to do with being mindful about preventing myself from being exposed to health hazards. Protecting myself means protecting my client. Both of us benefit.

So, for instance, I use clean sheets and towels for each client. I wash my hands, with soap and hot water, before and after a session. I try to be mindful about butt hygiene and scat germs, since probably at least half of the people I see for erotic massage enjoy some version of butt-pleasuring. I always have a supply of disposable latex gloves available for buttplay or use with toys, and dispose of them properly afterwards. Finger cots are also useful to have around, little rubbers that slide over a single finger — I get them at hospital supply stores. If I'm inside someone's butt with an unrubbered finger or anything else, I try to be mindful of where that hand goes next. If I do a session where I'm playing with someone's butt, and then I answer the phone, and then I pour a glass of water out of a pitcher in the refrigerator, I've left a possible trail of microbes that could expose me and any houseguests to parasites or hepatitis. Also I pay attention to lube containers and oil bottles — am I touching them with clean hands? I often use disposable gloves to slip over a tube of lube, for example. One last word to the wise about butt stuff: Clip your fingernails. These are basic safer-sex education things that I picked up from Body Electric trainings, and they're worth mentioning particularly to professionals who presumably have more sexual contacts than the average person.

One of the things I like most about being a professional bodyworker is the invitation to pay attention to my own body. Am I eating right? Am I exercising? Am I keeping my body clean and well-groomed? Am I getting enough sleep? If I don't get to a yoga class once a week, I feel tight and cranky in my body. If I don't get a massage myself every couple of weeks, I start feeling draggy. And I constantly have to be attentive to overworking. Body workers suffer all the emotional strains of people who are self-employed. I never know when the next chunk of change is going to come along, so I'm reluctant to turn down any work. But I have to be careful about burning out. Some signs of that are when I have trouble staying in my body. Do I find that I'm numbing myself out with food, or booze, or net-surfing? Maybe it's time to take a break.

Some of the most important issues of self-care for sex workers have to do with groundedness. Touching a lot of different people, especially on an intimate basis, can be fun and exciting and satisfying at times. It also means taking on extra energy from other people, emotional and spiritual energy, and you have to find ways to clear that stuff out. I remember when I started out, I thought it was my job to have sex with absolutely anybody who walked in the door, just because they wanted it. The third day, a guy came for a massage who was depressed and angry and a complete black cloud of negative energy. Visions of sexual healing dancing in my head, I got naked and gave him an extremely erotic session and was wide open with him — and promptly got sick and wasn't able to work at all for several days. It was like I'd absorbed a couple of gallons of toxic waste.

So I had to learn quickly how to assess people's energy, how to control how much of it to take on, how to maintain my own balance and my own values and my own mood. Taking showers is one way of clearing. Drinking a lot of water is important. I also got into the habit, especially after an emotionally intense session, of burning sage, which is Native American medicine for clearing and purifying sacred space for doing ritual.

Another issue for sex workers is emotional support. Unlike office work, you don't necessarily have a crew of people around you who do the same thing, whom you can talk to about your work. Unlike social work or psychotherapy, there's no tradition of supervision for sex workers. You walk around with this gigantic secret in your head that you feel like you can't share with just anybody. What happens when you feel overwhelmed, or troubled, or ashamed, or anxious, or conflicted, or you find your boundaries getting slippery, or your safe-sex standards flying out the window? What are your own emotional needs? What are your own sexual wounds that you might be acting out in your work? It helps to know these things about yourself, and if you don't have a friend you trust to discuss these things with, it helps to find a psychotherapist to explore these questions with. I know I have a tremendous amount of fear and trepidation about being judged or shamed by other people if I talk about my erotic bodywork practice, especially when I have conflicts or troublesome questions. I had an assumption that any therapist would fixate on this work as being illegal or pathological or compulsive or dangerous. Luckily, that's not turned out to be the case.

In dealing with clients, I've come to realize that almost everything I do becomes a model of behavior.

If I'm direct and honest and upfront with them, it's a signal that they are free to be direct and honest and upfront with me. Likewise, if I'm erratic about returning phone calls or slippery with them about the fee or manipulative about the transaction in any way, I'm issuing them a license to be erratic or slippery or manipulative with me. How I dress, how clean my bathroom is, how mindful I am about sexual hygiene — all of those things send a message.

I started my practice with an idealistic attitude about my ability to provide a sense of erotic abundance and sexual generosity. I was willing to get naked and interact with many of my clients. That period lasted about two years. In my experience and observation, many guys who go into sex work do it for a couple of years at most. What happens is usually one of three things: they find a boyfriend (which may have been the goal in the first place); they disappear into a self-destructive spiral with drugs; or they become completely drained of energy and move on to some less taxing occupation. Some version of the last category happened to me. Yet I was committed to offering loving touch and healing through pleasure, so I redefined my boundaries to make it clear to my clients that what I was offering was massage, not sex.

I want to put in a word about the value of massage, and specifically erotic bodywork. These days we have a lot of language to talk about sexual addiction and sexual compulsion. But we don't talk much about sexual starvation, erotic malnutrition, and touch deprivation. Being touched is a primary human need. Few of us get touched as much as we'd like. I know there's value to getting touched or massaged in an atmosphere that is strictly non-sexual; sometimes that's a welcome relief and profoundly healing in itself. At the same time, for me personally, I find it kind of strange for a massage therapist to touch every part of my body but steer around my genitals, as if they don't deserve to be touched and nurtured along with the rest of me. My sexuality then gets split off from the rest of my body. As gay men, most of us grew up having to compartmentalize our sexuality and keep it hidden, creating an unhealthy split inside us. In the work that I do, I'm specifically giving my clients a place to integrate their erotic energy with the rest of who they are. When you get a good massage, every part of you is touched and honored, often more completely and intimately than with sex partners.

A lot of the sex we have with each other is driven by a sense of deficiency: "I have to go outside myself to get something to make me whole or fill some lack." Or we think of orgasm as something that someone else gives you. Tantra is about cultivating your own erotic energy and orgasmic capacity, which is the same pool of energy that supplies your ability to love and to pray. With tantric massage, I'm empowering the person on the table to breathe and expand and experience his own erotic self, not mine. I'm the guide, not the ride. Modelling boundaries is one of the most important things I can convey to my clients.

For sex workers, one of the most important though trickiest aspects of interacting with clients is the area of sexual ethics. Negotiating what we're going to do together has several layers to it. Although on one level it can be a simple professional fee for service, there are always health issues in the picture. It is theoretically possible to have an erotic massage or a paid sexual encounter that is entirely free of risk of exposure to HIV or sexually transmitted diseases, and certainly many sessions are conducted with scrupulous adherence to safer-sex principles. But we all know that in the real world, there are many gray areas, and what one person considers acceptable sexual practice may be a red flag for someone else. This raises all the tricky questions. Do I disclose my HIV status? Do I ask for my partner's? What about rimming? What about sucking? What about swallowing cum? In any encounter, but especially for sex workers who have an added responsibility, what's important is frank and honest discussion so that if there are any risks involved, the risk is knowingly shared by both partners.

Another ethical issue for sex workers is getting tested frequently for sexually transmitted infections (STIs) and being mindful of exposing clients to communicable infections like crabs or herpes. It's embarrassing as hell to have to call up a sex partner and say "I have crabs or scabies or gonorrhea and you should get treated for it." Among sexually active gay men, this is an ethical issue that we don't address enough, in my opinion. But I think sex workers have an especially important responsibility to model integrity around sharing risks and contacting people about STIs if they show up. The advent of PREP (which stands for "pre-exposure prophylaxis") in 2015 transformed the gay world. Since then, anal sex without condoms has become possible again, since the medication – first Truvada, then Descovy – offers protection against HIV infection. In addition, most people who take PREP commit to being tested every three months. Originally, the bloodwork served the purpose of monitoring adverse kidney and liver reactions to the medication. Soon it became clear that many (not all) people on PREP chose to dispense with condoms as a safer-sex precaution, so the regular three-month check-ups became a community practice to manage the perhaps inevitable uptick in STIs (especially gonorrhea, chlamydia, and syphilis) by testing for and treating them routinely rather than haphazardly.

I know that many of the questions I've had to face come from the active imaginations of my clients. One of my clients who likes to ejaculate while having his prostate stimulated posed this question to me: "What if you got some blood under your fingernail from the last guy?" It was a perfectly reasonable question, and I assured him that I washed my hands after every session, but I made a note to myself to question any buttplay without a glove or a finger cot. Another client said, "I liked it when you sucked me, but what if the guy at 2:00 had gonorrhea or chlamydia?" Good question.

When I hear questions like that, I definitely have to sort through layers of guilt and shame and defensiveness in response. But I appreciate knowing that my clients are partners with me in looking at sex work as health care.

For anyone considering sex work as an occupation, you can look at sex work as an easy way to make money. You can treat it as something animalistic and mechanical and squirt-oriented and something to get over with as fast as possible. But you have to consider whether your attitude is supporting sex-shame and sex-negative messages from the culture and whether you're missing the opportunity to provide someone with a transcendent experience.

I've partaken of almost every possibility in the gay male sexual subculture and have definitely had ecstatic experiences in bathhouses and bookstores, parks and porn theaters. But I've also had plenty of experiences in gay sex venues that felt alienated and heartless, and I'm aware that sex workers are part of that landscape. I don't want my work to contribute to feelings of emptiness and spiritual deadness. I want more erotic abundance and sexual generosity in the world. And sex workers have the opportunity — maybe even the responsibility — to be community leaders in advocating healing through pleasure.

This book describes a particular journey that

began when I met Joe Kramer, who became my teacher. Everything about my sex life changed after I met Joe. It feels funny to say that, because it's not like he was my lover or even a casual boyfriend. I never had sex with him. But for years hardly a day went by that I didn't think of something he said or act on something he taught me. Like breathing and how it hooks up with sexual energy. Or the idea that you can get to a state of sexual ecstasy without cumming — and stay there. Or that most people's sex lives are paltry. That word often floats into my mind after the flimsy fleeting encounters that most gay men (most males? most humans?) call sex. Or the idea that what's most attractive about somebody could be something other than his face or his butt or his cock.

"My type was energy," I remember Joe saying to me. "It was about conscious touching. It was about presence. It wasn't about any one look. Certainly, there were parts that pleased me, but what I learned when I came out and started having sex in New York was to go for the vibrancy and aliveness. There are beauties who have no energy and no aliveness. They're like statues."

He was telling me about a life-changing experience he had at the baths in Berkeley, back in the days when they were called the Mayan Baths. He met an old man with thinning gray hair, wrinkles, and shaky hands. "This guy had me stand there. He said, 'Take some deep breaths.' He knelt down, and he started sucking me. Then his fingers started doing different things. He would push them into unusual places on my body and vibrate them. This went on for about an hour. I was flying. Finally I said, 'What is this?' He said, 'I was just doing acupressure, pulling the erotic energy around through your body.' Right after that I went and took four classes in acupressure."

That's another thing I loved about Joe Kramer. Even though he was pushing 50, he was a student of life.

When he encountered something that attracted him, he wanted to read all the books (well, skim at least some of them) and find out all about it. And he drew around him the same kind of people, thirsty for knowledge, hungry for experience, horny for God and sex with equal intensity.

In the context of Body Electric trainings, I and a diverse assortment of eccentric and magnetic individuals participated in a number of experiments in community, ritual, and intimacy. Some of these experiments were foolish; others were powerful. All in some way investigated the proposition, put forth by Joe Kramer and other esoteric practitioners throughout history, that human sexuality is not a sin or a step away from the self-knowledge and mystical union with the source of life some call God. It is, in fact, a direct experience of that inherent miracle.

I'd discovered my own vitality and connection to the earth and mythology — the hairy satyrs, Pan, Dionysus — by dancing naked around campfires at men's conferences and Radical Faerie gatherings. I felt liberated and at home in my body, more so than most people I knew. When I found in Body Electric a community that honored and praised my physical and sexual freedom, I got the idea that I could model sexual abundance for other men and increase the amount of love and self-acceptance in the world.

At the time I began these adventures, I was approaching the age of 40, and I was undergoing the phenomenon that people speak about with deceptive casualness as "a midlife crisis." A close friend had died. I'd quit a good job. I ended a 14-year relationship with the man I loved. With mystifying abruptness I lost all interest in the career as a journalist and theater critic I'd been pursuing since I was 20. It was a time of depression, separation, and reevaluating my life.

Inspired by my Body Electric training, I decided to launch a profession for myself offering erotic massage as a healing practice. Bodywork gave me something to do every day, a skill I could practice that would produce income. And I was grateful for the physical contact.

How did my home become a temple for healing through the body? It began a long time ago, when I was a mere lad rescued from trailer mentality and given access to the House of the Lord. By the time I was 10 I knew my way around a church. I was respectful but not overawed by priests. I was there for a reason. I had things to do. The world of priests and altar boys was one of hushed male camaraderie, ritual, costume, unquestioned obeisance to ancient instructions. Yet there was also a place for spontaneity (there was a congregation out there) and mystery (did everyone believe in the transubstantiation?). Hanging around backstage, knowing where they stashed the wine and wafers — only initiates to this secret world got to do such things. No kindly pater ever put his hands on me or showed me his wee-wee, though I ached for erotic attention from older men.

The first time I heard about the tradition of the sacred prostitute, Joe Kramer made it sound like the noblest calling in the world. "These are the people you go to when you want to have sex with God," he said. What an inflation: sex with me = sex with God. But Joe's original vision stayed faithful to the priestly function. The priest was not God Himself but the vessel that conjured and contained the object of worship. The priest was a go-between who channeled divine presence to us and channeled our devotion to Spirit. So did the sacred prostitute. But who ever called up and said, "I want to have sex with God"? Who knew it was possible to talk about or ask for such a thing?

When I started doing massage, I thought it was thrilling to take off my clothes to go to work. I loved observing men's sexuality, encouraging it, celebrating it, promoting it, admiring it, indulging it, extending it. I wanted to make up for the culture's lack of encouragement of gay men's sexuality and self-esteem. I thought it would be fun to dwell in the happy playground of enlightened sexuality and welcome others to share it. I discovered that outside the hothouse of Body Electric, sexual healing took on a different look. It was a long slow process, like cultivating a garden, rather than something to be accomplished quickly, like throwing together a tasty dinner.

Almost immediately, I was both dismayed and fascinated to find myself face-to-face with an array of the sexual wounds suffered by the men who came to see me. Body shame, sex shame, religious guilt, internalized homophobia, stunted desire, inability to speak of desire, fear of AIDS. And these wounds weren't experienced only by my clients. I had come away from my Body Electric training with an image of myself as a paragon of sexual health, a shining mirror of erotic vitality and wholeness for people to look at and model themselves on. It took two years for the message to begin to sink in that my clients were equally a mirror for me, reflecting my own wounds back to me, if I had the strength and the courage to see them. How do I feel about my body? How did I learn about sex, and how did that learning help me and harm me? How do I feel about my own desires? What do I want from intimate contact with others? Where do I deceive myself? Where am I struck speechless? And if I was initially blind to just how damaged many men are in their sexuality, I was equally oblivious to how strongly I needed something from them. Without knowing it, I turned my clients into Daddy surrogates and tried to get from them the unconditional approval of who I am that I always wanted and never got from my own father.

Somehow the shining vision of sexual healing that Joe Kramer held out had not prepared me for the reality of sexual wounds. The gap between the vision and the reality filled me with frustration, anger, and melancholy. I wanted to bridge that gap as soon as possible, to pave over that gaping hole. I am in some ways a typical product of a culture with a long history of embracing dazzling visions and avoiding messy realities, loving the quick answer and hating to contemplate the problem.

Upsetting as I found the gap between dream and reality to be, it did not destroy my faith in the value of healing through sexual expression, the value of good touch, the pleasure of erotic massage, the joy of accepting your erotic genius, and the sheer aesthetic/ spiritual pleasure of touching men's cocks and butts. There's a lot of pressure to "clean up" homosexuality and hide the sex. It's okay to be creative, funny, arty, religious, domestic, but not a shameless cocksucker. If you've had lots and lots of sex with lots and lots of people, it's okay to talk about it only if by the end of the story you've seen the error of your ways and you're willing to admit that it's bad to have lots and lots of sex with lots and lots of people.

The plot I've chosen to tell is a different story. It's a quest for self-knowledge through sexuality. Sex has been a positive force in my life as a gay man. I've written as truthfully as I can about all the obstacles but I leave no doubt about the essential theme.

What follows is a historical document, tracking my journey in real time. I'm always interested in reading about process: how things work, how people think, what funky things happen on the way to a finished product or a polished thought. I'd like to think that an unvarnished account of my unfolding discoveries will be illuminating and/or validating to past, present, or future practitioners, to seekers of sexual healing, or simply to sentient beings with an interest in the varieties of human sexual experience. It's an account of struggle, in many ways a catalogue of mistakes, not an unbroken string of pearls of wisdom. God knows I'd love to be Deepak Chopra and deliver "Seven Steps to Sexual Healing" — just think of the royalties I could collect! The narrator of this book is not that kind of beatific, know-it-all New Age guru. He evolves in the course of the book. He starts off angry and confused, and by the end he knows a few things he didn't know when he started out. But he spends a lot of time in the cloud of unknowing.

Ultimately, before there can be sexual healing, we have to name our sexual wounds and measure the distance between. If nothing else, I hope this book is an honest guided tour of the gap.

Note: In the pages that follow, I will be describing interactions that occurred in my sacred intimate practice. I have changed names and identifying characteristics of clients and certain other individuals to protect their privacy.

Also: I will occasionally introduce a Memo From the Future [MFF], a variation on footnotes, for the purpose of clarification.

PART ONE
The Dragons at the Door
(1993-1995)

Ancient spiritual traditions developed the sophisticated concept of "the dragons at the door." Any traveler who undertakes a deep exploration into the realms of wisdom and mystery will inevitably encounter, almost immediately, forces that will test the seeker with tricks, traps, ugly faces, and scary noises to see if you have the strength and commitment to face down the obstacles you will encounter along the way. The first section of this narrative provides a diaristic account of the early years of my sacred intimate journey. As I embrace the vocation of "sacred intimate," I aspire to manifest as the soul of compassion, offering skillful guidance and welcoming acceptance to anyone seeking sexual healing. But along the way I definitely make the acquaintance of the dragons at the door: my human capacity for impatience, frustration, insecurity, body snobbism, skepticism, fear, and ego.

Our story begins in a quaint bygone era, pre-Internet. Somewhere in the future there will be websites where practitioners attract customers with detailed descriptions of what they offer along with photos, videos, and testimonials. People will someday communicate via electronic mail (e-mail) and text messages written and read on expensive, multipurpose handheld devices. But for now, the year is 1993, and all that business is conducted over the telephone.

CHAPTER ONE

Complete with Release

The phone rings. His name is Jim. He saw my ad, the one in the weekly paper that says "Feed Your Body, Free Your Soul." He sounds middle-aged. His voice is low, as if there are other people nearby and he doesn't want to be overheard. He sits in his cubicle, and I sit in mine. It's sort of like confession. He wants to be touched by a stranger, by a man, and he feels guilty, ashamed, embarrassed. He asks what I do, and I tell him: a full-body massage with oil, on a massage table, Swedish-style with some acupressure. This is how long the session lasts, this is how much I charge. Then he wants to know, "Is there a release?"

This question instantly produces several emotions in me. The first one is dread: oh, God, here's someone who doesn't want a massage, he just wants to get off. Then there's judgment: you're not worthy of being on my massage table if all you want is a handjob. Then there's self-judgment: who are you kidding? You love to touch men's cocks, you've made erotic massage a specialty of your work, you often refer to it as "sexual healing." So who are you to get judgmental about this guy who wants a "release"? Somewhere in there is anger, anger at the indirection of guys like Jim, mixed with amusement. Yes, that's what I'm feeling: anger and amusement at the language of the massage trade.

Is there a release? Do you give a release? Is there any form of release? I know it's a code, but I can't help being literal-minded. Massage is, among other things, about releasing tension held in muscles and joints. It's possible to have an emotional release, to weep or laugh, when the tension dissolves and energy returns to some part of the body that has been blocked. Release is a technical term among dancers for certain kinds of free movement. Records are released. Prisoners are released. Significant public events are heralded by press releases.

When a potential massage client asks "Is there a release?" he means something specific. I don't know how, but those are the words that have entered the language as the way to ask the question most men seem to want to ask. A delicate expression, as euphemisms go. "Is there a ... 'release'?" There are a few other ways to ask the same question. "Is this a complete massage?" Innocent enough on the face of it. Mentally, I go coy as a geisha. Complete? Certainly. I massage the whole body. Is there some part that you're afraid will be left out, or some part that you wish me to skip?

"Is there a release?" Truthfully, most men who ask me that don't book appointments, no matter what I say. I can't help thinking they're the kind of guys who will pay a hooker $20 to sit in the car with them fully dressed and give them a handjob. That's a particular kind of sexual healing. It's not what I do. Not enough joy.

Even the men who never ask the question are thinking about sex when they come for a massage.

Almost all of them. What do I say? When people ask "Is there a release?" I often say, "I offer erotic massage, if that's what you're asking."

Here's what is being negotiated: are they going to get off? And I have an agenda about that. I want men to have great sex in their lives. I want people to live in their bodies — good practice for living in the world, living on the earth, loving it and holding it sacred. All this starts with your body, how you feel about it, how you take care of it, what you eat, how you wipe your ass, how you sleep, how you get rid of your stress and tension.

The thing is, I take both the massage part and the erotic part of my work seriously, which makes me feel like such a weirdo sometimes. Most "legitimate" masseurs steer clear of touching any part of your body that will get you aroused, and the ones who go straight for a guy's dick couldn't give a professional full-body massage if their lives depended on it. But then I didn't come into this business the usual way. I never set out to become a card-carrying member of the American Massage Therapy Association. Nor did I slide into it as another way of hustling, enticed by the taboo glamor of big bucks for fast sex. The first instruction I got came from erotic massage workshops taught by Joe Kramer, which were about breathing and ritual and raising erotic energy without ejaculating. Around the same time, I began massaging my friend Harry, whose body was increasingly ravaged by the effects of AIDS. He was so grateful for my touch that I was encouraged to seek at least rudimentary training. By chance I had an opportunity to study with Irene Smith, a former prostitute and drug addict who pioneered massage work for people with AIDS in San Francisco and created an organization called Service Through Touch. I learned from her both how to massage someone terminally ill in a hospital bed and how to ground myself emotionally while doing such delicate work.

Inspired by Irene's example to do volunteer massage in hospitals, I started my own practice. Clients showed up, but I quickly realized the training I'd had wasn't enough. I didn't want to go to the Swedish Institute in New York, partly because it would take a year to get licensed and partly because I didn't like their super-clinical approach, draping clients with sheets and towels and scrupulously avoiding the genitals (some call it "doughnut massage," because of the hole in the middle). Instead, I took an intensive course at the Body Electric School in California, where I could get state certification in a little over two weeks in a setting that was both gay-friendly and sex-positive. The training was Esalen-style — we massaged each other's full bodies without draping — but stayed away from erotic touch. Doug Fraser (who was quite sick and died of AIDS the following year) was an excellent instructor and taught me the basic skills that have served me ever since. I returned to my budding practice fully prepared, I thought, to be a professional masseur. But none of my teachers — not Joe, not Irene, not Doug — prepared me for that question that keeps popping up.

"Is there a release?" That sometimes means a handjob, and sometimes it means something emotional. What I mean is this: let's say the man asks for a "release," a specific sexual act, because we haven't developed a universal vocabulary to ask for what we actually want. He wants to be held. Or he wants me to be naked. He wants to look at a naked man. He wants to touch a naked man. He wants to be held while he cries. He wants to smell a man. He wants to have his butt touched, stroked, penetrated (often instead of saying that, he'll say, "I'd like you to work on my lower back"). I've never had someone say to me, "I want you to hold me like you're my father and I'm your child and you love me," although I'm sure that some men have wanted precisely that.

I came up with a rehearsed spiel that I would give people on the phone. I'd thought about every word carefully, although I worked hard to give the impression that I have not rehearsed this speech. When people call a masseur who advertises in a newspaper, they usually want to know a few basic practicalities: what do you offer, how much do you charge, where are you located. [MFF: A major blessing of having an online presence – a website or a personalized page on a listings site — is not having to repeat this basic information over and over again to potential clients.] Many of them assume that there will be an opportunity to get off, and they don't ask. Others have a real urge to get off, and that's what makes them call this Tuesday morning or Friday afternoon or in the wee small hours of the weekend, so they have their own set of questions, starting with: what do you look like?

What I used to say is "The work that I do is a thorough full-body massage with oil. I work on a table. I have a large comfortable massage table and shower facilities. The massage that I do is a Swedish/Esalen-style massage with some acupressure and conscious breathing. I do a session that lasts about an hour and a half, and I charge $100." [MFF: 1993 rates, which would be more like $300 today.] The language is clear and direct. Still some men comb through those sentences trying to find where I've hidden the sex. "It's a thorough massage?" "Full-body, head to toe?"

I do hide the sex in my work. I do so partly to protect myself. I guess it's left over from the coaching I got from my friend Wilson when I launched this whole adventure. An old pro at this work, Wilson advised me never to answer the question "Is there a release?" over the phone. "That constitutes solicitation," he said, "which is against the law." I've never been terribly concerned about police entrapment or legal prosecution, but Wilson's advice stuck with me, and I continue to follow his example. It is, after all, against the law to promise sex for money.

By avoiding the question, I'm also exercising my need to control the situation. I wouldn't go so far as to say the correct answer to "Is there a release?" is "Maybe — if I like you." But I do like to keep my options open. And I don't want to promise something I'm not able to deliver.

Those aren't the main reasons, though. I'm circumspect on the phone because I think sex is a great thing that deserves to be experienced with consciousness and high quality. Before I have sex with someone in my personal life, and before I engage erotically with a client on my table, I want him to be fully awake and in his body. I don't want him drunk or on drugs or numbed out, his brain full of office memos and household worries. I don't want his limbs and muscles frozen stiff with held tension and lack of exercise. I want him to be breathing fully with all his senses open.

Not many people walk in the door in that condition. So I have my work cut out for me.

How do I feel about men cumming on my table? To be perfectly honest, I love it. Even though my first training in massage was tantric and focused on postponing ejaculation, I have to admit that I like to see people get off. I feel privileged to be present with a man experiencing the pleasure of orgasm. Not every man who gets off in my presence is experiencing that pleasure. There are many forces at work against it: religious guilt, body deadness, the numbness of habit. A lot of men use ejaculation as a sedative at bedtime every day, or jerk off first thing in the morning to get them out of bed. There's nothing wrong with jerking off. It's fun. But when you start doing anything pleasurable out of habit rather than by conscious choice, it becomes

mechanical. It turns into a routine rather than a treat. The first drink you taste; not the seventeenth.
Even to ask "Is there a release?" takes a lot of guts. For some men, it's all they can do to get the words out, the code words for a deep and shameful longing. Some can't even manage that much.
My client last night, Patrick, sounded friendly and tired on the phone. He called me at least three times. I spoke to him twice, left him a message ... we had communicated several times before he arrived. I thought I had a clear picture of who he was and what he wanted. I wasn't prepared for how uptight he would be. He was a handsome guy, around 40, blond, tan. He told me he lives in Florida most of the time. He came in wearing black pointy shoes, jeans, a pullover shirt, and a jean jacket. He could barely bring himself to look me in the eye. He immediately stomped into the middle of the room and looked around, as if he were in a big hurry. I asked him to take his shoes off at the door, and I offered to hang up his jacket. He dropped his jacket on a chair and took off his shoes, then walked over to the massage table and started undressing.
I usually have people sit down and talk a little before we begin, but Patrick emitted such strange intense unsociable energy that I found myself unable to insist on that.
"Do you get massaged much?" I asked as he peeled off his shirt.
"I used to go to an Oriental woman," he said, "but she moved."
"Is there anything I need to know about your body," I asked, "any injuries or anything?"
"I injured my Achilles tendon years ago but it's mended now," he said brusquely. He seemed to want to get on the table immediately and have as little communication as possible.

He lay down on his back wearing his white jockey shorts. People don't usually keep their underwear on during a massage with me. I had a moment of wondering if he was a cop; cops aren't permitted to get naked on duty. I started the massage with him in his underwear, stretching his limbs and rocking his body to loosen him up. He was tense and high-strung. It was difficult for him to let his arms and legs rest. Breathing into a hip stretch was difficult; he wouldn't let all the breath out. He told me he didn't want me to massage his scalp or his face. And he emphasized that he didn't want any oil in his hair, even though I wasn't using oil at that point. His body seemed to be screaming fear of surrender: I want it/I don't want it.

When I turned him over on his belly, I said, "You can keep your shorts on if you want, but most people take them off." He said, "You use sticky oil?" I said, "I use coconut oil." He thought about it a moment and then slid his shorts off without turning over. He was hard to work on. His hyperdeveloped chest and arms felt like granite. He didn't register any particular pleasure at my touch. I stayed away from his butt and refrained from some of my more sensual massage strokes. When I turned him over again and started working on the front of his body, I decided to drape him with a towel, which I'd never done before. He seemed so uptight about being naked with me that I wanted to do whatever I could to make him feel comfortable.

When I worked on his belly and chest, and then again at the end of the session when I was toweling him off, his heart was pounding. That's when I got the feeling that he did want some kind of erotic experience. Maybe he'd taken a long time to get up his nerve to see a male masseur. Maybe he wanted me to touch his cock and get him hard. Maybe he wanted to touch me and experience his sexual attraction to men. If so, he couldn't bring himself to say it. Maybe he wanted me to read his mind. Sometimes I'm good at sensing when someone wants something and isn't saying it, or when something emotional is going on that he needs to talk about. But this guy was so uptight and so quiet that he scared me.

The only bit of conversation we had was about his Achilles tendon. I saw the scar on his left heel and wondered aloud, "Did you have surgery here?"

"Yes."

"How does that work?" I said. "I thought the Achilles tendon had to heal itself."

"No," he said, "they went in and sewed it up."

"How long were you off your feet?"

"Six months."

"How'd you do it?"

"Motorcycle accident."

"Do you still ride?"

"Uh huh."

That was as much information as I could pry out of him.

He did say it was a good massage. He thanked me several times without ever quite looking me in the eye. He pulled out his wallet and, instead of handing me the money, he put it on the massage table. This guy brought out the super-cautious, not-especially-talkative side of me. The session that usually lasts an entire hour and a half was over in an hour five. I couldn't wait to finish. I sensed that he, too, wanted it to be over fast. I felt that soon after he arrived he became stricken with guilt or remorse and decided he'd made a mistake. I wondered if he was made nervous by the altar prominently displayed in my living room. If the atmosphere were dimmer, more erotic, maybe it wouldn't matter if he didn't say anything; his desires would be assumed.

The session with Patrick left me quiet and a little shaky, thinking, "What was that about?" Every time I think I've surveyed the complete catalog of men's sexual wounds, a new variety walks in the door. Then my own unresolved questions pop up like loose floorboards. There I am, trying to be a ministering angel, and all my demons are dancing around the room, taunting me.

Okay, wise guy, how do you feel when you get on the table to get massaged by a cute guy? What do you say when you want sex and can't bring yourself to say so? How would you ask for sex if you were completely free of shame, if it were as simple as ordering takeout from a Thai restaurant? Oh, and by the way — is there a release?

CHAPTER TWO

Sex Work as Spiritual Practice

Maybe because I grew up Catholic and my first experience of community service was being an altar boy at Mass, I consciously conduct each session as a ritual. And anyone who does ritual knows that 90% of the experience is preparation. The first step is the invitation I put out to clients. In my advertising I use language that you don't usually see in the sexually-charged arena of massage ads — words like "Touch heals" or "Sacred Erotic Intimate" or "Erotic bodywork to nourish the soul." Nowadays my only advertising is a web page that talks about tantric massage and gives some possible intentions for an erotic massage ritual: Meditate. Pray. Rest. Be Grateful. Heal. Expand. Feel. Transform. These words are crucial in creating the context for how I work.

Preparing the space is another important part of the ritual. I've made my living room into a temple space that's clean, well-lit, inviting, and quiet. There are Balinese masks and framed original photographs on the walls, a candle burning, fresh flowers if possible, and on the mantelpiece of my (non-working) fireplace I've painted a sentence I once heard a West African teacher named Malidoma Some say: "Desire is a horse that wants to take you on a journey to spirit." Again, words are important to me, and a sentence that begins with desire and ends with spirit sets the tone for what I do.

Near my massage table is an active altar. An altar is an essential part of ritual space — it is a focus for reverence. My altar has a typical assortment of items: stones with various properties, a picture of my spiritual teacher, a picture of a loved one who's in the other world now, a picture of Krishna (the Hindu god of joy), objects representing both male and female sexuality, and objects representing the four elements (earth, air, fire, and water). Possibly the most important item on my altar these days is an icon of Marilyn Monroe with her skirt blowing up, which a friend gave me as a reminder not to take myself too seriously.

When a client arrives, I always have him (or her or them, but it's usually him) sit and talk for a minute, however briefly. The first time I see someone, I ask a few pertinent questions about any injuries or medical conditions I should know about. I assure him that he's here to be taken care of, first and foremost, and his feedback is welcome throughout the session. I go over the rough outline of the session, that it's a full-body massage that includes erotic touch. I tell him he can relax and soak it up as a pleasurable experience or he can make it a kind of meditation for himself. Again, just planting the seeds, so that by the time he gets on the table, the spell has been cast.

Every ritual has a beginning, a middle, and an end. I start and finish each session with a silent prayer, and the middle part is the massage, but in a way I'm praying continuously throughout the session. I start the session with a simple laying on of hands and asking my spirit guides and my client's to be with us and let this session be good for both of us. (That's a prayer I learned from a character in Alice Walker's novel, *The Temple of My Familiar*.) And then I set about touching every part of the person's body, blessing each part, waking it up with skillful loving touch.

To me one of the things that makes erotic massage a transcendent experience is activating the entire body with touch and breath from head to toe before zeroing in on the genitals. After I've done a thorough back massage, I'll turn the client over and do some light touching and hair-stroking on the front of his body, which usually raises some erotic energy. Then kneeling at his head stroking his nipples and speaking into his ear, I guide him through a visualization that might go something like this: "Take some easy big breaths from the base of your spine up to the top of your chest. With every breath, let yourself open and expand. Let your ribcage expand, let your heart open, and surrender to all the pleasure and freedom and joy and love that's possible for you in your life. Feel it in your body right here, right now, as you're breathing in a direct line from the base of your spine, up through your heart, all the way to the top of your head."

By this time I've been touching the person continuously for around 45 minutes, and only now do I begin to incorporate genital touch, using a variety of Taoist erotic massage strokes that I learned from Joseph Kramer, designed to raise and circulate erotic energy around the body without the goal of ejaculating. Whether the guy's cock is hard or soft, big, small or medium, whether he's prone to rapid ejaculation or has a hard time squirting at all, these strokes can be executed in such a way that builds energy that can be distributed around the body. I'm constantly coaching his breathing, moving energy up to his heart, down his legs, around his body, tending the flame of kundalini, letting life force penetrate every cell of his being, floating on the vehicle of breath and sensual erotic pleasure. Eventually I will talk him through a Big Draw, focusing on some faster conscious breathing and then a big held breath while simultaneously squeezing his butt and belly and pulling energy up his spine through his heart to the top of his head, and then exhaling.

What happens then is different for each person. Some kind of alchemical reaction occurs, and there is an opportunity for the person to have an internal experience of connecting the dots between the physical body, the emotional body, the erotic body, and the spiritual body. I can't direct what happens at this point — it's a free-floating, often peaceful moment around which the mind, body, and soul reorganize themselves.

Some people are content to contain this energy. Others are inclined to want to squirt, in which case I'm happy to assist, massaging and breathing and building erotic energy to a peak. Sometimes as that happens, the person will go into spontaneous prayer that goes something like this: "Oh God, ohhh God, oh God, oh God oh God oh God OHHHHH!"

In traditional tantric practice, retaining ejaculate is the preferred mode of healing, since ejaculating is seen as discharging precious energy. Another way of looking at it is that completely letting go and surrender of any control paves the way for a profoundly meditative state of "utmost relaxation, silence and stillness, a state of choiceless awareness and non-judgmental acceptance." (See Gunther Nitschke, *The Silent Orgasm*.)

For that reason, I always make it clear that orgasm is not the end of the session. Like the meditation at the end of a yoga class, I always do a series of finishing touches to end the ritual. That includes a centering and balancing sequence in which I touch chakra points and offer prayers, sometimes aloud but usually silent. Touching the crown of the head and the third eye: *May your vision of yourself be large and wonderful.* Touching the crown and the heart: *May your heart be open to the love that is possible for you in your life.* Touching the heart and the solar plexus: *May your power in the world always be connected to the things you love.* Touching the heart and the genitals: *May your heart and your genitals always be connected.* And as I'm holding the bottoms of the person's feet, my prayer is: *May the love you have inside you help to heal you and all beings on the planet.*

I would feel slightly awkward saying these prayers aloud. I usually don't share them with my clients, for fear that they sound corny or generic somehow. And yet most of the time when I've experienced praying in public, it's powerful. Whether I say them out loud or not, I know that these prayers have an impact on the person on my table.

One last item in this inventory has to do with payment. You might think that money changing hands would be outside the realm of spiritual practice. But in virtually every spiritual tradition there is some form of altar offering. Christians call it tithing or passing the collection plate. Buddhists call it *dana*. Hindus call it *darshana*. I remember attending a ceremony at a Thai temple in North Hollywood where in addition to paper money pinned onto a clothesline someone had contributed a six-pack of Pepsi. If all things are indeed sacred, then the body, erotic pleasure, and money all present opportunities to experience mindfulness, respect, love, and joy.

CHAPTER THREE

The Clock

Something I love about my massage practice is the structure of a session. It's one reason I started doing this work in the first place. I figured out the length of a session that felt right to me — 90 minutes, an hour and a half. I know where it begins; in the middle, a lot of things can happen; but I know where it ends, a rare treat in life. I even structure the timing of my sessions more rigorously than by their length: I prefer to make appointments on the even-numbered hours. So in my appointment book at the beginning of the week, I write down when I'm available. Sunday: noon, 2:00, 4:00, 6:00, 8:00. If it's a slow day, or if I have the time, I'll see someone at 5:15 or 7:30, but most of my clients sign up for those even-numbered hours. I always allow a half-hour between clients. I don't like rushing people out the door, and I think it's a little rude and potentially uncomfortable for clients to meet one another. Plus, I need time to change the sheets, dump the used sheets and towels in the laundry bag, burn sage to clear the room, replenish my drinking water, wash my hands and face, and shower if necessary.

I have noticed occasions when my sessions are controlled by the clock more than by my massage routine or by the client's needs. Occasionally the preliminary chat goes on for half an hour, if the client is going through some emotional crisis or is nervous or simply talkative. Then I have to weigh how to manage the rest of the session. How important is talking vs. touching, relaxation vs. erotic massage. I have an aversion to doing erotic work before someone has fully arrived in his body and seems awake and sensate. But I also resent it when the talking goes on for a long time, I spend an hour giving a great massage, and then the guy makes it clear he wants to be jerked off as well. A great erotic massage can easily take half an hour. I almost never give someone a half-hour erotic massage, though. Usually it's more like ten minutes. Some people can't take more than five minutes.

I started to notice a conflict inside myself. Sometimes I was willing to let the session go beyond the boundaries of a one-way massage and to interact erotically with my clients, but only up to a point and not beyond. There was a limited window of opportunity — after the one-hour mark and before 90 minutes is up, anything goes. If a client wanted to reach up and stroke my chest hair or nipples, or nuzzle his head against my crotch to see if I'm hard, and then slide a hand up to fondle my dick, this was the time to do it. But at the end of 90 minutes, I'm through. I wanted the session to be over.

This is where my professionalism intersects with my personality type. My first lover, Paul, once described the essential difference between us, using language from Buddhist teachings, which describe two forms of suffering: grasping (wanting something that isn't there) and aversion (pushing away something undesirable).

Paul was a grasping type, who hung on and didn't want to let go, and I was an aversive type, who found it easy to disengage and felt acutely uncomfortable letting things flow with no end in sight. Even with clients I like or feel attracted to, I rarely let myself go to enjoy their company or their bodies for an indefinite amount of time. Sometimes if it's the last client of the day, and I like the guy, I'll stop watching the clock, but only for a while. Then I'll start thinking about taking a shower, and getting to bed, and what time I want to get up in the morning, and am I going to get a tip for this extra amount of time, which I usually don't, which I resent ....

That's one of the liabilities of this practice as a modern-day sacred prostitute. If I were doing strictly massage therapy, everything would be clear cut, in and out, no one would expect more than an hour. If I were a temple whore, one of the *qadeshim* who served as priests to the Mother-Goddess Athirat in ancient Canaan, all my needs would be taken care of so it wouldn't matter how much men paid to experience union with the divine by having sex with me.

I do the best I can, I guess. Unconditional love, $100 an hour.

CHAPTER FOUR

Al (Part 1)

Sometimes I find it challenging to be patient and compassionate with clients who are aggressive, super-guarded, or unclear in their communications. Today I can't stop thinking about Al, whom I saw last night for the third time. He's short, self-confident, sexually confused. Sexually confused? That's being polite. There's no confusion. He's one of those guys who prefer to have sex with men, but they spend most of their lives cloaked in the comforts of conventional marriage and family, which looks better for business. They have sex with men on the side, and they suffer in secrecy. I'm reluctant to call them closet cases, because it sounds unkind. But that's what they are.

Al called me from the airport in Boston. He was on his way home from a business trip and made an appointment for later in the evening. When he arrived, he'd changed out of his monkey suit into a navy blue sweatshirt and jeans. He wanted hugging and kissing. Al is one of those clients I've "crossed the line" with.

The first time I saw him, he wanted erotic interaction, and I went along with it, not without misgivings. He relished our last session, which had three parts: he sat in my lap and I held him like he was a little kid; then we went to my bed and lay down together, eventually getting naked and increasingly sexual, until he squirted; then I put him on the table and massaged his back. This time we repeated part two of that session.

We did a lot of talking. The more time I spend with him, the more he relaxes, the more openly he talks about his life, and the clearer I get that he is a bit of a bullshit artist. When I ask him what he wants, he says he doesn't know, he wants me to be in charge. Ha! He knows what he wants, but he wants me to give it to him without asking, because then he doesn't have to take responsibility for it. He likes to play the helpless little boy. It's his mommy's fault, because she invaded him physically when he was a kid. It's his wife's fault, because she's frigid. He didn't use the word frigid. He said that she didn't like sex, and she's on medication that diminishes the feeling in her genitals, so she doesn't masturbate, and she doesn't like it when he touches himself in front of her. Her name is Marianne. They've been married 22 years. He never jerks off alone; he can only jerk off by getting on the phone sex lines. He says he likes to give back. It's important to give back. He keeps repeating the phrase "give back," in such a way that I can tell it's been pounded into him by someone else. Not good to take! Must give back!

He's like a lot of guys that way, unaccustomed to receiving touch or pleasure or help. It's mostly a control issue. If I accept something from you, receive something from you — take something from you — then I owe you something. I'd rather you owe me something. And because he keeps shoving away what others are trying to give him, he continues to feel needy, so he

complains that nobody ever gives him anything.
 Listening to him talk, I want to yell at him, or spank his butt, or kick him out of my house. But I recognize the pattern. I see it in myself. The universe has sent me someone who matches my wounds, so I can study them in detail. Al brings up my Daddy-Boy stuff, big-time. I'm a needy baby screaming, *The world owes me everything! I can't get no satisfaction!* What's going on is that I need approval and affection from other people and that makes me feel vulnerable. I'm afraid I won't get it. So I try to manipulate them by playing different roles. Then I get angry if they won't do exactly what I want exactly when I want them to do it. I know that song. I can sing it in my sleep.
 I don't want to let Al off the hook, though. We're lying on my futon, in my extremely alluring temple. It's just a regular sized queen bed, futon mattress on a wooden frame, but it looks like the size of a swimming pool. It's a real passion pit. It's centered in the middle of my bay window, so it's almost a separate room. I'm doing some Daddy practice, holding Al in my arms. He's wearing his red briefs with the white Calvin Klein waistband. I'm still fully clothed, wearing a white ribbed tank undershirt and black drawstring sweatpants and green socks. I'm lightly stroking his belly and his legs and his cock, which pushes up hard under his shorts. He's going on with his litany: no one ever touches me with tenderness, no one is ever soft with me. His brow is knit. He's put on his mask of victimhood. Talking About My Problems. Poor Me. Gotta Analyze This.
 But then he'll relax into being himself, and his demonic child comes out. "This is like a therapy session," he says.
 "Yeah," I say, "although your therapist probably doesn't hold you naked and stroke your cock."

He gets a sneaky grin on his face and says, "I went to a holistic therapist in the Village once." When he says "holistic" he widens his eyes, and his face takes on a leer as if everyone knows "holistic" means "anything goes." "We did everything!"

My next-door neighbor Vinny used to have a German boyfriend named Hans living with him for a while. Hans fielded all the sex calls that came in from Vinny's massage ad. Vinny didn't want to do sex work, but Hans was happy to take those clients. One day Hans and I got to talking, and he described having a session with a guy who I realized had to be Al. He came in, got naked, wanted Hans to lie on top of him, then turned over and jerked himself off, then got dressed and left. The whole session took 20 minutes and Hans got $100. I remember being jealous, hearing that story. I spend almost two hours with this guy, stroking him and listening to his stories and letting him believe he's an underloved, misunderstood man having a midlife crisis, and I get paid the same amount.

So why do I do it? Mainly because I can't do it any other way. I don't blame anyone for wanting to have sex. But jerking someone off and sending them away isn't good enough for me. That feels like vampirism, and the one who benefits is not me; the bloodsucker walks out the door, and I'm left with a small pile of cash, but my energy drained away.

So what makes the difference? If I give a guy a full massage and then jerk him off, somehow it's different?

For me, it is. Because in that space of time, in the hour it takes to do a full massage, we've been breathing together. We've been adjusting the rhythms of our bodies. And he's been relaxing, surrendering, letting go of muscle tension, turning down the volume of his mental chatter, opening up the channels of sensation. When someone comes in and you jerk him off as soon as possible, he hardly feels anything. It feels like a waste of my energy to do that. I'd rather my partner feel something. And if I can get him to breathe deeply and vigorously and let go of tension and build erotic energy for a long time, even better.

I realize that part of my job is to teach men how to have sex, how to enjoy their sexual bodies. After all, who teaches a gay man how to have sex? Heterosexuals are surrounded by love stories in movies, books, and TV shows that lead kids right up to the bed, and often beyond, so they have a good head start at knowing how the game is played. All that's left for them to do is to practice. Gay men have a deficit in that regard.

A whole literature of books and records and movies and videos and magazines has sprung up in the last 25 years so if you're sufficiently motivated, you can find what you need. But the kind of guys who patronize erotic masseurs often don't identify as "gay." They're clearly not 100% "straight." "Closeted" would be accurate if judgmental. I prefer to call them "undeclared."

These guys are likely to have experienced sex with men only in environments that are anything but conducive to great sex: movie theaters, porn shops, sex clubs, back rooms, bathrooms, rest stops, bath houses. It's possible to have great sex in these circumstances, but first you've got to know how to have great sex. You're not likely to learn in any of those places how to fully inhabit your body, how to breathe, how to connect your actions with your feelings, how to know what you want, how to ask for what you want, how to touch someone in the way they like to be touched, how to receive the touch you like, or how to negotiate all these things. You can study porn films, of course, but in porn movies, it's rare that people speak more than one or two sentences before diving deep into raw sex.

Let's face it, sex in porn movies is as much like real sex in bed with a real person as the World Series is like playing catch in your backyard.

Maybe I'm creating an elaborate rationalization for my line of work. It's true, though, that many guys come to me who seem completely prepared for me to get them turned on and get them off in no time flat — cut to the chase, get down to business. But I slow the whole process down, so by the time they feel dick-pleasure and cum (if they cum), they feel it all over their bodies. Some guys don't know how to deal with that because it's an almost revolutionary concept. Hardly anyone has sex that way, including me. But in my work, I try to offer the best experience of erotic energy I can imagine.

The work that I do is about erotic pleasure. As I mentioned before, one of my most faithful clients gave me the best name for my occupation: "pleasure activist." Pleasure is only part of the story though. Ultimately, it's about experiencing erotic pleasure without separating it from everything else in your life. That's the rare thing, the novelty, what you don't get every day: an invitation to connect your emotional body to your physical body to your erotic body to your creativity and your politics and your prayers and your imagination. The combination is what makes it a transcendent experience. In that state of openness, you can drop your social self-definition and let yourself expand to your full size, which is infinite. The erotic pleasure is a river that leads to the sea of spiritual experience.

It's so simple. It's so powerful. And it all starts with a boner.

CHAPTER FIVE

Boners

I like it best when a guy goes through several erections during a session. This is something those books on "The Art of Sensual Massage" never talk about. I love those books, but they're full of pictures of beautiful models posing in front of fireplaces and they hardly ever talk about boners. Here's the way it usually goes with me.

Boner #1 comes early on, sometimes as soon as he walks in the door, or as soon as he strips down to his underpants, but often it's when I first start touching him. He's lying flat on his back, I've put on some music, I rub my hands together to create some warmth, I ask him to breathe a few times, he closes his eyes, and I put one hand on his chest and one hand on his belly. Then I move the belly hand to his hip and start rocking him gently, from the hips, loosening him up. I rock his legs, one by one, then his chest, then move to his head and put my hands on his shoulders and rock him up and down. Then I stretch his arms out and massage his hands, and that's when Boner #1 goes down.

Boner #2 often happens when I turn him over on his belly and rock him again on that side. Guys will usually tuck their dicks between their legs out flat, so I can see their dicks peeking out from between their legs. Maybe it's a sign of guys who are anal-erotic, that when their bare butts are exposed to the masseur, they get turned on. That one goes away quickly and stays down while I do a thorough job on the upper body.

Boner #3 usually happens when I start on the legs by putting some extra oil on my hands and lightly running them up the inside of his thigh, letting the side of my hand slide up into the crack of his butt. This brings many sighs and moans, even sobs of joy. Many bright-red dickheads appear from under the folds of the scrotum at this point. Sometimes Boner #3 keeps going continuously from one leg to the other, sometimes it droops as I firmly massage the thigh and calf, and then move to the other side and work on the other buttock before moving down to the inner thigh. When I move to massage the feet, Boner #3 always goes away. Some guys doze off at this point. Foot massage is probably the biggest sedative in a massage session.

When I'm done with the feet, I kneel at the end of the table and work my way up the legs again and do some more buttock massage, pulling the cheeks apart and stretching the butthole open. I don't do this every time, but with people who seem to be up for an extremely erotic massage, I always do. Enter Boner #4. I sometimes lightly stroke the hairs around the butthole and then cup my hand over the butthole, with the heel of my hand on the sitz bones, and rock his body. You can move the whole body that way. Then I finish with some long strokes and say, "When you're ready, you can turn over." And often a pleasing sight greets me: big fresh Boner #4, or what's equally pleasing, the remains of Boner #4 with a thin stream of pre-cum trailing from the head of the dick to his thigh. There's always a relaxed smile of pleasure on his face at this point.

Boner #5 usually happens when I brush the full-length of his body along the tips of his body hair, from the neck to the toes and back, down the arms, then to the belly. Sometimes, if it seems right, and if I feel bold, I will continue this dry light brushing up and down the legs with one hand while the other gently strokes his nipples. For the nipple-erotic tribe, boneration is invariably accomplished tout suite. Then I will go into full-body oiling, belly rub, and then concentrated genital massage. For some guys Boner #5 stays up for the rest of the session. For others it will come and go for 20 minutes, as I work on distant parts of the body and coach them to breathe deeply. If they're getting close to squirting too soon, I slap their chests or thighs or belly to draw the energy away from the pelvis.

You get the picture. To spend an hour and 15 minutes in a state of almost continuous erotic arousal, with erections coming and going, makes for a different body state than one erection continuously stimulated until it squirts, which Kinsey reported takes most American men an average of 4 to 6 minutes from down to up and down again. When I'm done with an erotic massage, the guy on the table is in an altered state.

CHAPTER SIX

Al (Part 2)

What actually happened with Al? He told me about spending the weekend with an old friend of his who has a house out of the city. His friend has a jacuzzi, which they sat in together. They didn't do anything sexual or touch each other, but Al got a thrill purely from being naked with another man.

That's something urban gay men who are out of the closet and sexually active sacrifice after awhile — the excitement of near-sex that makes your blood run cold, that heightens your senses, that makes soft-core situations (locker rooms, showers, glimpses of male nudity) as good as actual contact. If not better. Your imagination polishes all the edges or roughens them up to your exact taste. It's been a long time since I've gotten excited simply being near another naked man. For me it's often a relaxing environment but not one where I have to make something happen.

Al was saying that his friends were on to him. They teased him one time, saying, "Do you like to suck cock or eat pussy?" He fended them off with macho bluster: "What, are you crazy?" But it made him nervous that they would even ask such a thing. He told his sister that he is attracted to men. His therapist knows, of course. He's in group therapy, as well, and the people in his group know. I wondered to myself if he told them all the details he was spilling right now — how often he goes to the dirty bookstore on West 81st Street, all the men's rooms that he's scoped out in midtown, at the Hilton, at the Marriott Marquis. I decided not to flatter myself by thinking I'm some kind of special confidant. This guy Al is such a motormouth. Despite his agonizing about being in the closet, he probably tells these stories everywhere he goes. He's begging for something to happen to break his life wide open, something that he doesn't have to take responsibility for, like someone calling his wife, or his wife catching him at something.

When I thought about Al objectively, I could see that his life has taught him to be manipulative and a bit self-deluded. In the moment, though, lying in bed, stroking his boner through his underpants, I found myself intrigued to watch where this encounter would lead.

There was a lull in the conversation, and it felt like some kind of request needed to be made. It would be easy for me to slip into sexual service mode, but for a change I wasn't going to offer anything. I wanted to see what Al would come up with. Finally, he said, "I want us to hold each other naked."

"Oh yeah?" I said softly. I paused and interrupted my usual impulse, which is to do exactly what a client proposes. "What would that do for you?"

"It would make me feel closer to you." I recognized this as a learned script, guaranteed to manipulate a partner into sex, usually a guy talking to a girl. Why can't he just say, "I want my dick in your mouth"? Instead, he says, "I want to feel closer to you."

DADDY LOVER GOD 53

I noticed how nothing could ever please Al. We were lying chest to chest, touching intimately and tenderly. I felt a little bit like Groucho Marx with Margaret Dumont: "If I get any closer, I'll be on the other side of you."

Al's chatter was making me listless, though, and I was ready for some action myself. I didn't want to feel guilty when an hour and a half was up and all I'd done was listen. That's the difference between psychotherapy and erotic bodywork. A therapist is willing to sit for years, listening and sympathizing and collecting fees. I know there's a time for listening. And probably what Al needed most was someone to listen to him, not just touch him and make him squirt and squash his pain back in the can. But look, I'm a human being. There's only so much pretending I can take.

Without a word, I knelt over Al and pulled the waistband of his underpants down. He lifted his butt and then his legs as I pulled his shorts all the way off. I raised the shorts to my nose and sniffed them ostentatiously. They smelled clean. I put the shorts down on the comforter nearby. I looked down at Al, now completely naked and hard. Not a huge dick, kind of a little boy dick — average length, not especially thick, pointy at the end, tightly circumcised, no extra skin. I leaned down to lick his cock. I kissed the head of the cock, and then took the whole thing in my mouth. After a couple of strokes up and down, I automatically reached down between his legs and stroked his hairy balls, and then I stroked behind his balls. He had his feet flat on the bed with his knees up. I let my hand glide down farther, beyond the perineum and lightly touched the hairs in his buttcrack, and then pressed down with my fingers.

I stopped for a moment, then stroked Al's butthole again.

That confirmed it.

Sometime after Al took the car service home from the airport, before or after he changed into casual clothes to come see me, Al had taken care to lube up his butthole.

CHAPTER SEVEN

Looky-Loos

The phone rang in the afternoon. It was someone calling for information. I recognized the voice. It was a young Asian man who called himself Martin. He spoke broken English in a peculiar accent that never quite landed on a consonant. He wanted to know everything about the massage, and how much, and where was the location. He wanted to know when I was available. I did have some time in the evening. He wondered if 6:30 was okay. I said it was. He said he would call back. I put it out of my mind and went about my business. Later he called to ask if I was available at 7:30. I was. It was a slow day, and I was eager for work.

In the meantime, I had consulted the log I keep on my clients and refreshed my memory about the previous session I'd had with Martin. He was young, in his early twenties, a student at the Fashion Institute. He was a plain-looking lad with a pronounced overbite and thick black-framed glasses. Most of all, he was completely dead in his body. No muscles, no energy, shallow breathing. Still, he wanted an erotic experience. I remembered the session vividly. It wasn't fun. Drawing Martin into any kind of conversation had been difficult. I sort of dreaded seeing him again. But I needed the money, and he needed to be touched. So.

He called again, the third time in one day, to say he would be about ten minutes late for his 7:30 appointment and was that okay? "No problem," I said, although his inability to commit to a time was starting to get on my nerves. Then he asked, "What do you look like?"

This surprised me and annoyed me. That question usually comes in the first conversation if it's important to a client. When the client books the session and then asks "What do you look like?" it sounds like they're insecure. I'm sufficiently confident about my looks to figure that no one is going to be unhappy showing up for a massage and having me answer the door. So I rattled off for Martin my standard description: "I'm in my thirties, I work out at a gym, I'm in good shape." Never mind that I turned 40 recently. I felt comfortable with that description. I used to be more descriptive of my appearance: "I'm half-Portuguese, so I'm dark and hairy." But that's one big step onto the slippery slope to giving your height, weight, and penis dimensions, and I'm not going to engage in that level of body-shopping.

I know why people ask questions about what masseurs look like. Sometimes it's pure phone sex talk, to which the standard answer is "I'm 27, blond, buff, with a 10-inch dick." On the other hand, when you're going to a total stranger for touch, especially if you want sexual touch, you want to know more about who you're hiring for the occasion.

I assumed that Martin was satisfied with the description I gave. But when 7:45 rolled around and he hadn't rung my bell, I began to suspect he would be a no-show. By 8:00 when another caller wanted an appointment, I didn't hesitate to book it. Martin was obviously a goner.

It's part of the practice, but people who don't show up for appointments always piss me off. I've developed a few methods of reducing no-shows over the years. First of all, with a new client, I always book on a same-day basis. When someone answers an ad in the paper and wants a massage, he usually wants it within the next couple of hours. If he can't get it, he either loses interest, goes to the gym, beats off, hires someone else, gets drunk, or goes to sleep. Then, with a new client, I always try to get a phone number before booking the session. Before giving out my address, I'll call the guy back to verify the call. This has saved me several times, when I've called back to a number where there's no answer, given by some asshole – excuse me, some frightened individual who had no intention of booking a massage and was just whacking off while pretending to gather information.

Some guys are shy about giving out their phone numbers, out of paranoia that a masseur will suddenly start calling his home or workplace and letting it be known that he's (uh-oh!) getting a massage (wink wink). These are basically closet cases, or they have a wife or a lover from whom they want to keep their massage appointments secret. This attitude challenges my sense of compassion as well, but my strategy in those situations is to have the guy call from the nearest corner at the appointed time. Then I'll give him the address. The rule of thumb, which I learned from my massage mentor Wilson, is that two communications are a good sign that the guy is going to show up. In other words, if he calls for information, then calls back to book an appointment, you don't necessarily need to get his phone number. And obviously, if you've seen the guy before and he calls again, he's sufficiently motivated to keep the appointment.

Looking back, I realize I should have started smelling a no-show as soon as Martin asked, "What do you look like?" My experience is that most people who ask that question (as with those who ask "Is there a release?") do not make appointments. Maybe they do with other bodyworkers who are willing to talk more explicit phone-sex talk — "I'm hot, I'm hung, it's a complete session, I'll get you off." I suspect, though, that when people are shopping for their ideal fantasy sex-god, no mere mortal ever lives up to the fantasy. Porn stars, maybe, but not masseurs.

Another liability of the massage trade is the people who book a session, show up, take one look at you, invent some excuse why they have to leave, and don't come back. That does wonders for a bodyworker's self-esteem. I call them "looky-loos." They have the most plausible reasons for stepping out: gotta find a parking space, gotta go to the bank machine. Some haven't even bothered to invent an excuse. The first time it happened to me, I went to the door, and there was a tall white-haired senior executive type who took one look at me in my cut-off shorts, tank top, and bare feet and said, "I don't think so." I felt like going straight home to Dogpatch.

The scariest was the guy who marched into my studio, looked around, and demanded to know, "What's the story here?" I pointed to the table. "That's a massage table. I'm a masseur. You called me for a massage, remember?" The guy, a bundle of nerves in a bad suit with a potbelly and a goatee, craned his neck around, inspecting all the corners of the room. I could only imagine that he was expecting to get massaged by a broad and assumed that the guy who answered the phone was her pimp. He didn't stay.

Then there are the people who call up to stare at you over the phone. They don't say anything, they don't even breathe, they just listen to your voice and hang up. Whenever that happens, I usually spend the next half hour worrying that my voice isn't butch enough. I'll sit at my desk practicing, making my voice lower. Or maybe I need to cram "Hello" into one syllable: "H'lo." Maybe I need to add a few more suggestive syllables. Be more friendly, more effusive? Or more butch — sound like I just crawled out from under my pickup?

Sometimes working the phone is harder than doing the massage.

CHAPTER EIGHT

The Vampires

In the same day I encountered two different versions of what I think of as The Massage Vampire. These are the guys who study the bodywork ads in the *Village Voice*, and when a new ad appears they immediately call and book a session — once. They never return.

One version was Dr. Barry, notorious among masseurs in New York. He'd been to see everyone. He was a giant bald guy who had a jaded attitude about masseurs. He made no bones about checking you off his list. Maybe one reason he didn't go back to anyone a second time is that no one would have him, because he behaved so badly the first time. When I started my practice, Dr. Barry was one of my first clients. Since I hadn't yet solidified my boundaries, he crashed right through them, fondling me throughout the massage whenever he could sneak a grope.

At the time I felt conflicted. I'd gone into a bodywork practice with the loftiest ideals, inspired by my Body Electric training: to offer erotic touch and sexual healing to all men. So how could I object when men came to me wanting sex, or wanting to touch me? When I offered to massage someone's cock, how could I object or be surprised if the guy took it as an invitation to grab my cock? Why should you be the only one having fun? The truth is, I didn't like having Dr. Barry touch me. It wasn't just that he was morbidly obese. It was everything about his shifty demeanor, the way he wouldn't look me in the eye when he walked in the door, the way he never spoke or asked for anything but tested the waters with his hands to see how far he could go.

That's it, that's the challenge for the Massage Vampires — they want to see how far they can go. They have little mental checklists: will he let me feel him up? will he get naked? will he touch my cock? will he let me touch his cock? will he jerk me off? will he let me jerk him off? They're not satisfied until they've tried everything and succeeded.

In that first session I made my standard offer of erotic massage, and he said yes and proceeded to take license with me, even though I was fully clothed. I finally directed his hands back to his own body, but he wanted to see my dick, wanted me to get hard, wanted me to shoot. I wasn't interested in cumming but allowed myself to be talked into putting on a show, as if I were a dancer at the Gaiety Burlesk. He had to ask me to fetch his glasses so he could see the show properly, twisting to the side and jerking his own floppy uncut dick until he squirted.

When the session was over, he asked to use the phone to call his office and check his messages. Listening to his side of the conversation, I deduced that he was a pediatrician at a hospital on Long Island. A pediatrician! This slimy space-invader taking care of little kids?! My mind reeled.

After I moved to a new space with a different

phone number, Dr. Barry called again and booked an appointment, apparently not suspecting that he'd already seen me once. I wondered if these guys kept the phone numbers of masseurs in a database to make sure they never called the same one twice. I had figured out before he arrived that it was the same guy, so I was prepared this time. We made the same small talk as before. He talked about his house in Italy where he takes two week vacations several times a year. This time whenever he got grabby — lying on his belly, slowly creeping one hand out to stroke my leg or arm or crotch — I quickly put myself out of range. It was awkward trying to massage someone with a 90-inch waist at arm's length, but I accomplished it without ever having to get schoolmarmish — "Now young man, don't you try that kind of thing with me!" — or suffering in silence.

Whenever possible I would take his arm by the wrist and pin it down while I worked on his back or leg with the other hand. It seemed a bit extreme, but I reminded myself that he was truly one of those people who doesn't respect other people's boundaries, so you have to treat them like incorrigible children. He didn't complain, which made me suspect that he almost expected to be corralled and contained that way.

He kept lifting and waving his butt whenever I got near it. At first I thought, "I'm not going near that." But standing at his feet, I calculated that I could massage his butt and inner thighs without ever coming into his grope-range, so I relented and offered to put on gloves for some butt massage. This had the intended effect of pleasing and almost sedating him, though I was surprised when he murmured, "No penetration." I had gotten the impression that he had a hungry butt that like to be plowed and rarely got satisfaction. But he did seem satisfied indeed with my expert porch work.

By the time I turned him over, the allotted hour-

and-a-half was nearly up. As I started the neck-and-shoulder sequence I usually end with, he reached down around his giant pot belly and started fondling his dick, ignoring the calming meditative touch I was offering. I said, "We have to stop in a couple of minutes, but if you want to jerk yourself off, be my guest." He tensed up his legs, twisted his head to the side, almost jacknifing his body while he furiously pumped his cock.

"Whoa, whoa, whoa," I said, resting a hand on his giant belly. The behemoth halted his paroxyms. "The way you're tensing up your legs, you're blocking any of the sensation you might get from stroking your cock. If you keep breathing all the way down to your toes and relax your shoulders and your legs, you can circulate the good feeling from here" — I touched the underside of his balls — "all over your body."

He opened one eye, looked at me, closed his eye, and went into his seizure again, whacking his dick wildly, his thighs and feet locked in rigor mortis, his shoulders squeezed up to his ears.

Great, I thought. I've just given you this thorough relaxing massage, and now you're undoing the whole thing. I was momentarily furious. I may as well have stood back, lit a cigarette, and watched. It was all over in a minute. I laid a warm towel on him and wiped the oil off his skin. He rolled off the table and got dressed. He seemed to be perfectly satisfied and took my card. As if, I thought.

Later the same day, Dexter showed up. I recognized him at once and said so, but he didn't remember seeing me before. "I wonder if the massage was any good," he wondered aloud tactlessly. He was a middle-aged man with the overdeveloped pecs of a long-time gymgoer, but his muscles were covered with skin gone slack with age, and his flesh was entirely hairless. He was hard of hearing and wanted me to turn off all the lights in the room. I turned down all but the most basic work lights. He still complained it was too bright. I offered him a blindfold, but he declined.

As I started working on his back, he kept talking about how tight his hamstrings were, sighing any time I touched his buttocks. It dawned on me that this was one of those guys who is ashamed of what he likes about his body, who says "I'd like you to do some deep massage on my hamstrings" when he means to say is "I want you to massage my butthole." These guys are so ashamed of their erotic desires and having them fulfilled that they can't go see any masseur more than once.

Once again I found myself in a quandary. After giving Dexter the butt massage I knew he came for, I turned him over to massage the front of his body. We got to talking about the massive clump of fatty tissue on his abdomen, and then time was up. After I toweled him off, he started fondling himself and stretching voluptuously on the table.

"Oh, I feel so aroused," he said, wiggling his limp dick in his hand.

"You're feeling open and relaxed," I suggested, ostensibly trying to give him other words to describe his sensation, but also correcting him in that overbearing, you're-not-feeling-what-you-think-you're-feeling way.

"Yes," he said, clapping a hand onto my butt.

"How 'bout if we sit you up so I can towel your back off?" I said evenly.

"Oh, is it over?" He looked confused and surprised, but then recovered quickly and did as he was told.

I felt a pang of guilt. I knew Dexter expected that this massage would come "complete with release," and I could have suspended the backrub in time to incorporate cock massage to ejaculation. I told myself I was doing Dexter a service by manipulating the session so that he would have a strong erotic charge in his body without dissipating the feeling by ejaculating. I doubt if he'd agree, though, so who am I kidding?

Sometimes I act like a spy on a secret mission to induce spiritual experiences in men without them knowing it, but I don't think it works that way.

CHAPTER NINE

Full-Body Orgasm

Every so often I have a session that reminds me why I do this work in the first place.

Gerald arrived directly from the office, on his way to a business dinner. I hung up his navy blue Hugo Boss jacket, and he put the rest of his clothes on a chair. He left his fancy white boxer shorts on while we did some preliminary stretching. "Let your eyes gently close," I said. "Take a few big, easy breaths especially into the lower part of your body — your belly, your butt, your legs." This gave me a chance to check out his body, his alignment, his breathing. He was tall with shiny blond-brown hair, stocky, a little overweight. His head was small for his body, and he was starting to get a double chin. His shoulders were narrow. His body was okay, not unattractive, covered with a healthy coat of reddish-blond fur. I couldn't quite tell through his boxers, but I think he was half-hard at this point.

I talked him through a guided visualization that involved breathing and pulling solid-earth energy up the body — through his legs, hips, belly, chest, arms, shoulders, neck, to the top of his head. I had him stretch, shake, and bounce a few different ways before he lay down on the table. As he was undressing, he noticed the material on my information table and asked me, "What is Body Electric?"

"It's the school in California where I did a lot of my training," I replied. "They offer a state-certification training in Swedish/Esalen massage. But their distinction is that they also offer trainings in erotic massage as a healing practice."

He said, "Oh."

When he lay down on his back, he immediately got hard. He had a beautiful dick. His erection grew upwards in a graceful curve, tilting toward the left side. At full height it stood away from his body at a roughly 45-degree angle but curved upwards. I could tell that he had a lot of erotic energy in his body. He had exactly the kind of cock that I love to look at and especially to suck. It was smooth and pink, darker at the head, substantial in size without being huge, well-proportioned with a thick shaft and a bulbous head, circumcised as most of my clients' are.

I tried to ignore his boner and went about my business not saying anything for a while. After stretching out his second arm, while massaging his hand, I knew I wanted to broach the subject of erotic massage. I thought of all the times I didn't speak up and regretted it afterwards. I let a beat pass. Mustering my most casual voice, I asked him, "Do you want any erotic touch as part of the massage?" I looked at his face. He was lying with his eyes closed, and he didn't open them.

"Umm, well, yes, I think so. I don't know," he said, sounding a little flustered. "It's not the main thing I'm here for. I want to relax. I get aroused easily, though, and when I go to a regular masseur, I get embarrassed

about it. So I sometimes go for an erotic massage, but it isn't always what I want. They just ... " He trailed off.
"All they want to do is get you off," I suggested.
"Right."
"Yes," I said. "Well, when I do erotic massage, the intention is to raise and circulate erotic energy around the body without the goal of ejaculating. How does that sound to you?"
"Good. That's fine." He kept his eyes closed. He seemed embarrassed to be talking about this, but as I continued stretching him, I noticed that his cock had gotten a little harder, vibrating with arousal in anticipation of being touched by me before too long.

I turned him over and gave him a good, thorough back massage, from the tops of his shoulders to the bottoms of his feet. He had a small scar on his lower back that looked like a jellyfish, a glob in the middle surrounded by small dots. He had tucked his dick upwards rather than back, so I didn't have a chance to monitor the state of his erection through this part. He had hair all over his meaty buttocks as well as along the moist pink crack. I stretched his buttcheeks apart and did some firm massage with my thumbs along his sitz bones, which made him sigh: "Ohhhhhh." I cupped my palm over his butthole and rested the heel of my hand on his pelvic bone and then rocked his whole body back and forth, putting light pressure on that first-chakra point. "Ohhhhhh."

When I turned him over, he was fully erect. "How you doing?" I asked. "Fantastic," he said, opening his eyes for a second and then sinking back into his pleasure. I wiped my oily hands on a small towel and then went to the head of the table to do a neck-and-shoulder release. This is a Jin Shin Do move, touching five acupressure points in sequence: points in the armpit, the corners of the shoulder blades nearest the spine, the tops of the shoulders, along the neck, and at the base of the skull. This is a soothing, extremely relaxing sequence that never fails. If I meet someone who complains of achiness and needs a five-minute massage, I'll do a neck-and-shoulder release, and they'll often feel like they've had a full-body massage.

And usually, if a guy has a hard-on, it completely goes away during the neck-and-shoulder release. Gerald was no exception. Applying firm pressure to designated acupressure points draws energy away from the pelvic area and directs it to other parts of the body. Now his glorious phallus, which minutes ago strained toward the ceiling like a riled-up dog at the end of its leash, was just a penis, nestled softly in his pubic hair like a sleeping puppy, drooling clear liquid.

Not for long, though. I ran my hands lightly across the tips of his body hair, down to his feet, then back up to his chest. Gerald's nipples responded to the lightest touch by stiffening, so I ran my fingers back and forth, lightly plucking one nipple, then the other, as I trailed my fingers in a U up and down his thighs, featherdusting the hair on his balls as I went. By this time, the swannish upward curve had returned to Mr. Boner, which throbbed and twitched with his pulse.

I reached for a new bottle of warm oil and anointed the front of his body, starting with his belly, hairy chest, and arms. I was tempted to oil up his cock immediately, but I knew that he would remain charged up whether I touched his cock or not. Instead I followed my usual route, oiling up the legs. Then I put some more oil on my hands and applied it to his dick, which had softened slightly. He moaned when I first touched it. "Ahhhh." I stroked up once and down once, and then did the move that Joe Kramer calls "Cock Shiatsu": starting at the base of his cock I squeezed on either side with my thumb and forefinger, working my way up to the tip and back. By this time Gerald was again completely erect. With my right hand I lifted his balls, which were already tightening against his body, and circled my left hand around his scrotum where it attached to his body, so I was holding his balls tightly in my fist like a bouquet of flowers. I lightly ran the fingernails of my right hand over the bumpy surface of his scrotum, brushing the hairs and stroking the skin. I could tell this felt good by the way his dick jumped and turned a deeper shade of red. One of his balls seemed to be retreating into his body.

I let go of his balls and took his cock in my hand again. "As I mentioned before, Gerald," I said, looking at his face, "when I do this kind of erotic massage, the intention is to raise and circulate erotic energy without the goal of ejaculating." He opened his eyes for an instant, looked at me, and nodded. His face was flushed, and he seemed transported, high. "So if you feel yourself close to cumming, and you don't want to, be sure to let me know, so I can back off and keep working on you in other ways. Okay?" He nodded again. I reminded him to continue breathing and feeling all the sensations in his body. I massaged his belly and his chest, and then I knelt by his head, breathing into his ear and stroking his pebble-like nipples. He tilted his head toward mine, breathing along with me. I stood up and continued massaging his chest and belly, never neglecting his cock for more than a few seconds. I did a few of Joe Kramer's delicious Taoist erotic massage strokes: pulling the length of the cock in every direction ("Rock Around the Clock"), sliding both thumbs side-by-side on the sensitive spot just under the corona (the spot Joe Kramer calls "the gates of consciousness"), holding the stiffy in my left hand and running the flat of my right hand in circles against the tip ("Hairy Palm Sunday"), rubbing the cock quickly between my two hands as if it were a stick of wood ("Fire").

"Gerald," I said, "we have to stop in a few minutes. I want to let you know that you're welcome to squirt if you want, and you're also welcome to hold onto this energy and enjoy how it feels in your body." He nodded, "Uh huh." He kept his eyes closed. He seemed to be deliberating.

I waited a few seconds and then nudged him. "So what would you like to do?"

"I think I'd like to cum," he whispered.

"Okay," I said. "So keep breathing and keep feeling all the things you're feeling." I ran my hands down his chest and belly and began stroking his cock in a more traditional way, trading hands, running a hand along his inner thighs, all the things I know contribute to getting a man hot enough to shoot. I noticed that he kept tightening his legs and squeezing his butt. When he'd do that, I would put my hand against his hip and rock him from side to side until he relaxed his butt. Then I would return to stroking his cock. After he'd done that a few times, I said, "Gerald, try not to tighten your butt or lock your legs. Keep breathing all the way down to your toes." I had him take 20 faster breaths along with me while I stroked his chest and his cock, and then I instructed him to take three big deep breaths and make an "Ahhhh" sound on the exhalation while I rocked his body from side to side. Then I knelt at his head again and breathed into his ear while stroking his nipples.

This time I noticed that something had changed. His erection was starting to droop, and no amount of touching his nipples seemed to make it bounce or twitch. But he continued to breathe strongly. Slowly he lifted his hands and started to shake them. I was just about to say something when he beat me to it. "My hands feel so tingly, and my face, and my belly!"

"Uh huh," I said. I hung out near his head, resting one hand lightly on his shoulder, watching his body breath and move.

"Oh my God, it feels fantastic," he said. "As soon as you said 'Don't tighten your butt,' I realized I'd been holding in my belly and it was starting to hurt. As soon as I let go, I felt all this feeling move up my spine into my head."

I scanned his body and saw that his erection had totally dropped off to the side. He'd passed his peak. There was no point in squirting now. "What you're having," I said, "is a full-body orgasm without ejaculation."

"Yeah," he said. "I'd heard about that from watching a videotape on 'The Art of Erotic Massage,' but I didn't believe that it could happen."

Afterwards, Gerald was full of questions. He wanted books to read. He wanted to hug me and have sex with me. He wanted to tell me his life story. He wanted everything to happen at once. His life required him, though, to hop in the shower, slide his vibrating sheath of kundalini back into Hugo Boss, and rush off to dinner.

CHAPTER TEN

The Feeling Is Mutual

At first, I felt resentful when my clients didn't automatically view erotic massage as an inner journey to spiritual self-knowledge but just wanted to have sex with me. Eventually, I had to face that fact that, despite my fantasies of being a sort of detached and beatific ritual priest, sometimes I had the urge to merge with my clients. But I was suppressing those urges as low or inappropriate. A psychotherapist might point out that by "disowning" my own desires, I was "projecting" them onto my clients and judging them harshly for having the exact same feelings I was having.

When I came down off the Sacred Prostitute pedestal and trusted my own instincts, I realized that loving touch is something I need to give and get as much as any of my clients. And although I honestly never set out to be a prostitute selling sex, I found it surprisingly easy and natural to slide over the line from erotic massage to mutual interactive sex.

Especially if the client is as attractive as Wayne. He's

a red-haired Irishman who works as a personal trainer at a fancy gym downtown, and his body is a fantastic compact bundle of muscled masculinity. Working on him the first time, my heart pounded the whole time. I felt like Michelangelo's David had appeared in the flesh on my table.

When he called to book his second session, Wayne told me I give the best massage in town. I could tell he was also turned on by me, though he acted shy and modest about it. He leapt onto the table before I could see him get hard. When I turned him over, he had a giant erection. I did a lot of work on his arms, hands, neck, shoulders, etc. Then did the hair-brushing sequence — running my hands lightly across the tips of his body hair, from his chest to his feet and back — which got him hard again. Oiled him up, including his cock. When I stood at his head leaning over him, he started nuzzling my cock. I gave him permission to touch me back. I knelt on the table with my crotch in his face. Then I asked permission to taste his cock. "Go for it," he croaked, and I did.

We 69'd for a while. His cock was so big that I couldn't push it too far down my throat without some of it scraping my molars. But I took a lot of it in. I got the feeling that isn't what gets him going. Maybe he likes to get fucked. Or maybe he's squeamish and mostly like to jerk himself off.

I turned around and lay down on top of him. He wrapped his legs around me, and I nibbled his neck. We slid into lovemaking, and the temperature soared. But we only allowed it to go on for 60 seconds or so. Then I pulled back and got a little athletic. I spread his legs and buttsurfed him — running my hard cock up and down the crack of his ass — until he told me he was on the verge of cumming. "Me, too," I said. We jerked ourselves off spectacularly. It was exciting but over fast, and he had little interest in lingering. "You've got to get ready for your next client," he said. He was concerned that he'd nicked himself shaving his balls and some semen passed over them. Highly paranoid about HIV.

I'd love to see him again and again, for sex. But I suspect for Wayne I'm more valuable as a masseur, and in that situation I'm holding the space for him to have his experience. Therefore I can't let go and feel my feelings and ask for things. So where do I go to get healed? Have I maneuvered myself into a situation where I'm the giver and never the getter?

The thrill of mutual sexplay with massage clients is so often momentary. I like that excitement a lot, but there's somewhere else I want to go with it. I want to offer love in my work, the experience of love, to be in the room of love. If I "have sex" with someone — kiss, suck, fuck, squirt squirt — is that automatically love? Is it automatically not-love? Is it more loving to withhold sex? When does love look like sex, and when not? I keep thinking, "It's not enough to Just Have Sex." People can have sex every day; it's almost routine. But to have a powerful experience of your own body and soul and your potential, through breathing and connection and intention — that's something you don't get every day.

On the other hand, I give these sessions 8 or 10 or 12 times a week. The people who come to me have this experience once in a great while. For them, often the intimacy and touching and eroticism does have a big impact.

Gary arrived late for his first appointment. He'd called a few times and seemed nervous. Originally he booked only an hour, then he quickly decided he wanted an hour and a half. He requested dim lighting. He was jumpy at first. He had driven in from New Jersey and was still mentally racing to get here.

I got naked when he did. His butt seemed erotically active. He sighed when I massaged near it. So after working on his feet, I got up on the table and massaged his back. I did some buttsurfing. He said, "Don't stop."

After a while, I asked him if he wanted me to put on a glove and do some butt massage. He said yes. As I was doing it, he said, "I've never been ... you know."

I said, "Penetrated?"

"Yes," he said, "but I have fantasies about it." He described wet dreams where someone is just about to fuck him — then he cums and wakes up. I moved into him slowly and carefully. We talked through the whole thing.

"One part of me likes it and another part is scared."

"What's scary?"

"I wonder if it's safe."

I said, "I've got a glove on, and I'm massaging you with one finger."

"Can you see my asshole?" he asked. "Tell me what it looks like."

"It's beautiful," I said truthfully. "Masculine and hairy."

That was thrilling for him to hear.

I worked on him for a while, then withdrew my finger. He asked me to lie on top of him. As I rested the weight of my body on his, he wondered aloud, "What is the part of me that likes this?" He told me he's married and has two kids. He had tried to suppress the part of himself that likes to be with men, but it's coming out stronger now, and he's fighting the shame of it. He said he feared being judged by God.

"God created your sexuality," I told him, "and what God creates he doesn't judge." I recited the lines from Mary Oliver: *You do not have to be good/You do not have to walk on your knees for a hundred miles across the desert/ You only have to let the soft animal of your body love what it loves.*

After he left, I thought: *Great advice. If only I could act on it myself.*

CHAPTER ELEVEN

Daddy Practice

Having a massage practice altered the dynamics of my own sexuality, specifically my relationship to fucking, to being a "top." I'd never felt comfortable before as the active partner in fucking. I was always looking for the ideal eroticized Daddy, an older and more powerful man. I was accustomed to giving all the power in any interaction to my sexual partners. I must have unconsciously imitated the role I watched my mother play with my father. Though she was older, more educated, and more thoughtful than he, she did what society has programmed women to do. She made herself subservient to him, never challenged his authority, and bit her lip when she disagreed, the better to avoid his hot temper and alcoholic rage. On some level, I must have understood that she reaped erotic rewards for submerging her power and authority. And although I admired neither one as a child — I considered him tyrannical and her ineffectual — I identified with my mother as a co-victim of my father and learned to be accommodating as a survival strategy.

As a young man, then, I usually identified myself sexually as a bottom. My erotic life revolved around servicing my partners orally. It wasn't easy for me to surrender into being penetrated anally, but the fantasy held me in its strong grip. What I loved was the feeling of being surrounded, held, comforted, protected, taken care of, wrapped in a blanket of warm breathing large loving hairy male flesh. What I loved was the idea of surrendering, of opening, of being entered, of uniting with another, of cellularly dismantling my boundaries and merging in a rough sensual riverbank dream of masculine passion. What I didn't love was the fast flip, hard power, a hasty slap of cold lube, being punctured, and a brief brutal jab sawing my sphincter against which involuntarily I clenched my bowels and held my breath.

When I became an erotic masseur, I was the one in control of the session. I was responsible. I became the Daddy. If I neglected to take charge of the session, trouble was likely to set in. It took a while, but I warmed up to it. I began to assert myself as a "top," a power I'd been afraid of before. Working with my clients was Daddy practice to me, and I liked it. It was healing for me to reclaim the power I so readily gave away to other men. Luckily, it seemed to be healing for my clients as well.

A major part of taking the dominant Daddy role with my erotic massage clients involved proceeding beyond genital touching to anal penetration. I knew from my own experience that buttplay could be extremely pleasurable. I was also aware that many (if not most) gay men first experienced anal sex with a partner who was insensitive at best and often downright abusive — rape masquerading as routine gay sex. I made it my business to reclaim men's assholes as a site for deliciousness and ecstasy rather than shame and violation.

Of course, I had the benefit of being trained in anal massage by a master. Chester Mainard, a psychotherapist and bodyworker of Cherokee heritage, was on the faculty of the Body Electric School, where his specialty was conducting rituals and trainings around anal massage and the pleasures of the butt. Joe Kramer affectionately dubbed him "the Avatar of Assholes." Chester had a history of being raped, and he'd also worked at a medical school where he served as a demonstration model for physicians learning to give prostate exams. He'd devoted more time and love to the study of anal eroticism than anybody I'd ever heard of, with the possible exception of Dr. Jack Morin, the San Francisco psychologist who wrote the Bible on the subject, *Anal Pleasure and Health*.

In a week-long certificate training in "Advanced Anal Massage" (aka "Historic Butt Camp") at a retreat center in California, Chester insisted on a protocol of scrupulous hygiene for buttwork. Gloves were required for any anal contact; they weren't to touch anything else after touching someone's butt, and they were to be disposed of properly. His other cardinal rule was: buttplay should never be painful; if it is, you're going too fast or doing something wrong. In contrast to the primitive male programming — stick it in and keep pumping 'til it shoots — Chester demonstrated the distinctly different sensations attached to the external anal area, the sphincters (both of them — who knew?), and the internal area, including the prostate. He gave many people, including me, an invaluable education in relaxing, teasing, and pleasuring a man's butthole so it opens as naturally as a rosebud.

My clients became the overjoyed beneficiaries of my expertise in this field, though it often took them by surprise. Leonard, for instance. Apparently, he'd met me before, though I didn't remember him. Perhaps he was referred by another masseur, or he came to a massage class that I taught. Anyway, he was a giant fat guy, sexy in his way (his big-butt, I'm-wearing-a-wedding-ring way). After giving him a full backrub, I offered buttwork. He readily accepted. I worked on his butt for some time, and he loved it. His dick didn't seem particularly hard. He seemed to be enjoying butt massage as its own reward, which I was happy to observe.

Once you start pleasuring someone's butt, though, you're going to find you've got a hungry hole on your hands (or vice versa). When I stopped fingering his butt and peeled off the gloves, Leonard reached back to stroke my cock, which started to stiffen. I could have drawn a boundary right there. I could have reinforced the concept that buttwork could be an end in itself (so to speak) and didn't have to escalate to anything else. Instead, I asked him if he wanted me to put on a rubber. He said yes. I slid into him a little too fast. He said, "Ooh, it's been a long time." I slid out, put on some more lube, then eased into him again. He said it felt great. And I gave him the works, banged his butt, stroking his back, holding him around the enormous waist, holding his hand over his shoulder. It was hot, but I knew I didn't want to cum. Ejaculating dissipates my energy, and if I'm doing several sessions a day, I need all the energy I can get.

It got close to stopping time. I mentioned that to Leonard and asked if he wanted to squirt. He said, "I don't know. It feels so good having you inside me." But I started to wilt, so I pulled out, turned him over, and oiled up his belly and dick, which lay limp against his curly hair. I positioned myself at his head and played with his nipples and dick. Then I did my fail-safe move: I squatted over him, brushing his face with my balls and cock and hairy butt and tweaking his nipples, while he jerked himself off big time.

As he got dressed, he said, "This is not what I expected, but it was a pleasant surprise."

For me, too. I've often had the fleeting desire to merge with big sexy guys I massage, and I'm glad I got the opportunity to do it.

Before he left, he said, "I learned something about myself. I always thought I needed poppers to relax" (i.e., to get fucked) "and now I know that I don't."

Maybe I took Leonard farther down the road to erotic interaction than he wanted to go. He said he had a good time and I believed him. It's always possible, though, that my own need to satisfy my sexual curiosity overrode what was best for him. I notice how easy it is for me to shed my BVDs and step right into a pornographic movie.

That's what I did with Oscar, another sexy fat boy. I always enjoy seeing him because I know he likes to suck me and nuzzle my butt. Tonight his stubble scraped my ass. That didn't feel so hot, but him sucking me and me butt-surfing him felt glorious. Then he asked me to fuck him. The request turned me on. I was rock-hard and close to shooting. I put on a rubber and lubed him up. He was tight. "It's been a long time," he said. I slid my finger in first. "That feels so good." Then he wanted my cock. By then he was more relaxed. It felt good to both of us.

Oh! I thought to myself. I love this! I love fucking a big fat sexy dude in the ass, bouncing my hips against his butt.

After we were done, I toweled him off (we'd already gone 10 minutes overtime), I initiated a conversation about the erotic play we'd fallen into. I'd gotten a little concerned because we had never directly discussed it, and this session went farther than ever. What he told me was surprising.

He said he'd been off sex for about a year or so.

He hadn't felt like having sex at all even though he thought about it a lot. It had become a problem in his relationship. He and his lover had been to counseling about it. Finally, his therapist suggested Oscar go to a masseur for erotic massage. He said that I had jump-started his libido, and that his sex life with his lover has recommenced. He said that I've been like a sexual surrogate for him.

I was flattered, disconcerted, and happy to hear this. I made it a point to say I couldn't guarantee that I'd feel up to being erotic with him in every session. He readily agreed. And I said, "You seem to enjoy rimming me, but I do want to point out that it carries some risks of transmitting bacteria." He said, "Yeah, I know. It's a risk I choose to take."

I felt satisfied and clear about the transaction.

In sharp contrast to my session with Wayne last night. In our previous session, we'd upped the ante on our mutual attraction. I maneuvered things so I wound up slurping the crack of his clean, muscled butt while he sat on my face and sucked my dick — it was heaven! So last night I assumed we'd do some equally intimate playing.

This time he wanted to be fucked. By the time I got the rubber on, I wasn't hard enough to penetrate. I finger-fucked him for a while but ended up taking the rubber off. I thought he knew that, so when I got hard again and he guided me into his ass, I thought he was consenting to being fucked without a rubber. I asked him a couple of times, "Is this OK?"

This was taboo territory for me. Fucking without rubbers is the single biggest no-no in all the safe-sex literature. I'd never done it since the AIDS crisis erupted, except within the confines of a long-term relationship. Fucking with Wayne seemed dangerous, especially because he was my client and I felt responsibility for his safety. However, common sense told me that for HIV to be transmitted, it has to be present in the first place. I'd repeatedly tested negative for HIV, and I clearly communicated that to Wayne the first time I saw him. Although no safe-sex literature dared to say it at the time, I felt justified in believing that two HIV-negative men could choose to have unprotected anal sex without risking their health. Would I consent to being fucked without a rubber? Only if he didn't come inside me. My own personal safe-sex mantra was: As long as I don't take cum into my body, I'm okay. That meant that I only had sex with people I trusted not to cum inside me. [MFF: As previously noted, the emergence of pre-exposure prophylaxis, or PREP, transformed the gay world in 2015, making anal sex without condoms possible again, since the medication – Truvada or Descovy – offers protection again HIV infection. In the early 1990s, when these encounters occurred, everything about buttsex was surrounded by fear and caution.]

When Wayne and I stopped fucking (without cumming), he noticed I didn't have a rubber on my dick and got upset. Not upset enough to stop playing, though. He begged me to shoot all over his face. I obliged while he jerked himself off. But he immediately groped for a towel to wipe off his face and pronounced the feeling of cum on his face "disgusting." Then he said, "You fucked me without a rubber! I'll kill you!"

He was loud and angry at first, which frightened me. We had a long talk. He settled down. In addition to genuine surprise/fear about fucking without rubbers, he seemed to have a lot of guilt and shame about sex and a tendency toward freaking out afterwards. The whole episode left an extremely bad taste in my mouth.

It made me lay down the law with myself: Never fuck anybody bareback without explicit verbal approval acknowledging shared risks. [MFF: The term "bareback" evolved from being a renegade activity favored by men who already have HIV, to an edgy practice among knowledgeable players, to normalized behavior signifying "I'm on PREP."] And today I'm thinking: why have sex with massage clients at all? It seems to be messing me up, psychologically/ emotionally/spiritually. I can offer erotic massage without engaging in sex with people. Just stay clothed. Don't let people grab my dick or suck it. Don't get up on the table.

That sounds reasonable and professional. The thing is, I'm only now starting to enjoy my studliness, the powerful Daddy/top aspect of my sexual nature, which lay buried for so long. And I know with some people, and in some moods, sticking to the outline of Taoist erotic massage, with all the conscious breathing and refraining from ejaculation, seems sanctimonious and almost ludicrously inappropriate. Sometimes all I want to do is lie down on top of them and hump them to delirium. And sometimes I love to have my cock sucked.

When I take a step back and look at these intense, psychologically slippery erotic interactions with clients in the context of my whole practice, I realize I've strayed far away from the kind of conscious healing-and-teaching session I had with Gerald, which is what I'd like to be doing. Without a teacher, without a tradition, without anybody looking over my shoulder, I see how difficult it is to separate the "higher consciousness" of sex-as-healing from the alluring chaos of sex-as-sex.

CHAPTER TWELVE

Four Sessions with a Friend Who Has AIDS

I.
Scott learned today that he has an untreatable spinal ailment. He hadn't yet told his lover David. He needed to feel his grief and anger and sadness about that. He cried during the massage. He wanted to touch my hard cock and for me to hold him naked. It was a precious experience.

II.
I gave him a full body massage. His legs were tense and protective, his shoulders tight (especially the right), also his neck. I went into erotic massage as before, without asking this time. He started touching me back, groping me through my shorts. I got hard. I stood at his head, massaging his torso, brushing my chest hair against his face. He reached behind to stroke my butt. I took off my shorts. After some more massage, I laid down on top of him. He toyed with my butthole (which surprised me). He got semi-hard. He was happy to hold and hug and nuzzle and hump. We

kissed a little without tongues. Mutual j/o, no squirts. Next time I want to discuss this erotic work. Music for the session: Jan deGaetani singing Wolf, Dawn Upshaw singing Goethe lieder.

III.

He was feeling down. He was diagnosed with Pneumocystis Carinii Pneumonia (PCP) last week, and the first medication didn't work. He started today on pentamidine. His spinal condition is better, though, he said. His only precaution was that he couldn't breathe deeply.

I felt a little tentative massaging him, my fragile friend. And I suspected that he wasn't up for erotic work. Wrong. He was absolutely up for it, more than ever. When I asked if he wanted me to massage his cock, he nodded and started to touch me. I had a T-shirt and shorts on. It was a muggy, humid day. I asked if he wanted me to take my clothes off. He said yes. I said, "I warn you, I'm sweaty." He said, "Good."

We proceeded to have quite a romp. He stroked himself a lot, and he even sucked me a little. I perched over his face as he nuzzled and licked my balls and tasted my cock. I lay on top of him and did a little frottage. He held my hard cock in his hands while I moved my hips, so I was fucking his fist. He loved that. He jerked himself while I jerked myself, bumping my hand against his butt. I raised his legs and humped his butt a little bit. He liked it all. It felt hot to me, too.

I considered cumming with him, for historical purposes. But it was time to stop.

I invited him to keep feeling his feelings. "Remember, Scott," I said, "that it's possible to have PCP and feel this good."

He said he felt better than he'd felt in weeks. There was a thunderstorm raging outside, and he said, "Do you think the gods disapprove?" I told him the rain was a blessing — they were cheering us on. (But I notice his sex shame/guilt.)

IV.

He's mending well from PCP; the pentamidine works. He has another week of therapy to go.

When he got on the table, he said that something had happened after our last session: he'd managed to get a firm erection and have good sex with David, and he attributed it to me. He said what meant the most to him was my saying "You can have PCP and still feel this good." He said he's been so serious about taking care of himself that he sometimes forgets he can also have fun and feel good.

I was moved by what he said.

He also rather somberly mentioned sucking me in our last session and wondered if it was okay with me. I told him I like it if people ask first, but it was fine.

"I take it from what you're saying that full-body massage with erotic work is a good combo for you."

He said, "Yes." So that got clear.

Much like before: he sucked me happily, jerked himself, I stroked his cock, his nipples, some frottage, some kissing. Hot, loving, holy.

Afterwards he told me he's never been happier in his life than he is now.

*

Sweet as these sessions were, I can't let them stand without acknowledging an awkward undercurrent. After I'd seen Scott twice, David called me and arranged to buy four sessions in advance as a birthday present for Scott. I couldn't tell if Scott had discussed with David the erotic component of the massages he got from me. The evening after our fourth session, I found a single crab louse on my hairy belly. In a spasm of professional integrity, I decided I should share this information with Scott, lest he come down with crabs and give them to

David. When I called Scott's line, David picked up. I asked for Scott, who was standing nearby, and blurted out my reason for calling. He thanked me calmly and we hung up without any further conversation. I immediately felt that I'd put Scott in an awkward situation of having to answer David's question, "What did Don want?"

I never found out how he handled it. Although his health went up and down until he died several months later, he never used the remainder of his gift massages. I still socialize sometimes with David, whom I consider a friend, and I'm haunted by the fear that he resents me for having sex with Scott. I wish we could talk about it. I give erotic massage to numerous men with wives or spouse equivalents, and I wonder: do their partners know? Would they be upset, or would they give me their blessing? I choose to believe that they want the same thing I want: the spiritual health and erotic well-being of my client.

CHAPTER THIRTEEN

Oral Hygiene

"Let me ask you a question," said my writer friend Vito. "When you're doing an erotic massage, and somebody cums, how do you control it?"

"What do you mean, control it?" I wondered.

"Well, let me put it this way," he said. "I've never masturbated a man, so I don't know quite how it works. But I don't think you always know where it's going to land. I mean, aren't you afraid of it flying all over and getting on your furniture?"

I love it when Vito questions me about my massage practice. Though he's straight and in some ways endearingly square, he's not judgmental or squeamish. (Well, maybe a little squeamish — he kept saying "it" rather than "cum" or "jizz.") He has a thoroughly energetic and mildly titillated curiosity about the ins and outs of what I do for a living.

I laughed at Vito's image of semen flying uncontrollably around the room. "It's a pretty scientific process," I said. "You'd be surprised. Some men shoot over their heads, but that's rare. Usually it lands on their bellies, and sometimes it just kind of drools out and forms a puddle on top of their pubic hair."

"But what if it hit you in the face or got in your eyes?"

"Aha," I said. "Now I see what you're getting at. You're worrying about HIV transmission and the safety of all this cum flying around."

Vito admitted that he was. I remembered that Vito was conscientious about HIV transmission. His brother died of AIDS, and Vito nursed him during his final months, when he had to have daily injections of ganciclovir to prevent him from going blind. One day after Vito injected the medication into his brother's Hickman catheter, he accidentally dropped the used syringe on his bare foot, sticking himself on the big toe so it bled. Vito spent the rest of the day calling every AIDS hotline in town to discuss what happened and to seek advice. He immediately got tested for HIV. Waiting for the results to come back, which took a week, he considered himself doomed. He contemplated whether to spend his last few months plotting political assassination or to commit suicide outright. It took several months and a second HIV test to quell his panic and assure him that he didn't pick up HIV from a syringe that, after all, never made contact with his brother's blood anyway.

That's another difference between gay men and straight people. There are many questions about HIV no one knows the answers to. But gay men have spent more than a decade on the battlefield, nursing the sick and dying and burying the casualties. Meanwhile, we've been renegotiating how to have touch and sex and affection with one another. Every gay man has gone through a period of pondering all the questions and mapping out all the gray areas: is it safe to kiss? to suck cock? to swallow cum? to fuck with rubbers? to fuck without rubbers if you don't cum? Sometimes it takes a week, sometimes a year, sometimes ten years, but eventually we all figure out what level of risk we're comfortable with and go about our lives accordingly.

Probably the biggest lesson anybody learned from this experience is that life is never risk-free. One of the most frequently mouthed cliches of the epidemic has to do with the foolishness of living your life trying to protect yourself from every teeny-tiny sliver of a risk: "I could get hit by a bus tomorrow." People do get hit by buses, and gunned down on the Long Island Railroad, and pushed in front of subway cars by deranged adolescents. Hijacked planes topple 110-story buildings, burying 3000 people at a time. But most people ride the subways and walk the streets and tongue-kiss lovers and go to work without suffering dire consequences.

After lunch, Vito and I stopped and browsed at the used book tables in front of the NYU library across from Washington Square Park. Vito found a D.H. Lawrence paperback he'd been looking for. I impulsively bought it as a present and gave it to him. We walked to the end of the block and parted ways, Vito to his apartment in Soho and me to the subway. On the way home, I realized I never spend any time thinking about the risks I take in my sex life. I thought I'd enumerate them, for my own edification if not for Vito's.

"I'm not afraid to kiss." The first person I had sex with that I knew had AIDS was Bob. We had an ardent love affair, but Bob was scrupulous about HIV transmission. We never kissed with open mouths. We did a lot of rolling around and hugging. Most of our sex was frottage. He loved to lie on his belly while I humped his butt from behind. He loved it when I shot my load on his back, and then he often liked to cum inside his own jockey shorts. The few times we engaged in cocksucking or buttplay, we always used rubbers, but that was rare.

Since then, and probably before, I've kissed numerous lovers who were HIV-positive. There were a few scattered days when I was aware of having a sore in my mouth, so I refrained from kissing, but mostly I accept that kissing is safe. What are the scary edges of that? Sores in the mouth are the main possible entry for oral transmission of HIV, but it's not like I have root canal work done every other week. I can't imagine feeling up to tongue-kissing if I had.

There were times, though, when I had a date scheduled that I would get upset if I accidentally bit my lip or the inside of my cheek. I would worry about it beforehand, but it would rarely prevent me from kissing. I do make it a point not to floss my teeth right before having sex with anyone — cuts in the gums are probably another major entry point in the mouth for HIV. Instead of brushing my teeth, I sometimes rinse my mouth with Listerine before a date, although a safe-sex educator once told me that the alcohol in mouthwash brings all the blood to the surface for a period of time, which may not be the greatest thing in terms of safe sex. Basically I decided long ago that a life without kissing is a life not worth living.

"I'm not afraid to suck cock." That wasn't always the case. I remember the time at a Radical Faerie gathering when I was having rambunctious sex with an artist from Seattle who'd casually mentioned in the morning circle that he was positive. I suddenly lost my hard-on sucking the guy because I started worrying about how safe it was to be doing that.

The arguments about unprotected oral sex go around and around in circles. Basically, the authorities have no idea whether it's safe, or how to make it safe. Apparently HIV does show up in samples of saliva and pre-cum, and apparently people have been infected who only had unprotected oral sex. It obviously doesn't happen every time, or there wouldn't be a single gay man left alive in New York City. I considered all the evidence and weighed the risks. I hated the thought of revising my own private safe-sex guidelines over and over again. I also wanted to avoid the habit that so many people fall into — relaxing safe-sex guidelines ("in the heat of the moment," as the cliche goes), then freaking out, then hysterically getting tested, then living in dread until the results came back, swearing and praying "God, please, let me test negative and I'll never put another raw cock in my mouth again, I swear it, I swear it, I promise on my stack of Barbra Streisand CDs." And then beginning the whole cycle all over again, from the top.

So I suck dick. Mainly, because there isn't anything else in the world I love more. Not listening to music, not spending money, not eating a delicious meal at an Italian restaurant, not lying on a grassy hillside on a sunny day. Nothing beats cocksucking. Truly, if it's a choice between dying from a blowjob or living without oral sex, I'll go to my grave an unrepentant cocksucker. In truth I believe it's a low-risk proposition if I never swallow cum. All the safe-sex literature makes it abundantly clear that HIV is transmitted through blood and semen. If infected blood or semen never enter my body, I'm safe. I don't worry about precum. I've clearly swallowed gallons of precum in my life, and I've tested negative eight years running. [MFF: the advent of PREP has made swallowing cum an ostensibly safe pleasure again.]

There are other risks I take. I like to eat butt — a taste cultivated only recently. No problem with HIV, as far as anyone can say, but there were always those pesky parasites. I've never had amoebas, as far as I know, though sometimes I've had stomach ailments and near-diarrhea that made me suspect I'd eaten a dirty butt. Even though I've been thoroughly trained in the 100% safe art of using Saran Wrap to eat butt, I never do. I eat it raw.

What other risks do I take? I sometimes engage in the dangerous borderline dickhead-at-the-butthole maneuver, both as top and bottom, where the dick never slides all the way in, but there are moments when the head is definitely past the sphincter. This is a situation that I find indescribably arousing, and much more pleasurable than full-body butt-banging, without a doubt. I'm not so much worried about doing this butthole-teasing when I'm the top; I'm confident about my HIV status and know I'm not endangering my partner. But I occasionally ride the tip of someone's dick, and a few other guys have slipped it in. I usually felt nervous and thrilled at toying with this taboo, but I haven't been fucked without a rubber in ten years, and I'd never let anyone cum in my ass. [MFF: It was absolutely a red-letter day when PREP made it acceptable to fuck without rubbers and take cum up the ass.]

Other risks? I never worry about handling the shit or piss or blood or vomit of friends who are sick. I'm careful enough and wash my hands a lot, but I almost always feel I'm more likely to pose a health hazard to an immune-compromised person than vice versa.

In truth, I'm not afraid of AIDS. I don't live in fear of it. I take much bigger risks emotionally, and I keep coming back for more.

CHAPTER FOURTEEN

The Client-Husbands

Sunday is often a busy day, but yesterday was slow. Two sessions, neither of them strictly speaking a massage. It was an afternoon with what I call my client-husbands. There are several of them now among my regulars, men with whom the work has gone beyond erotic massage and into the realm of sacred intimate work, where anything is possible. Sometimes it's a dilemma when more than one of my client-husbands call to book sessions on the same day. They take up a lot of energy, and I prefer to see no more than one a day.

But these two yesterday, Eugene and Lester, were so vastly different that I didn't mind seeing them one right after the other. In fact, it made the afternoon fun.

Eugene is one of my most intriguing clients. A handsome, rich, and successful African-American book publisher with two kids and a soon-to-be-ex-wife, Eugene turned 44 recently and decided it was time to do some of the things he'd always dreamed about but never done. Being with a man was one of those things.

He'd gotten massaged at his health club, but he called me for a private session out of curiosity to see what might happen. I quickly discovered Eugene's pleasure spot was his butt, especially the tender pink skin around his butthole, stroked by a finger or a tongue or the firm head of a hard cock. What surprised me, though, was how eager Eugene was for hugging and kissing and friendly affectionate interaction. He didn't seem to have a shred of sex-shame or body-shame. I couldn't bring myself to think of him as heterosexual; he was just sexual, period.

Our first few sessions set a pattern. I would stretch him out and massage his back thoroughly, relaxing him and working out the kinks. Eugene was fairly relaxed anyway; he took care of his body and always stopped at his health club to shower and groom himself before a session. I would work my way down his body to his butt and legs, applying firm pressure when kneading his buttocks, sliding my warm oily hands lightly over his inner thighs (always producing a beautiful cherry-red boner), working on his feet to let the erotic energy subside, then stroking back up the legs to spend time on his butt.

After some stretching, stroking, and rocking, Eugene would be loosened up and ready for further exploration. At first, I put on gloves and gave him a full-scale internal prostate massage. But after a few sessions we discussed it, and I learned that Eugene preferred the external butt stroking to penetration. What he liked the most was for me to lie on top of him, resting the full weight of my body on his back, and tease his butthole with the head of my dick. I would wrap my hands around his pecs and pull him close, nuzzling the back of his neck with my lips and teeth, while he writhed and pushed his butt back against my hips. Sometimes I would get so hot doing this that

I would squirt prematurely onto his back, which he never seemed to mind. In fact, he said it turned him on. Inevitably he would roll over and pull me on top of him for some deep tongue-kissing. He would let his huge warm hand slide down my body until it rested over my hairy butt, and we would proceed from there until he was ready to climax. I didn't bother trying to convince Eugene to contain his erotic energy. He was so highly charged, there was no stopping him from cumming.

Eugene was full of euphemisms. I enjoyed hearing them and liked to torture them out of him by asking point-blank, "What is the experience you would like to have today?" Eugene was much too polite and respectful to say, "I want you to chow down on my joint" or "Put it up my ass, baby, the way you know I like it." No no no no no. He'd say things like, "Well, I like part one of the massage, and then I'd like to move to part two." Or he'd say, "Depending on how you're feeling, I'd like to have an 'interesting' session rather than a conventional one."

Yesterday, when I asked the question, Eugene dropped the expression "role play." This puzzled me. In the gay world, role-playing generally takes place in SM relationships and the roles are severely defined. Dominant and submissive are the most common, but they can also be as benign as big brother/little brother. Somehow I didn't think that's what Eugene had in mind. Then it dawned on me that for a straight guy accustomed to taking the initiative with women and always dominating, simply to lie back and have someone else take care of you is a role-reversal. What to me seemed like a natural, reciprocal interaction — two guys rolling around together, alternating top and bottom — Eugene considered a psychologically risky abdication of male gender behavior. Ideal recipe for good sex.

The breakthrough session with Eugene came when I asked him to close his eyes and think for a minute and tell me exactly what experience he wanted. Eugene hesitated and said shyly, "I want to make love." I rejoiced that he had stated his desire so directly. That night we abandoned the massage table. I pulled down the comforter on my futon, and we spent a lovely hour in bed together. It was the first time Eugene ever had a penis in his mouth. Looking up from between my legs, where he'd been attentively stroking my cock, he murmured, "Can I taste it?" When he got permission, he was trembling. I ran my hand across his short curly hair. "Take your time," I said. "Enjoy it. Let yourself taste my cock. Feel what it feels like in your mouth."

Getting blowjobs from novices isn't the most exciting thing in the world, especially when they get hasty and frenzied and their teeth get in the way. That's why I like to slow them down, to get more tongue, more spit. There's a sort of regression that takes place. Sucking dick is like nursing, and it takes a few minutes to relax and get into it, to go back to the infantile pleasure of sucking for the sake of sucking. For grown men, I notice, infantile feelings often bring up a lot of shame. It feels too good to be that helpless, and that's not permitted. It's a macho thing, too — the man has got to be in control, and one way that shows up in cocksucking is the sucker feels he has to work hard to make the guy cum, so the pleasure of simply sucking gets lost in the mechanical function and the power struggle.

I watched Eugene sucking me with the peaceful detachment of a mother watching her child nurse. "This is what it's like to be a sacred intimate," I thought. "I don't feel the urgent need to cum or control the situation. I'm content to be present and let Eugene try on this behavior. There are harder ways to make a living."

Yesterday we had one of our "interesting" sessions. Eugene called earlier in the day than usual and arrived for an appointment at noon. We undressed each other and proceeded to sprawl on my bed. The early afternoon sun joined us. In the direct sunlight his skin changed colors. Where I licked his thigh, the wet spot shone yellow against brown. I loved seeing the clear sparkle of precum on the tip of his undying erection in direct sunlight. And the blanket of skylight added a layer of warmth to the crush of our hairy chests together.

"I missed you," Eugene murmured in my ear as he lifted his knees and wrapped them around my waist.

For a fleeting moment I wondered how I felt about Eugene. I know this will sound funny, but I try not to have personal feelings toward any of my clients. It's specifically because I have no future with any of the men I see that I can bring to them a radical presence. In a way, I treat all my clients the same way – as a combination of Daddy, lover, and God. Sometimes I get lonely after they leave. Sometimes I entertain fantasies that a relationship with a client could expand into something larger and more unpredictable — if not a domestic partnership, then some kind of glamorous or romantic partnership of courtesan and patron, with free trips to exotic destinations. But I know I can only get hurt if I expect anything from them. The last time Eugene had visited, he was on his way to a blind date with a famous black opera diva. When he didn't call for three weeks, after a pattern of coming to see me every week, I assumed that Eugene had clicked with the diva and decided to terminate his exploration of mansex.

So my heart lifted and opened at Eugene's tender confession.

"I missed you, too," I said.

In some ways this is the best kind of lovemaking on earth. Both of us set aside time to be together, devoting ourselves to pleasure and connection. All the sex manuals and marriage counselors advise couples to set aside time for lovemaking, but how many people actually do that? In my experience, scheduling lovemaking usually creates anxiety and resentment and imitations of arousal. In the context of a sacred intimate session, both parties rise to the occasion. Of course, there is a financial transaction — the client wants to get his money's worth, and the professional wants to earn his keep. Marxists might call this the commodification of desire, and Puritans might frown on the sale of what should properly be given freely. Sometimes I feel cynical about the work and observe myself going through the motions. I'm performing work-for-hire masquerading as unconditional love. I'm peddling counterfeit romance to men too deprived or depraved to complain. Those are the accusations I fling at myself.

But in the best of times, the work feels not like consumer carnality but focused ritual. Ritual in the sense of creating time out of time with a specific intention. We are here not to talk about the weather or the stock market, or to run power trips on each other, but to do something we don't get many opportunities to do — open our hearts and bodies to someone else.

I must have been getting a little corny and overly spiritual in my reverie because Eugene suddenly raised his head and looked me in the eye. "When are we going to go all the way?" he asked. Then I remembered that I was dealing with a straight man, whose experience of sex centers on intercourse-to-ejaculation, in contrast to which everything else is hors d'oeurves.

"Going all the way" with Eugene tempts me. If there is any scenario that justifies fucking without rubbers, here's a good one — a "straight" guy who's never been fucked, a wealthy businessman with no drug habits.

I'm as certain as I can be that I'm HIV-negative. What would be the harm of going in bareback? He'd love it. I'd love it. Skip that awkward moment of freezing the pelvis while struggling with the condom pack (not easy to rip open with lube-smeared fingers), trying to stay hard while putting the rubber on, inevitably putting it on upside down to begin with, reservoir tip UP so the rest of it rolls DOWN the shaft, and then aiming for the hole and hoping it yields immediately so the friction of sliding in and out can rejuvenate any diminishment of erection...

I wondered what Eugene did with the women he slept with. Did he use rubbers? Did they insist? Eugene clearly has no trouble staying hard. He's usually hard the entire time he spends with me.

The angel choir of Safe Sex Precautions and Professional Integrity danced in my head, with some semi-legal language about the "slippery slope." I have a responsibility! To educate guys who are out of the safe sex loop, exactly like Eugene! At the moment, I didn't feel like educating. So I avoided the whole question by positioning myself so he could feel my cock pulsing against his butthole, and I rocked my hips against the back of his butt and thighs, for that all-important first chakra awakening sensation. For me, hardly anything feels better than butthole-surfing. Still, I knew Eugene craved the sensation of penetration, if only out of curiosity.

Maybe it would happen another day.

CHAPTER FIFTEEN

Lester

When we were done, Eugene dressed slowly, chatting all the way. I didn't want to rush him, but as soon as the door closed, I had to rush around like a madman. I didn't have to put a fresh sheet on the table, because we'd skipped that part. But I saged the room, hopped in the shower, closed the curtains, and then changed clothes. Out of my sweat pants and T-shirt, into my leather pants, white tank-top, leather vest, and high-top Timberland boots: an outfit that predictably brought a sigh of pleasure from Lester when he came in the door.

Lester looks more like Humpty Dumpty than anyone I've ever met. A middle manager in his late 50s, he recently shaved his mustache and cut his white hair short, so his large head looks paler and more egg-like than ever. Over six feet tall, he probably weighs 250 pounds, including a big soft white under-exercised belly.

He walked in the door and handed me a black plastic shopping bag. Inside was a white plastic shopping bag with the handles tied in a knot. In addition to his usual

wrist and ankle restraints, he brought some new toys that he'd picked up cheap from a one-man bazaar at the Eagle: a black leather dog collar and a black Spandex hood with a single mouth-hole for breathing.
"Have you tried them out?" I asked.
"Yes," he said.
"How do they feel?"
"They feel great. I can see through the hood, though."
I instructed him to remove his black turtleneck, and I fastened the dog collar around his neck. I pulled the hood over his head and then went to my bureau drawer to get a foam-padded blackout blindfold and strapped that over the hood. I restrained his wrists behind his back, noticing drops of anxious sweat already trickling along his flabby sides. Unfastening his belt, I roughly yanked his denim pants to his knees and smacked his ankles until he spread his feet wide. Then I tugged his white cotton underpants down as well, freeing a big fat smooth-headed boner (already drooling precum) and giant balls. I walked across the room to fetch a length of clothesline from a drawer, and when I turned back I stopped for a minute to take in the sight in front of me: a giant schlumpy black-hooded white guy with a deserted patch of scraggly graying hair on his droopy chest standing with his pants around his knees, sporting an erection, wearing a dog collar with his hands tied behind his back, and gulping shallow breaths through his goldfish mouth. *This is truly sacred work*, I thought.

I stood in front of him and tied the clothesline to the largest ring on his dog collar. I let the other end of the clothesline fall to the floor and then wrapped it around his cock and balls several times, which made his dick bob toward the ceiling higher and harder. Now a long line of liquid dripped from the tip of his dick down to the carpet. (Good thing I'm not Suzy Homemaker, hysterical about spills and stains.) I grabbed the rope at chest level and plucked it gently, tugging his neck and balls at the same time. I let myself enjoy playing with Lester in this state. No rush.

I knelt at his feet and one after the other lifted his legs and removed his trousers. Then I walked behind him and, sliding a hand down one arm after the other, I unsnapped the wrist restraints. Walking in front of him again, I unwrapped the clothesline from around his balls and said, "I want you to get down on your knees."

As he lurched forward, I added, "Slowly!"

Grunting, he dropped first to one knee, then the other.

"Okay, now get down on all fours." I adjusted the dog collar so the ring the line was attached to slid around to the back of his neck. "We're going to go for a little walk."

I led him across the room, steering him with slight tugs on the rope. When I got to the hallway, I didn't say anything but let him find his bearings between the radiator (going full blast) and the wall. Leading him down the hall, I realized we would be passing the window in the hallway and wondered if anyone in the adjacent apartments happened to be standing at their windows looking this way. If so, they were getting the kind of show urban voyeurs long for and rarely find.

I herded Lester into my small bathroom. I pushed the toilet cover up against the tank with a loud ceramic crack. Then I pushed the toilet seat up so it also made a distinct sound.

"Are you thirsty?" I asked the figure on the floor.

"No, Sir," came the faint reply.

"Are you sure?"

"Yes, Sir."

After a few rounds of boot-kissing and sitting-up-

and-begging, I walked him back to the living room and had him kneel on a pillow on the floor while I attached the wrist restraints to the end of the massage table. I took my wide leather belt off and gave Lester the strapping that he eagerly anticipated at every session. This turned out to be a good position. Usually I tie him down to the table on his belly. On his knees, he could stick his butt way out — a sign of pleasure and a request for more — and lengthen his back for the strokes on the upper back and shoulders that he seemed to like even more than lashes across his expansive white butt. I also noticed the strapping made him rock hard, a fact that lying on the table usually concealed.

Finished with that, I had him crawl up onto the table and lie on his back, still blindfolded, hooded, and manacled. I opened a bureau drawer and took out my braided nylon bondage ropes. I secured his feet to the end of the massage table and pulled his arms up over his head. Then I wound the longest rope I had around his mountainous belly and under the table and tied it up tight. Then I brought his arms down and secured them to the ropes. I got out a set of Walkman headphones, plugged them into the stereo system, positioned them over Lester's ears, and turned on some spacy and vaguely sinister electronic music quite loud. His shiny red apple of a dickhead pointed straight up to the ceiling.

I stood back and examined my work and saw that it was good.

My experience in tying people up is laughably limited. Lester would have been surprised to know that he was my only BDSM client. He repeatedly marveled at my ingenuity and expertise at taking him on journeys through intense body play. If the truth be known, I surprise myself almost every time I see Lester. Although the practice of massaging someone centers on being radically present and paying attention to the individual body on the table in front of you, most of my massage sessions follow the same routine, touching the same spots in the same order each time. Even lovemaking sessions with my favorite sex partners tend to follow the same pattern after a while, once we've worked out what we like. These sessions with Lester, though, permit and even require much more spontaneity than I'm used to.

It actually terrifies me. I hate having to be spontaneous. I much prefer having a script in front of me, a road map. But more and more I find myself having fun in these sessions with Lester. Working with someone who is blindfolded, restrained (no touching back), and often sound-sealed, I can operate without being seen. Sometimes I feel like a scientist working in a laboratory, mixing this chemical with that chemical and observing which makes the liquid turn green and which produces clouds of vapor. There is a lot of Frankenstein involved, too — I measure the effect of my actions by how much the creature on the table twitches and jerks.

I often find myself thinking, as I'm feeding Lester a ripe strawberry or a teaspoon of his own copious precum, or as I'm stroking his engorged penis with the blossom of a rose, *This is as intimate as I've ever been with anybody. I've never done this even with a lover.*

I had about 15 minutes left to play with Lester in this state. I rummaged around in my basket of playthings and pulled out a handful of clothespins. I fastened one to his right nipple, which made him jump, and then another to the left. He rocked slightly from side to side, and his fleshpole danced with pleasure. In quick succession I attached three clothespins to his scrotum, starting at the bottom near his perineum up to the base of his shaft, the wooden clips forming a kind of peacock's fan spreading out over the top of his balls, which were as big as a juice orange. Aesthetically pleasing.

After a pause, I stuck a few more clothespins on some other sensitive areas: the sides of his belly, just below his armpits, his inner thighs. Then I hung back and let the endorphins kick in. I knew that, far from being tortured, Lester was having a ball. Not only was he feeling sensations in parts of his gargantuan body that usually spent their days numb and dead, he was also being closely attended by a hot studly leatherman. It was like having a Broadway show performed just for you.

I reached over and fiddled with the stereo system, hiking the volume up and fucking with the fast-forward button so the music sped up and slowed down.

It was getting to be time to stop. I quickly pulled the clothespins off of Lester's body in reverse order. At each removal, a shudder would ripple through his system. When I got to the nipples, I squeezed each clothespin harder until I got a whimper of response, and then unfastened it. I walked into the kitchen and plucked a pink plastic-handled feather-duster off a hook. I took it to the massage table and lightly brushed each of the spots where a clothespin had been. I lingered at Lester's balls. Brushing up and down the scrotum, barely touching them with the feathers, made his slightly drooping dick harder and redder. I returned the feather-duster to its hook and began untying the ropes. I took my time, coiling each rope and knotting it for storage before going on to the next. Cleaning up while I go saves me time later, and it gives Lester a few more minutes to stay in his trance. I could tell that he had gone deep this time, because his body was relaxed and his breathing was quiet.

Once the ropes and restraints were removed, I had him sit up on the table. "I'm going to count backwards from five to zero, and when I get to zero, we'll be done." As I counted down, I kneaded his shoulders and unhooked his dog collar. I slid the blindfold off, and as I got to "Zero," I pulled off the hood.

He looked up at me with the docile, shining eyes of a newborn chick. A puddle of gratitude and satisfaction, he seemed more like a five-year-old child than a middle-aged man.

"Sometime," he said, "you're going to have to figure out what your overnight rate would be."

Lester almost always makes a comment like that when the scene is over: he wants it to go on and on. He once even proposed marriage, pointing out the excellent health benefits his company offered the spouse equivalents of employees. I take these comments as compliments to my work, but they also make me a little nervous. I guess I recognize in Lester my own aggressive instinct to concretize my desires. Sometimes, though, fantasies are more potent when they remain in the fantasy realm. That's why I've never taken off my clothes in front of him and never given him a "release." I want him to consider me a guide along the journey of coming out (as a gay man and as an BDSM practitioner), not the destination.

When he made his half-joking request for an overnight session, I felt a little badly, because I knew that as much as Lester enjoys the kinky play, he wants to be held and loved. What are the chances of a schlumpy bald middle-aged guy who's just come out of the closet finding a lover? It's not impossible, but it takes as much inner work as getting out there and hunting. I wanted to give Lester a pep talk about self-esteem, to urge him to look inside himself for validation rather than outside. But that seemed tricky coming out of a session that revolved around wearing a dog collar and having clothespins fastened to his nipples.

I recently flipped through a paperback book of SM fantasies called *Sir*, looking for new ideas of what to do with Lester. I was getting a little tired of the routine we'd established — dog training, strapping, bondage. I read through the stories. They didn't interest me. Most of them involved teenage or college-age boys having their first experiences with a man. None of them involved a schlumpy middle-aged bald guy seeking experience in the hands of a professional masseur.

I tried to remember what I'd been like as a kid, full of yearning for experience. When every physical encounter felt like a judgment from heaven on my worth as a person. In high school I knew for certain I was queer. I was in love with two of my friends: tall and talkative Lenny Meltzer, whose mother was the art teacher at school, and dark, handsome Ron Garrett, whose father was an Air Force general and who wanted to be a priest. I would go for long walks in the woods with Lenny, talking about the pseudo-philosophical stuff young intellectuals discuss, while fantasizing ripping off his shirt and holding him to my heart. Ron and I would sit in his family car late at night after school-play rehearsals, talking for an hour when, to my mind, we could have been making out.

My fantasies about Lenny and Ron were less sexual than romantic. It was the jocks at school who stirred up my beastly fantasies. Listening to them brag about the number of times they'd fucked girls, I conceived hot scenarios in which I'd be alone in the locker room when tall, long-legged football star Jack Mundy would wander in from his shower with half a boner and sit on the bench drying his crotch over and over again, looking at me with an attitude of pugnacious challenge mixed with a vulnerable curiosity ....

I was 19 before I ever had a dick in my mouth, and I felt like I was years behind then. Imagine being 57 and never having sucked a cock. "Why bother coming out?" Lester complained. For him it would mean taking on all the stigma with no guarantee of social acceptance.

When I began my massage practice, I unthinkingly assumed that everyone in the world had the same images and associations with being gay that I have. For me, coming out as a college student during the mid-1970s in politically active Boston meant entering a community, gaining self-knowledge, finding a place in the world, and enjoying almost limitless sexual opportunities. Seeing so many clients who are married, closeted, or coming out late in life, I've come to realize that their associations with being gay are much more negative and frightening. Embracing a gay identity for them means jettisoning another that, for better or worse, has served them for a lifetime. Being gay is just as likely to conjure a sense of loss and shrinking horizons as to spell freedom and expansion. And for many of them, sexual satisfaction will only occur through encounters with professionals. Admitting these realities makes me sad and angry, and it increases my compassion for older guys who didn't have the same chances I had — a compassion I'm not always able to show. It does make me wonder what my life will be like when I'm 60. I assume that I will be partnered and sexually satisfied, but for all I know I'll be just like Lester, investing my emotions in unrequited affairs with young erotic masseurs. [MFF: When I was in my forties, I could never have guessed that in my sixties I would be happily married to another man. Nor could I have foreseen that niche porn and websites like SilverDaddies.com would turn transform schlumpy older guys like Lester into a sought-after constituency.]

CHAPTER SIXTEEN

Self-Service

After Lester left, I decided to give myself a sacred intimate session. I turned off all the electric lights in the apartment, leaving the candles flickering on the mantelpiece and on the ancestors' altar. I put on my favorite ambient music, a spacy disk with unpredictable eruptions of bass-heavy sex-groove riffs. I peeled off my leathers, and I gathered supplies. One bottle of coconut oil was still warm from the session. I dug around in the middle drawer of my supply bureau and brought out my personal-use dildo, which was slightly smaller, more friendly, more human than the somewhat imposing dildo I used with clients. Grabbing a tube of K-Y, I climbed aboard the massage table, still slightly cool and damp with oil.

I lay on my back and slid the cushioned face plate under the middle of my back, which pushed my chest out while my shoulders relaxed backwards. I took deep breaths. For all my coaching of clients, I knew I didn't breathe as much as I could either. Breathing brings up all kinds of feelings and sensations. It opens you up to the possibility of pleasure, but it also makes you acutely aware of aches and pains in your body as well as whatever emotions you've been avoiding all day.

I registered the dull ache that usually shows up in my lower back on the right side at the end of a day. I felt the heaviness in my balls and wondered if it was related to my lower back pain. Kidneys? Backed-up jizz? I hadn't cum for two weeks and had experienced raging hard-ons practically every day. Sure, some Chinese practitioners could go for ten years without cumming. But I felt quite certain that my own body was getting a little fried with frustration. I am my own cocktease, I thought.

My cock had been gearing up to shoot every day now, all the neurons and pistons and hydraulics on alert and ready to spring into action. I had a moment of understanding why the United States was always getting drawn into conflagrations abroad. If you spend half the national budget on defense, employing a million hot-blooded American males to be ready to fight, they're going to get antsy if they don't get to blow off some steam every now and then. Hey, maybe I should write a grant application to the Pentagon, proposing a giant annual orgy, a week-long sexual Olympics, in lieu of invading some tiny foreign country populated by non-white people. This would primarily be aimed at servicemen between the ages of 18 and 25. There would be physique competitions, how-many-times-can-you-cum contests, how-far-can-you-shoot matches, circle jerks, blowjob booths. I would personally volunteer to supervise the festivities. Yes, I would write that proposal.

Later, though. Right now I was oiling up my half-hard cock and thinking about Jacob. He was one of the few clients I had crossed the cocksucking barrier with. It was an extraordinary experience to play with Jacob.

DADDY LOVER GOD

I always gave him a good thorough massage. He was relaxed, tan (maintained by frequent trips to South Beach and the local tanning salon), and well-groomed. He trimmed his body hair closely. I prefer untrimmed body hair, but the way Jacob attends to his seems to have no purpose other than erotic. I'm pleased to inspect the careful way he shaves his balls and razors his pubic hair up to the top of his beautiful fat dick, which begins to swell as soon as I lay my hands on his body.

The routine is that I don't introduce any erotic touch for the first hour, until Jacob has gotten stretched and pummeled and all the kinks worked out of his back. Then when I roll him over onto his back again, I lightly stroke the tips of his close-cropped body hair, from his clavicle to his big toes and back. After stroking the full length of his body, I do another length with one hand while using the other to lightly brush his nipples, which I know sends him through the roof. Before long, his cock is rock-hard and pointing at his chin. I stand at his head and brush both nipples while breathing quietly into his ear, encouraging him to fill his body with oxygen, to feel the erotic energy all over his body. He tends to catch his breath, hold it for a while, take in a little bit at a time. I have to keep reminding him to breathe all the way down to his toes.

I lean across his face to stroke his chest and his belly. The curly hair on my chest and torso tickles his nose, and he begins to nudge my body, keeping his eyes closed, like a newborn puppy blindly finding its way to sustenance. I climb onto the table, carefully kneeling on either side of his head, and proceed to plant a line of soft kisses down his belly, to his shaved balls, and eventually to the dripping, bouncing head of his dick. Opening wide, I invite his cock into the warm wetness of my mouth. After a couple of preliminary strokes, I take him all the way into my throat, like a key going into a lock. And I rest there, lying flat on top of Jacob, our warm hairy bellies smushed together, and I breathe through my nose, while he moans softly, his cock twitching, the full length of it buried in my mouth. I've almost never experienced this ecstasy before. It's a cocksucker's dream: the Perfect Fit.

I replayed this scene, lying back on a maroon bedsheet, my oily cock in one hand. It didn't take much to get fully stiff, thinking about Jacob. If only he were here right now. If only he and I could permit ourselves to indulge in an hour-long blowjob, rather than a few minutes snatched at the end of a massage session. I felt down between my legs and ran a fingertip around the bulging pucker of my asshole. I snapped open the fliptop tube of K-Y and squeezed a drop onto my forefinger, and then smeared it over my butthole and easily slid the finger in up to the first knuckle. It wasn't so often that I played with my own butt, so I decided to go all the way.

I got up on my knees and faced the mirror over the fireplace. I extracted another gob of lubricant from the long white tube and slathered it on the head and shaft of my rubber husband. Then I positioned the dildo at the opening to my butt. It immediately slid in just past the head. I stopped and took a breath. My cock had wilted a little bit during these maneuvers, so I stroked myself again. My hands were gooey from the K-Y. I wiped one hand on the sheet and returned it to my cock. With the other hand I pinched first one nipple, then the other. Concentrating on my breathing, I opened my ass to receive more of the dildo. Suddenly, a rush of heat spread all over my body, down my legs, through my hips and butt, up my spine to the back of my neck. I slowed down my cock strokes, then sped them up. I was so close. I loved this fullness. I thought of all the cocks I'd loved sitting on, and the ones I'd fantasized sitting on, filling me up and rocking and rocking and holding and pushing and heat hot full hot gasp stop stop can't stop oh oh oh oh. I spilled a torrent of thick white juice onto the blood-red sheet. It looked like a map of all the Great Lakes: Lake Michigan, Lake Huron, Lake Ontario, Lake Erie, Lake Superior.

PART TWO
The Daddy Variations
(1964-1993)

CHAPTER SEVENTEEN

Altar Boy

Being in church was vastly different from living in a trailer. In church things were maintained with reverence and wonder and mystery. People wore special clothes and used a different language. Incense and candle wax dressed the air. I learned that behind the solemn ceremony there was humor and humanity. Kindness was available to a boy like me. All the priests looked at me and remembered when they too were sensitive homosexual children who didn't belong to their families. They took me in and accepted me without question.

From the moment I first saw them, I envied the altar boys who got to be part of the theater of church. They had roles to play, a few lines, they got to carry things for the priest, they got to dress up in special robes. I wanted to be one of them. I was in third grade when it started, this craving not unrelated to my later craving to act, to go onstage, to get attention, to participate in a larger more colorful world that existed partly in the visible and partly in the invisible. My mother knew I wanted it, but I didn't launch my career as an altar boy until we moved from Texas to Japan.

My mother grew up in a Portuguese family in Massachusetts. Maybe that's why she felt perfectly at home talking to priests. One day after Mass on the Air Force base in Japan where my father was stationed, she took me up to the sacristy — I almost said stage door — to meet the priest and declare my interest in being an altar boy. The priest's name was Father Donahue. He was tall and bald with slow blue eyes and a long birdlike nose. I got nervous standing on the carpeted steps next to the altar, waiting to talk to the priest. My mother didn't seem nervous at all.

"Father Donahue, I'm Mizzuz Shewey," she said, holding her worn leather pocketbook in front of her with both hands. "This is my son here, and he's interested in becoming an altar boy."

"Oh, you are?" the priest said, looking down his beak at the skinny little boy with the crewcut standing in front of him in his short-sleeved white shirt and creased gray trousers.

"Uh huh." My throat was so dry I could barely speak.

"And what's your name?"

"Donny," I mumbled.

"And how old are you, Johnny?"

"Donny!" I said sharply.

"Donny. I'm sorry," the priest said, ruffling his vestments and exchanging a look with my mother. "How old are you, son?"

"He's ten," his mother said. She took over the negotiations and between them they arranged for me to start altar boy practice.

It was definitely an initiation, my first separation from my family. At the beginning, I would only serve at the Mass my mother and sisters went to, but eventually I got on a schedule of serving other Masses, sometimes more than once on Sunday.

I actively wanted to be an altar boy, to be in the show every Sunday morning rather than sitting in the audience. I don't remember ever craving to be a Cub Scout or to play Little League baseball, though I ended up doing both. Those were executive decisions made without my consultation. I wasn't an enthusiastic joiner. If there wasn't anybody else around to play with, I wouldn't pout or parade sadly from door to door asking, "Can Joey come out?" I would rather sit in the library reading books or climb trees by myself. In Little League, I played shortstop. I wasn't good at hitting the ball. The best I could hope for was getting on base by walking. I was a short, skinny kid, a pipsqueak. At the plate I would crouch down and bend over so the strike range was tiny as possible. The first summer I played in Japan, my team was the Tigers. We lost every game.

I did like the uniforms. That was what all three of my ten-year-old hobbies had in common. As an altar boy, a baseball player, and a Cub Scout I got to wear three different costumes. Altar boy was the raciest costume, of course. It meant wearing some version of a skirt. I couldn't wait to get into a cassock and surplice. The surplice I wasn't so crazy about, a gauzy, see-through white polyester pullover. But I liked the long black cassocks with snaps down the front. All the priests and altar boys wore them over their street clothes, but I fantasized about wearing nothing underneath my cassock. Partly what enflamed me was the idea of being a monk full-time and never removing the costume, taking a vow of poverty and not having another set of clothes to change into. The thought of being naked under a long loose-fitting garment made the blood rush warm up my neck and behind my ears.

Naked. Naked. Naked. Seeing people naked was the most exciting and most forbidden thing possible. Just saying the word "naked" or even reading it produced the same tilting sensation. I lived in a house with five other people and we never saw each other naked. Whenever my parents or my sisters took a bath or used the toilet, they would close the door and holler if anyone walked in. Big Sister and I would sometimes play sexy games, pretending to strip, but we would never take off our clothes. We would sit in the bottom of the closet in our room playing Stripper. We would take turns holding a plastic toy telephone receiver over our chests and pretending it was a brassiere. What was everybody covering up? I longed to see what was hidden.

Sex appeared first in the form of jokes. I heard about *Playboy* magazine from other kids who laughed and snickered about it before I ever saw one. I saw the magazine on display in the BX — the base exchange, the all-purpose department store for servicemen and their dependents — but it was always on the top shelf. I had a hunch that the cashiers kept the *Playboy* rack in their line of vision and would yell at any underage boy trying to sneak a peek at the naked pictures inside. Besides, I usually went to the BX with my mother, and what would she say if she caught me looking at *Playboy*? I was afraid to find out.

When I started being an altar boy, I gained a new mobility and a new excuse for travelling around the base by myself. The chapel where I first served Mass was in the hospital, and the hospital also had its own small store with a magazine rack. It was here that I devised my own scheme for looking at *Playboy*. I would move a copy from the stack of *Playboy*s to a lower rack and hide it behind the top copy of a movie magazine. I would pretend to be looking at *Modern Screen* and when I was sure no one was looking I would leaf through *Playboy*. I had trouble breathing as I did this. My heart pounded so hard it would block the breath from my throat. I could only scan the thick glossy pages for a minute or two before I'd have to turn back to the black and white pictures of Ava Gardner getting out of limousines until my pulse slowed down.

After a while I became familiar and more comfortable with the dangerous thrill of looking at *Playboy*. Though it never stopped being exciting and naughty to see women with their big pink tits exposed, I discovered an even more terrifying thrill: seeing naked men. It was rare in *Playboy*, which made each one even more tantalizing. The first socially acceptable skin magazine was so overwhelmingly hetero that the only nude men on display were glimpsed in a regular section called "Sex in the Cinema" featuring color stills from the raciest movies of the day, usually made in Europe. I was always thrilled to see these pictures because the only other source of information about sexy movies available to me as a child was the newsletter of the Catholic League of Decency, which was always posted at church — backstage, as it were. The League of Decency rated all new films according to whether they were suitable to be viewed by practicing Catholics. The ones that enflamed my curiosity the most were those rated "C." The C stood for "Condemned."

Somehow I knew that the movies I wanted to see, the ones that could tell me what I wanted to know about sex and love and bodies (titties and pee-pees), fell in that category. Certainly, any of the movies spotlighted by *Playboy*'s "Sex in the Cinema" department must have been "Condemned." Even there, though, the most I could hope for was a peek at the hairy chest of some actor ravishing a buxom pink blond. A rear view of naked man was considered outrageous and the outer limits of daring. "Full frontal nudity" was so taboo that even the expression seemed enough to frighten the horses. You would no more expect to see such a thing in a national magazine than you would expect to see a statue of the Virgin Mary dripping tears of blood.

Such miracles did occur, however. One day at the magazine rack I laid my sweaty palms on an issue of Playboy that devoted several pages to color stills from a new movie called *Can Hieronymous Merkin Ever Forget Mercy Humppe and Find True Happiness?* The film starred Anthony Newley, who seemed to spend at least part of the movie running around bare-assed because there he was, letting it all hang out on the pages of *Playboy*. The pictures were tiny, and they were mostly taken from behind, but in one or two of them I could discern a dangly piece of flesh framed by a ruff of pubic hair. Besides my daddy, whom I would glimpse showering when we went swimming at Battle Lake, Anthony Newley was the first grown-up man I saw naked. For years he danced through my dreams, a curly-haired Fred Astaire with no top hat, no white tie, and no tails.

Ordinarily my parents kept me on a short leash. They had to know my whereabouts at all times. If I wasn't within earshot when they called me for dinner, my father would be waiting at the door with his belt off to lash my butt and legs as punishment. In the service of my roles as ten-year-old altar boy or Cub Scout or Little League baseball player, though, I had much more license to travel unsupervised around the base, riding my bicycle or taking the shuttle bus (a classic yellow school bus painted ignore-me navy blue). Of all those spring and summer afternoons of Little League practice and Saturday morning games, of Cub Scout meetings and outings, I have retained few detailed memories. What sticks with me is the romantic melancholy solitude I enjoyed moving around the base in Japan, waiting endlessly for buses, gazing into the canal that ran along the bus route, contentedly accompanied only by my bookworm dreaminess.

It was hot and sunny, whatever season it was I spent selling tickets for the Cub Scout Jamboree. The Jamboree itself was a forgettable festival of crafts-peddling and food-vending held in a vacant airplane hangar, over in a day. Ticket-selling stretched out for eons. Somehow I was sufficiently earnest or aggressive or maybe just pathetic to succeed at hawking these tickets. My mother and father thought it was cute that I would stand in front of the BX buttonholing passersby and saying, "I'm selling tickets to the Cub Scout Jamboree — how many would you like to buy?" They encouraged my Willy Loman Jr. instincts and amused themselves by thinking up new populations for me to hit with my runty salesman tactics. One untapped market they sicced me on was the GIs living in the barracks. Young single guys without families to support always had a dollar or two to spare. They didn't have much contact with kids, and they'd probably either identify with me or take pity on me.

So there I was in full Cub Scout regalia, navy blue khaki suit and mustard yellow bandana fastened under my collar with a cheap brass slide, marching around the barracks on a broiling Saturday afternoon selling fifty-cent tickets to the Cub Scout Jamboree. Hardly anyone was home. I got sweaty and discouraged fast. This felt stupid and pointless. Then I walked by a door that was open. The room was dark and cave-like, compared to the bright sun outside. I peered into the cool dark and saw a guy lounging on the lower bunk in his skivvies. "Come on in," he called in a friendly voice. Tentatively I stepped over the threshold and instantly felt surrounded by an overwhelmingly sensual masculine environment.

The small room seemed to be jammed full of furniture. There were two bunkbeds, just like the bedroom I shared with my sisters. The difference was that three grown men shared this space, and they were all walking back and forth, showering, shaving, talking and joking. The other two guys were friendly and greeted me from faces that seemed to tower over me, miles away. But my host, the one who beckoned me in, invited me to sit next to him on the bunkbed and engaged me in conversation. I felt tongue-tied and intimidated being the focus of his attention. I liked it but I didn't know what to say. I was titillated and alarmed and curious about what was going on in the room. I wanted to stare and stare at all of it. The muscular white men with white towels wrapped around their waists. The tiny steamy bathroom where they showered and shaved and did other private business. The pinups on the wall of luscious women wearing little or nothing at all. It didn't seem right to stare, though. I wasn't supposed to look. I felt nervous and torn. My host did everything he could to put me at ease. He called my attention to the music blaring out of the phonograph.

"Do you like this song?" he said. "It's called 'Baby Elephant Walk.'" Of course I'd heard Henry Mancini's theme song from the movie *Hatari*. It was unavoidable that year, with its circus-y clarinet melody and comic-sexy bump-and-grind trombones. I didn't care one way or the other about the song before. But I liked it now. I liked him. He must have been 20 or 21, a kid from Wichita or Jacksonville or Pocatello exhilarated to be away from home, seeing the world, serving his country and having all his needs taken care of, nothing to do on a white-hot-sky Saturday afternoon but hang out with his buddies and be nice to a Cub Scout starved for male attention. He was probably a lot like my father was not so long before.

He turned 36 in 1965, a young man still good-looking, still fit. He had a little fat wife at home and four young children. He didn't feel completely himself with them. Too many responsibilities. Too many questions. Too much pressure to know stuff he didn't know. He preferred being at work with the guys, wearing his flight suit with all the zippers. Sitting in his engineers' booth, joking and cooperating with the pilot, the co-pilot, the rest of the flight crew, the ground crew — it felt like being at home with his brothers. He didn't have to worry if he didn't know how to do something. There was always someone higher up in the hierarchy who knew, a lifer, someone more experienced who would be glad to show him. That's what it was like to work with men. We're men getting a job done.

But at home there are no men. He slipped into the house, quiet and looking sheepish. His green clearwater eyes looked shy and scared, as if he wasn't sure he was welcome in the house. His mind reeled with guilty memories of Thai whores, their thick perfumes, their alien flesh, their long straight hair, their raucous voices. Could he fit in at home after such luxurious sinful pleasures?

At home there was a woman and a bunch of little girls and a son who might as well be a little girl. He only liked to read books. Face it, he was a little sissy. He came running to the door, though, and took Daddy's flight bag away. He rummaged through the pockets of Daddy's flight bag, looking for the treat, the present, the proof that Daddy had been thinking about him, that he cared — and there, behind the navy blue plastic toilet article bag, next to the pile of clean V-neck white T-shirts and the extra pair of shiny black dress shoes, the little boy found the treasure, the thing that opened his heart wide and gave hope to the world, the evidence of Daddy's love — the silver package with the yellow paper band around it that said "Butter Rum Life Savers."

CHAPTER EIGHTEEN

Home Leaves

Okay, I admit it. The reason I started doing erotic massage for a living is because my parents didn't love me enough. Therefore, I can never get enough love. That's why I'm a slut and a whore.

Maybe there were too many kids in my family. There were four of us, which is plenty for a trailer and one income. Or maybe there were too many kids in my parents' families. They grew up in broods of eight apiece, where there was no such thing as individual attention to the needs and dreams and desires of each one. They were neglected, abused, and abandoned, denied pleasure and safety and loving touch. For them it was normal to run the family like a military regiment, or like a field of cattle. Head 'em up, move 'em out, Rawhide!

I have a photograph of myself on my father's lap when I was a few months old. And I have another snapshot of him leaning over and kissing me on the cheek when I was about three. But in the kissing picture he's holding a can of beer in his hand, which to me cancels out the kiss. Afterwards, in the race for his affection, the beer always came in first. By the time I was ten, when I accidentally knocked over the beer he was drinking while barbecuing in the backyard, and my father hauled off and kicked me in the ass in front of a yardful of visitors, the priorities had been firmly established.

I don't remember either of my parents being any more affectionate with my three sisters. They all grew up like me, starved for affection. When we visited my grandparents' farm in Kansas, my sisters were pathetically grateful for the attention they got from Grandpa. He loved to take them into his lap and hold them and hug them and bounce them on his knee. He would do that with all the granddaughters and none of the grandsons. Only after he died did I learn that he also had a clever way of slipping a finger up their shorts to play with their little-girl pussies without anybody else noticing.

Meanwhile, I would be downstairs in the cool basement with the boy cousins, rough-housing and rolling around on giant family-size beds, trying to get some action going, without any success.

My parents were physically affectionate with each other. Even though they were tiny roly-poly peasants, and I can't imagine wanting to have sex with either one of them, they acted with one another like they were legendary sexpots. Not in any gross way, but in my mind's eye I see them standing in the kitchen in San Antonio embracing, and my father slides his hand down the back of my mother's blue polyester stretch pants and pats her butt affectionately.

I wonder if I would have had better friends, more touch, earlier sex if I'd grown up in the same town with the same group of kids. We moved all the time: Texas, Japan, Utah, Colorado, Texas again, New Jersey. At least

I finished the last two and a half years at the same high school. The school was a combined junior and senior high, and the students were half military dependents ("base kids") and half from the rural farming community in mid-Jersey. It was tough changing schools in the middle of the year. There was another new kid after Christmas break. His name was B.C. O'Reilly, unavoidably known as B.O. We were bonded together from the start as New Kids, even though the first day we got into a mock-fight and he broke my glasses. He was the kind of bad kid that I always seemed to attract. We were an unlikely pair, because I was so clearly a "good kid," but I was lucky that way. I learned a lot from bad kids.

B.C. once told me that he was walking home from the base one day and a GI stopped his car and offered him a ride home. He got in the car, and the airman gave him a blowjob and $20. I was envious. I wanted that blowjob. But no GI would have given me the same treatment. B.C. was a classic tall beefy ruddy-cheeked teenage version of Jon Voight in *Midnight Cowboy*. I was a runty kid with a bad haircut and ugly glasses. No one wanted to touch me.

I already had my strategy down. I was the brain, the genius. That was my way of getting attention. I related to people through my mind, my burning curiosity, my dark serious eyes, my formidable memory, my precocious tastes in reading, and my artistic pretensions. Kids like that usually get the shit kicked out of them by rowdier boys. Girls with long nails and teased hair humiliate them or ignore them altogether. I managed to escape that fate. I knew better than to be arrogant. I wasn't a squealer, and I didn't suck up to the teachers. I fell in with the artistic kids, the ones who edited the newspaper and created the literary magazine and put on the school plays. They weren't all goody two-shoes;

they were the same kids who smoked pot and listened to the Grateful Dead. Being tolerated (if not accepted) by them provided me with protection.

But none of it got me love or touch or kissing. I overheard the cool jocks talking about the notches on their belt, so I knew there was fucking going on (though I could never figure out who the girls were). I even heard that some of the cool jocks had sex with each other. I wasn't in on any of that. I was a eunuch, putting out the school paper, talking about Baudelaire with the French teacher, taking fourth-year Latin as an independent study so I could translate Ovid, and playing the lead in the senior-year production of *Carousel*. Thank God for Mr. Sakach, who directed the plays. He was handsome and swarthy, balding with a mustache. He always smelled of coffee and cigarettes. He collected around him the smartest, most romantic and artistically inclined kids in the school.

This is where all my erotic fixations developed. There was Tina Truscott, who played Antigone in Jean Anouilh's version of the Sophocles classic, while I played the chorus. There was Ron Garrett, the one who wanted to be a priest. There was Lenny Meltzer, the art teacher's son, who was some kind of Jesus freak, but he was my St. Sebastian — I wanted to pierce his creamy breast with kisses and bites. And then there was Lucy Manuel, a suicidal poetess who carried a torch for me the whole time. I was in love with all of them and never touched any of them, though I masturbated furiously imagining Ron's thighs and Lenny's chest.

How did my parents express their love for me as a teenager? They came to see all the plays I acted in, sat in the front row, and slumbered throughout. I was such a responsible kid that you would think the leash would slacken as I got older. But my father got more restrictive the older I got and imposed tight curfews and ridiculous demands. He wanted to know where I was at all times, who would be there, and when I would be back. He had such a ferocious temper that I didn't dare disobey or the already high temperature in the house would become unbearable. My senior year in high school he developed gout and had to stop drinking for several months. He couldn't go to work, so he had nothing better to do than sit at home with a swollen foot and scrutinize my every move and criticize my choice of friends.

Walking down the stairs one day, I heard angry voices in the kitchen, my youngest sister begging my father for permission to go somewhere or do somewhere, him saying no, her crying and complaining. She rushed past me on the stairs. Behind me, I heard her bedroom door slam. "Young lady!" my father yelled, charging across the carpet on the living room floor. "Young lady!" Standing at the foot of the stairs witnessing this scene, I stepped in front of the staircase, blocking my father's path. I did this without thinking, Prince Valiant hoping to prevent another rage-driven beating. Suddenly, I was flat against the wall, my father's hands tightening around my neck. When he realized what he was doing, he stepped back, breathless and tense. We were both shocked. Nobody ever mentioned this incident aloud.

Where was my mother? I see her doing endless drudge work — cleaning house, doing laundry, fixing meals — in order to earn the right to do what she wanted to do, which was sit at the kitchen table drinking coffee, smoking cigarettes, and doing crossword puzzles. When I was home, I stayed in my room reading or listening to albums with my headphones on. I didn't want them to know too much about me.

Here's how I knew that I succeeded. My father retired from the Air Force the same month that I graduated from high school. He and my mother and my two younger sisters packed up the house to move to Colorado. I had a summer job so I was staying in New Jersey with friends. The morning they packed the last few items in the pink camping trailer (our claustrophobic vacation vehicle) to head west, my father sat me down for the first and only heart-to-heart talk of our father-son career.

We couldn't sit down because all the furniture had been shipped to Colorado. He perched on the windowsill. I was standing in front of him. I looked at his creased red face and his wide green eyes, the bristle-length regulation Air Force crewcut, the short-sleeved baby blue Ban-Lon knit shirt that gathered in a fold under his flabby breasts and stretched tight over his beer belly. I was curious to see what kind of advice he wanted to give me, although I think I was hoping that he would hand me some money before they went off and left me behind. We both felt like this was a momentous occasion in which important words needed to be spoken. As he stumbled his way through a few sentences, I realized that he felt like a complete fraud as a father. No one had ever given him wise and kind fatherly advice. He didn't know what the hocus-pocus words were to convey manhood on your adolescent son when the time comes for him to leave home — or, in this case, for home to leave him. And now, if I wasn't mistaken, he was trying to give me advice about girls.

"And, you know," he said, his face getting a little redder, "if you get a girl pregnant, why, you'll do the right thing."

I stared at him and nodded my head. At that moment my soul split in half, and a ghostly double stood next to me in the room. I was in the body of a boy who desperately needed his daddy — to see him, to show him the way, to give advice, to commiserate about disappointments, to celebrate triumphs. And I knew in that moment that I never had and never would have a daddy like that. And everything I needed I would have to get from myself.

When my family drove away, I waited on the sidewalk waving and watched them disappear. Then I got on my bicycle and went for a long ride. I listened to the birds whistle as they flew from the top of one Jersey pine tree to another. Cool air whipped by my ears. I felt like an open window. My body sang a song with no words. The muscles in my legs stretched and ached and felt good as I stood on the pedals, cycling up and down the sloping asphalt streets of the neighborhood, quiet and deserted in that summer midmorning.

CHAPTER NINETEEN

Library Hours

My sexual education began by reading books, the most arousing if not quite practical being the novels of Jean Genet. I came across *Our Lady of the Flowers* in the public library at the age of 13. I read this book a chapter at a time, crouched in the aisle on the gray linoleum to hide the boners I got reading about French queers in prison sniffing each other's farts.

The next phase of my sexual education took place in bathrooms. Did I read in some pulpy novel a reference to sex in bathrooms? Or was it a sixth sense that drew me to the basement men's room of the library on my college campus?

This was a world unto itself. Two stalls and two urinals surrounded by salacious graffiti. Men who travel as much as I had by the time I was 19 have used a lot of public toilets. Somewhere along the way I'd picked up the idea that "Show hard for blow job" was the way it worked. I was more interested in seeing hard cocks and taking them in my mouth than getting blowjobs, though. All it took to get initiated into this quiet, forbidden, secret world was one episode of going into a stall and reading all the graffiti and waiting 15 minutes.

The basement men's room in the campus library was my first experience of adult sexuality. Nothing innocent here. Desperate men having perverted sex in public a few feet from unsuspecting straight folks — heigh-ho, that's the life for me.

The graffiti in the bathroom had obviously been there for some time, possibly for years. The bathroom was surely cleaned and maintained every day or two by a custodian who mopped the floors and replenished the toilet paper. Did he ignore the graffiti out of shame and embarrassment, avert his gaze, do his job, and leave? Did he report the defacement and the signs of homo sex activity to some authority? Did he try to scrub away the scribbling in Magic Marker and ballpoint pen but found himself thwarted? Were bathroom cleansers not strong enough in those days to cut through ink? Or did the custodian enjoy the alluring self-descriptions, the carefully dated advertisements of availability, the phallic iconography, the succinct and astonishingly literate capsule reviews of assignations posted for toilet-seat reading? Perhaps he got off on it, his sphincter tightening as he confronted the range of sexual possibilities this tapestry of handwriting samples revealed.

Like any temple where many people have prayed, this bathroom had a distinct aura to it, even when no one else was there but me. It was cool and quiet. The air stood thick with sexual memory and possibility. When I entered this sanctum, all my senses changed and became more attuned, as if I were back in church, stepping into the confessional, preparing to receive the sacrament. I slowed down (everything but my heart, which leapt and raced until I thought it might pop out my ears and bounce against the walls). From the basement stacks, you entered the men's room through a door with a handle. That door opened onto a tiny vestibule. To get to the toilets, you had to walk through a swinging door. The double-door configuration was crucial. It made all the difference between an ordinary lavatory and a prime meeting ground for anonymous sex.

What thickened the air was the presence of two levels of realities, the sexual and the non-sexual. The non-sexual reality had to be maintained at all times, at any cost. If anyone walked into the men's room, by the time they were through the second door, they had to be greeted by the appearance of nothing more remarkable than men going about the mundane business of relieving their bladders, moving their bowels, washing their hands, or combing their hair. Any number of things could happen between two men standing at the urinals or, more commonly, in the toilet stalls, but they had to be simple enough to be hastily concluded at the two-second warning of the outer door — the mechanical revolution of the doorknob, the whoosh of air breaking the vacuum seal of the closed quarters, the thump of a hand on the swinging door.

The first time I took a stall in the men's room, I dropped my pants, sat on the toilet, and waited. I didn't know what would happen. *Bless me, Father, for I have sinned.* I looked around at the graffiti. My eyes wanted to gobble it all up at once. In my memory all three surfaces I could see were covered with writing as dense as a Chinese story painting, from knee-level to the top of the stall. I needed this information. I needed to know that other men had desires for other men and that it was possible to satisfy those desires. I needed to know that satisfying those desires could take place in a location within my reach, not some other time and place. I couldn't wait for it to happen to me.

How did this game work? There were no active indications, no positive steps to take. The overriding rule was: don't get caught. But how do you connect in this underworld? How do you know the difference between the guy who interrupted his chemistry homework to take a dump and the guy who right this minute is fondling a thick boner you'd like to be tasting? Sitting in the toilet stall was like being in a prison cell, in isolation, fantasizing about the other prisoners, whom you could hear cough, breathe, whistle, hum, tap, fart, but you could not see. You had to imagine who he was, what he looked like, what he wanted, if he knew the scene, if he wanted to blow or be blown. All of this took time. But in this furtive public space, ever-vigilant for trouble or danger, time got compressed. A minute of waiting to determine the intentions of the guy who just stepped into the next stall felt like eternity. How long could I spend in this limbo? I was in a trance. I was under a spell. From the moment I knew I was going to the tearoom — which might have been in my room, or walking across campus, or in the middle of Latin class, or when I walked through the front door of the library, flashing my student ID card, or while reading the newspaper, or when I felt the urge to pee — the spell would descend. I would not speak. I would switch from a verbal input-output mode to sensory mode, danger watch, sex-vibe radar flipped on.

I forgot to mention an essential flavor of the gumbo-like atmosphere in the men's room: guilt. I felt crushed with guilt 'til I could barely breathe, walking into that men's room looking for sex. Nowhere else on campus was there any indication that men might want to get together for sex. This was 1973. There was no gay students' league yet. The extracurricular theater company with whom I spent every spare minute and the architecture department were hotbeds of closet cases. I took the only women's studies course offered on campus, where we read smart feminist texts like Shulamith Firetone's *The Dialectic of Sex* and *Toward a Recognition of Androgyny* by Carolyn Heilbrun. Ten years later, a course like that would be a haven for brainy queers; back then I was the only guy in the class.

The only open appearance of homosexuality on campus occurred in Sociology 102, the second-semester first-year course commonly referred to as "Nuts and Sluts." Each year the instructor would bring a gay person to speak to the class. It was usually the first time any of the students had come face-to-face with someone willing to admit to being homosexual. I wasn't enrolled for the class, but my roommate was, and I went with him on The Day of the Homosexual. The specimen on display was a friendly, attractive, bearded young man who bravely weathered the awed and ignorant questions that class put to him. I remember that he said, "I don't spend all day thinking, 'I'm gay, I'm gay, I'm gay.'"

The guest slot in Nuts and Sluts class satisfied my intellectual curiosity about the existence of other homosexuals. But homosexuality in action was still a mystery. My brief, one-sided grapplings with my roommate didn't count. What did men do who wanted to have sex with each other? Again, this was 1973. Home video didn't exist. Pornography must have been available somewhere in Houston but as a 19-year-old college student I'd never laid eyes on any gay porn.

All I knew were the cryptic, largely imagined movements of the denizens of the library bathroom. The nondescript man with dark-framed glasses and navy blue windbreaker looking over his shoulder repeatedly while standing at the urinal, for instance. I could see him through the crack between the door and the doorframe of the toilet stall. Was he looking at me? Could he see me? What did he want? What do I do? Should I open the door and say, "Right this way"? I want something to happen. I'm not exactly turned on. In fact, I'm so scared my hands are shaking, and I don't think I could even stand up. My dick is not hard. If he wanted to come into the stall, I'd be curious to see what would happen. How is he supposed to signal that to me? I intuit that he wants something to happen, too, but he's just as frustrated as I am. He doesn't know how to make it happen, either. So he leaves.

Most of my experiences in the library bathroom were like that. It took a rare brave forward soul to connect. One day I sat in the stall next to an occupied stall. I tuned into my radar and determined that we were on the same wavelength. We'd edged our shoes close enough to the marble divider between us so they were nearly touching. My right-foot white sneaker cruised his left black loafer. Suddenly a hand appeared under the divider. I took it in my hand. That felt ridiculous, holding hands under a marble wall between toilet stalls like Pyramus and Thisbe. I was a smart boy, 5th in my high school class, in the top 1% of intelligence tests. I figured out that the hand wasn't looking for my hand.

I slid halfway off the toilet seat so the hand straining up from under the wall could grip my erect penis. The hand communicated to me wordlessly that I should kneel next to the wall and slide the lower half of my body underneath the divider, as if I were doing the limbo. There I was, lying on the cold tile floor, my pants around my ankles, leaning back on my elbows. It was as if I had volunteered for some strange magic act, strapped into a box to be sawed in half. The unseen bottom half of my body was completely naked. The magician on the other side of the divider quickly made my cock disappear into his mouth. I couldn't see anything. I could only feel it.

I'd never felt anything like this before. It felt silky, his smooth mouth descending onto my cock. The attention he paid to the few inches between my legs flooded my body with unprecedented sensations. The isolation of the sex organ from every other stimulus — visual, verbal, manual, the coordination of other muscles — heightened the intense sensation in my groin.

He hadn't taken more than two or three good sucks when suddenly the hinge on the outside door squeaked. Faster than Elizabeth Montgomery could wrinkle her nose on *Bewitched*, I was back on my side of the wall, perched on the toilet seat, my heart pounding, hoping we hadn't been discovered. The intruder went about his piddly business — tinkle, flush, zip, adjust, running water, splash splash, screech of the faucet, silent preening — which gave me time to catch my breath.

As soon as he exited, the hand motioned underneath the divider. Without hesitation I assumed the position once more. The silky sucking wetness ministered to my pulsing phallus, shocked and ravenous for this kind of attention. I felt a lock of his hair brush against my belly as he skillfully swabbed me with his tongue. Our interruption had slightly diminished the fierceness of my erection, yet it had also underscored the preciousness of every second. It couldn't have been more than a minute or two before I exploded into his mouth. I slid back into my stall. I don't remember if there was an opportunity to reciprocate on my part, or even a desire. I fastened my pants and left the men's room in a daze of complete ecstasy, joy, wish-fulfilment, and an exquisite feeling of shame that assured me that I could not speak of this experience to anyone I knew on earth.

In the few months I spent at that school after discovering the men's room in the library basement, I must have revisited this chapel to pray for sex 20 or 30 times. *Bless me, Father, for I have sinned. It has been two weeks since my last confession.* I almost never succeeded in connecting with someone there. I clearly remember only one other occasion. It was a rare face-to-face encounter. A handsome, craggy-faced man with dirty blond hair and thick fingers — I decided he must have been Scandinavian — accepted an invitation into my stall for a few frenzied moments of wordless groping, kissing, and relief. The other times may have left me sick to my stomach with nervousness, fear, unmet desire, and shame. Still, they fed me in some way. They were opportunities to practice my homosexuality. You know, practice makes perfect.

Whatever guilt and shame my bathroom exploits brought me, they also triggered a kind of cocky pride. Leaving the library, I would look around at the other students walking through the quad and think, "How many of them can say they've just had an orgasm at 2:35 on a Wednesday afternoon? Ha! None of them!" I got a kick out of belonging to a secret brotherhood, an underworld. I liked the exclusivity of it, much as it thrilled me as an altar boy to hang out "backstage" with the priest before and after the show, I mean, the Mass. I enjoyed the radicalness of my library basement adventures and the freedom of choice that I got to exercise. No one gave me permission to suck cock in a library bathroom. I seized the opportunity myself. I knew that most people didn't behave this way. I didn't mind. I didn't want to be like most people.

Looking back from the perspective of an adult sacred intimate, I think, "That's it? Fumbling around with terrified strangers, contorting yourself in toilet stalls, investing all that emotion into a two-minute standup handjob? Is that the Joy of Gay Sex?" It seems sad to me, and (to use Joe Kramer's word) paltry. I'd been listening religiously to pop music for ten years, eavesdropping on 150 flavors of boy-girl romance. John Lennon and Paul McCartney, Diana Ross and the Supremes, smooth Smokey Robinson, and those bad bad Rolling Stones had drilled my generation of teenagers with chapter and verse from the Book of Love — how to date and how to flirt, how good it feels to kiss for the first time and how rotten it feels to break up. I'd been going to the movies for the same amount of time and watching TV shows even longer. I'd seen dozens of cute and tortured love stories. I'd never seen two guys kiss. I'd never been handed the first clue about how to act on desire for another guy. I certainly identified with the swoony yearning of boy-girl romance, but I couldn't see where I fit in. I wasn't Wally Cleaver borrowing Ward's car for a date, and I wasn't Little Miss What's Her Name on *Father Knows Best* flouncing her ponytail down the stairs whenever the doorbell rang. I didn't have any images to guide me or suggest there was any other way to be gay besides the world I stumbled upon in the library basement.

It was in some ways sordid, smelly, unpleasant, like the inevitable bookends of "perversion" and "deviance" that bracketed the mention of homosexuality in *The Sexually Adequate Male* and other pop-psych paperbacks of the time. But like the word "homosexuality" in the dictionary, those graffiti-covered stalls were a granite-and-Magic-Marker mirror that allowed me to see my existence as a sexual being, to experience it, and to accept it.

CHAPTER TWENTY

Steam Room

You weren't supposed to have sex with a lot of different people, and certainly not all at the same time. You were supposed to find one person who you loved and settle down with that person and only have sex with that one person for the rest of your life. That's what anybody would say if you asked what was right and good. From the first time I encountered the word "orgy," though, I knew I wanted to participate in one. It was the most exciting thing I could imagine doing.

Sex with more than one person always made sense to me. It was different from sex with your boyfriend, and the two weren't mutually exclusive. My first lover, Paul, seemed eager to teach me that.

I met Paul at Boston University. I moved from Houston to Boston after my sophomore year. The official reason was to pursue training as an actor. My life in Texas revolved around doing shows with the campus theater group, but it was all extracurricular; there was no theater department. It would be equally true to say I had to leave Houston to come out as a gay man. I had scandalized my friends by having a brief but blatant affair with the Greek Orthodox priest who was the musical director for our campus production of *Zorba!* (Given my raging Daddy wound, my unsatisfied longing for parental acceptance, it seems perfect that my first reciprocal sexual relationship was with a man whom everyone called Father.) There were a number of fags in my social circle, including two of my roommates, but nobody was definitively "out." They were either quiet about their homosexuality, or there were women in the picture to make things look normal. I'd played along with that game, too. I had three women friends who were madly in love with me, two of whom I'd slept with. For me, leaving Houston meant putting an end to my bisexual experiment. No more sitting on the fence.

Boston University had a campus gay group, which I immediately joined. That's where I met Paul, who was in his second year at the law school. Within a few months, I moved into his apartment in Cambridge, and we stayed together for five years. He was a recovering alcoholic, 12 years older than me (again, a perfect Daddy substitute), and much more sexually experienced. We'd only been together a few months before he took me down to the Esplanade along the Charles River late at night. Paul talked about having sex in the bushes as if it were one of the routine aspects of gay life. You wouldn't read about it in *Gay Community News* unless somebody got arrested doing it. You wouldn't talk about it over dinner necessarily. But you accepted it as a matter of fact: gay men cruise the Esplanade and have sex in the bushes. When he took me down there, though, I didn't understand why the men seemed to be running away from each other all the time. Why didn't they stay in one place and have sex, if that's what they came there for?

Another fixture of gay life that Paul introduced me to was going to the baths. The idea of a place where men walked around naked and made themselves available for multiple sexual encounters sounded unutterably exciting to me. I never got touched when I was growing up, except when I got punished. I was too much of an egghead intellectual even as an eight-year-old to roll around with the boys. After having surgery when I was 11, I was too frail to play sports. I liked being friends with girls, and I was able to simulate enough romantic attraction to have girlfriends in high school. They were profoundly unphysical relationships. It was all I could do to get up the nerve to hold hands and deliver the occasional chaste peck on the lips.

In college I gravitated toward the theater crowd, perhaps specifically because they were so touchy-feely. Cast parties would involve a lot of heavy drinking and bodies sprawled out touching nonchalantly. There was always an air of decadence and polymorphous sexuality, but if it ever turned into actual fucking I missed out.

Before I went to the baths in Boston for the first time, I made Paul sit down and draw me a diagram of the premises and explain to me how it all worked. I couldn't afford to buy a membership, and I was borrowing Paul's membership card, so I felt I had to pretend to know where everything was or they would discover I wasn't a member and kick me out. Later, I could see that I was simply petrified for fear of doing something wrong. Not morally wrong, but not knowing how to act like a gay man. Paul was a kind and patient teacher, even if he was motivated by his own insecurity. He thought he wasn't attractive enough to be my boyfriend but that if he showed me the ropes I would be grateful and love him anyway.

Most details of that first time at the baths are a blur. I remember running into somebody from school in the locker room. Both of us felt embarrassed but covered it over with breezy chat. The place was seedy, with wall-to-wall carpeting that felt slightly damp. I paced the hallways and peered into a few rooms, but the men in them struck me as sad and unattractive. They were either way too skinny or way too fat, and they draped their white towels over their crotches as if what Carol Merrill was hiding behind door #3 would compensate for the parts I could already see.

Then I discovered the steam room. It was tiny, only wide enough for a bench along one wall. It was jam-packed with men. I had to wait until the door opened and expelled someone before there was room for me to squeeze in. Movement in the steam room happened by peristalsis. Suddenly I was surrounded by flesh — hot, wet, hairy, naked male flesh. I wriggled my way as far into the steam room as I could get and turned around to face the door. The temperature was high, and the claustrophobia was alarming, but the excitement of being mashed together with naked men openly acknowledging their horniness sent me into such a state of intoxication that I could barely see or speak. In this intensely sexual environment, no one spoke anyway. Hands glided over my skin and into my crevices. Tongues lolled against my neck, my belly and below. I reached out with every cell of my body, welcoming each touch. I found myself in a position I had conceived only in my wildest dreams — I had a cock in each hand, someone was kissing me, someone else was sucking me, and someone was standing behind me rubbing a hard-on against my slippery butt.

That was my first experience of ecstatic sex. It must have lasted for a minute or two, possibly less. I loved it. It thrilled me. It fed me.

Yet I didn't go back to the baths for two years.

If it was such an exciting experience, why didn't I

pursue it every day, every week, every month at least? It was expensive, of course. For a poor boy working his way through college, every ten dollars was precious. And I was in a relationship. Though non-monogamous out of principle (we were proud participants in the gay liberation movement and its critique of heterosexism in its many guises), my "marriage" with Paul for the most part satisfied my needs for sexual, affectional, and intellectual companionship. But that wasn't the whole story. Anytime I started hankering for sexual experimentation, my Catholic upbringing asserted itself. You could have fun, but not too much, or it'll all be taken away from you.

Fifteen years would go by — and hundreds of sexual encounters in bedrooms, bathrooms, saunas, steam rooms, sand dunes, and movie theaters — before I crossed paths with Joe Kramer, the first person I met who suggested that an abundance of sex was not a sin but a gift from God.

CHAPTER TWENTY-ONE

New York Jacks

By the 1970s when I came out, gay men had created a culture for themselves with many opportunities to plunge into sex without preliminaries, introductions, or negotiations. We'd been ready-to-go anytime, anywhere. In public parks, in bathrooms, in backrooms and bathhouses and dark balconies of discos, we'd been prepared to snatch a moment of love where we could find it. We were starved and impatient. We were oppressed and kept ignorant and isolated from each other. We grew bold and resourceful. The ready availability of sex didn't necessarily feed us, though, emotionally or spiritually. The first sex club I visited in New York was the Anvil, a legendary after-hours establishment in the West Village meat-packing district second only to the Mine Shaft in its reputation for sexual revelry. I must have hoped to revisit the orgiastic joy that I encountered at the baths in Boston. But this was a different scene, more shadowy and alienated. Stumbling around the pitch-black basement, fumbling with awkward and smelly shapes in the dark, spurting into a void — it was one of the most depressing experiences of my young life.

The path that led me to Joseph Kramer and the Body Electric School started at the New York Jacks, the safe-sex club for queer men that pre-dated the AIDS epidemic. This club was different from the Anvil or the Mine Shaft or other backroom bars. Strictly a jerk-off club, the Jacks held regular meetings in a bar where men stripped down to jockstraps, underpants, or bare skin and walked around socializing and drinking beer even as they played with each other's dicks. It was fun and extremely liberating to skip several layers of social convention — the meeting, greeting, dating, dinners, conversations over drinks — and get right down to the boyish fun of playing with each other's cocks. The handshake was replaced with the cockstroke. You could have extended, fiery, passionate, explosive stand-up sex with someone — or a whole group of someones — without exchanging a word.

My peer-group sex-fantasies had been marinating for decades before they finally materialized in the fall of 1985, when I was 31. I'd been in a relationship for six years with a man I loved with tremendous devotion. I'd met Hardy Wilcox in New York while I was still living with Paul. Within a year I'd moved to New York to be with him. Physically he was an erotic ideal for me: blond, balding, and (like Paul) a dozen years my senior. That he was another loving Daddy-surrogate was so obvious that I was embarrassed to admit it.

My love for Hardy did not prevent me from feeling horny and curious about sex with other men. I found ways to fool around that didn't seem to intrude on the relationship. I'd slip off to the St. Mark's Baths or to the back room of the International Stud on nights that we slept apart. I tried to be discreet and thoughtful. When I came down with hepatitis B, I had to re-think my strategy.

I didn't want to endanger my lover's health by bringing home communicable diseases. Plus, with a deadly virus lurking in our midst, I had to look out for myself. When I heard about the New York Jacks, it seemed like an ideal way to act on my frisky libido without having an affair, which would threaten Hardy emotionally, or engage in the kind of anything-goes sexuality at the baths that could expose me to STDs or worse.

Back then the New York Jacks was strictly a membership club. Bathhouses and sex clubs like the Mine Shaft were threatened by the authorities and eventually closed down. AIDS paranoia ran high. The only way you could get into a Jacks meeting was as the guest of a member. To join the club, you had to get signatures of support from three members. I didn't know anyone who was a member. One Monday night I simply went down to the meeting place, which was, in fact, the Mine Shaft, a few months before it was padlocked. I stood out front hoping to talk some friendly soul into escorting me inside. When a guy rode up on his bicycle and locked it to a street sign, I approached him and hesitantly asked if he would take me in. He looked at me sideways and said, "Are you a po-lice man?" He was a good sport and walked me in.

I was nervous and shaky. I didn't know what to do. Danny showed me how the clothes check worked. He handed me a clothes hanger from a pile on a table and told me to hang my shirt and jeans on it. "Guests have to check all their clothes," he said, leering at me as I peeled off my underpants and draped them over the hanger, too. I kept my eye on Danny and played follow-the-leader. He took off all his clothes except for his shoes and socks. When he gave his clothes to the coat-check — a skinny guy with a Snidely Whiplash mustache wearing a leather vest over his bare chest and jeans — he got back a numbered ticket, which he stuck inside one of his socks. I did the same.

Standing butt-naked in a gay bar, I felt terribly exposed. Of course, everybody checked me out. I couldn't decide where to look. The men seemed intimidating to me. They looked older, leathery, lots of facial hair. It was a bar full of the daddy types that appealed to me, in an awestruck, love-hungry little-boy way. Danny showed me around and introduced me to guys who reached out to fondle my dick with hands frosty from clutching beer cans. I had no boundaries. I felt like when I walked in, I'd given up any right to my body. I felt obliged to have sex anytime anybody else wanted to. I desperately wanted to be accepted in this den of radical sexhounds.

The club's front room was the socializing area, a typical leather-bar simulated corral with stools and benches to perch on. There was also an aggressively unfurnished backroom and an open-air roof deck. That's where serious sexplay tended to happen. My wide eyes took it all in. I loved most of all seeing clumps of guys — three, four, five — their heads leaning together, whacking off. This was my teenage fantasy, only populated with grown hairy men with tattoos and goatees and leather vests and nipple rings and big veiny cocks sprouting out of thick pubic bushes. Kissing seemed to be permitted, and some discreet fingering of buttholes. But when I dropped to my knees to nuzzle Danny's balls with my tongue, a stranger's hand clamped around my jaw and pulled me to my feet. A calm voice whispered in my ear, "We don't do that here." I was deeply embarrassed. My first time at the Jacks and I'd already broken the rules. Danny laughed and assured me there was no harm done.

My experience with the New York Jacks initiated me to erotic interaction on a communal level. The group energy filled me with an ecstasy I'd glimpsed in the steam room at the baths in Boston but had never experienced during one-on-one sexual encounters. I notice that I'm reluctant to say what excited me so much: I liked not having to be personal, not having to talk and bring my intellectual life into the encounter. I could just be a body, interacting with other bodies. What I liked most of all was being in a cluster-fuck at the Jacks, interacting with a group of men all tangled up so that you lost track of whose hand was whose, whose hairy arm, whose protruding nipple, whose greasy dick, whose stubbly neck you were kissing, whose tongue you were sucking. You were all part of the same erotic body, a jumble of parts working together as an erotic machine. You were co-celebrants in a rite honoring Dionysus, the god of drama and fertility and intoxication, the god of ecstasy, that disorienting burst of intense, even frenzied feeling that signals the presence of something more-than-human, something divine.

The image of an erotic machine triggers conflicting feelings in me. How can good sex be so impersonal and mechanical? How can it be satisfying to have interchangeable partners? Another part of me recognizes in these encounters traces of ancient spiritual traditions. Carnivals and festivals from a dimly remembered collective past where the whole point was to get outside your self. To abandon your strict, limited definition of your self. To escape the tyranny of the intellect. To surrender to the passionate possibilities of the flesh. To merge not even with other dancers but with the dance itself, the formless energy that runs through us all. It's at least as mystical a practice as the rites of those who seek God (or insight or nirvana) by denying the pleasures of the flesh, by practicing negation, by rehearsing non-existence. For what is this communal sexual ecstasy among men but "their eagerness" (in the words of poet Mary Oliver) "to be wild and perfect for a moment, before they are nothing, forever?"

Something in men loves to be erect, quite apart from the desire to copulate or procreate. It's a primal thing. The phallus is a shining mirror of one's own ideal of masculine divinity. Phallos, the spirit of masculine sexuality. Not phallus as the symbol of the destructive power of men — but phallus as pagan symbol of life, action, sex, divine spark, the invisible energy that turns a flaccid, tame, unassuming penis into a proud, stiff, throbbing organ with totally different powers and functions. Phallos doesn't always require something else to complete it, a hole to stick it in, anymore than a vagina requires something to stick in it. Sometimes it is simply to be worshipped.

You glimpse this in tearooms, shower rooms of gyms, porn theaters — phallic worship wearing a mask of furtiveness, shy about eye contact. Sometimes men get hard to squirt or to fuck. Sometimes they just feel in touch with life force, consciously or unconsciously. When it's unconscious, other forces can rush in — compulsion, codependence (needing someone else to be complete), anger at isolation or loneliness. But this is the force that lures an ostensibly hetero guy into a game of "show hard" with a gym buddy.

When I emerge from a mini-orgy in the sauna at my gym, having been erect and stoking myself in the presence of other guys doing the same, I feel refreshed and energized. I've woken up some part of me that sends blood and breath and energy around the body, encourages action, sweeps away sluggishness, timidity, self-doubt, and self-criticism. Sometimes I squirt in those play periods, and sometimes I feel slightly guilty that I've discharged my energy rather than containing and building it. Then I have to laugh at my Catholic-boy reaction, as if I'm disobeying the catechism and counting up my sins for confession. Certainly, there's pleasure in ejaculation. There can be pleasure, too, in holding off. Pleasure is the ultimate goal. You can use it for other things in your life, like stimulating action and cutting through blocked feelings. But it's also useful all by itself, like beauty is.

The glory of naked men, the beautiful and the ideal, the peculiar and the individual — AIDS has heightened our appreciation of this miracle. During the dark days of the epidemic, some of us found ourselves doing unexpected buddy work, hospice care, tending and loving sick people. You can only do it by taking great interest in the human body. Not looking away but looking even closer, with matter-of-fact curiosity at every scar and sore. This toe is sacred. This rash is sacred. This Magic Marker cross where they aim the radiation — that too is sacred. Slipping a suppository up the rectum of a friend, holding a plastic hospital urinal so he can pee lying down ... such are the further intimacies the '80s and '90s taught gay men who never expected to study nursing.

There's societal pressure to couple up. But most humans don't mate for life. Few men remain monogamous. That's a fact of life. There's something holy in that. Likewise, in the gay world, there are lover relationships modeled on marriage and other improvised forms of family and household. But there's also a tradition of orgiastic group sex. It can sometimes be rightly seen as sleazy and compulsive, like those times when you emerge from a smelly dark backroom with crud under your nails, cum stains on your shoes, and an empty feeling in your heart where the love was supposed to be. Sometimes, though, the god is present. A deafening dance floor and the dead-silent revelry in the bushes at night are both domains of Pan.

The love in men for charging sexual energy in the presence of other men is separate from (though not opposed to) other forms of sexual contact — romantic sex, domestic sex. I thought of it as warrior sex. Sometimes I was drawn to sexual encounters with others out of loneliness or anger or because I wasn't getting enough love/sex/attention at home. Sometimes I was getting plenty at home, and yet my soul craved this warrior sex for wholeness, to feel in my body. (I could get the same feeling sometimes by running or dancing.) In fact, my experience was that a lot of guys who went to the New York Jacks were in relationships and sought this tribal tantric experience to enrich relationships. Not all men are equally charged sexually. Sometimes a hot guy can charge up his lover. Sometimes not, and the hot guy needs partners to charge himself but in a setting that doesn't threaten the relationship the way a more conventional affair might.

This is largely why men go to prostitutes. Sometimes, yes, for companionship, for basic animal instinct coupling, and also to get it up and feel virile. This is the part of male sexuality where the gay/straight distinction virtually doesn't exist. Gay men tend to accept more easily than straight guys the desire to be sexual in the presence of other men, though you see traces of that desire in lots of all-male activity. Violent manifestations may be caused by frustration of that sexual expression. Ritual spaces that lift the taboo might temper men's pent-up anger that gets channeled into needless war, woman-beating, and destruction of the planet.

The reason there was such a fuss about the prospect of gays serving openly in the military is that war-makers don't want warriors to be erotically satisfied. Then they're full of Eros, in debt to Aphrodite, and they don't feel like killing. Deprived of Aphrodite, they're more likely to be cranky, mean, brutal. It may be good for war, or at least good for the war machine that profits financially from the perpetuation of warfare (Mars, after all, is said to be satisfied by the first drop of blood), but it's not necessarily good for the warrior.

Reading about various esoteric spiritual practices, I came to understand that the soul-nurturing aspect of these group-sex episodes was not impersonal but transpersonal, a direct experience of being part of something larger than myself. That is the goal of almost all spiritual practice, a longing surely felt by every soul. It's especially healing and powerful for gay men to acknowledge that sense of communion through the vehicle of sexuality, which has been so repressed and tarnished by the disapproving Judeo-Christian culture. Randy Conner's book *Blossom of Bone* documents dozens of textual references to "cultic homoeroticism" — religious festivals in which queer devotees of reigning deities expressed their devotion and worship through the feelings and behavior they valued most: sexual desire and pleasure with other men.

Not every gay man enjoys communal sex ritual or exhibitionistic public jerk-off parties, of course. Perhaps those of us who do are remembering our ancestry, our racial memory of serving as temple dancers, priests, and ritual participants.

In retrospect, I can see that the New York Jacks, like the cruisy bathrooms of my college days and the steam rooms I so loved in bathhouses and YMCAs, constituted a kind of ritual ground. Dare I call it a sacred space, this dank, unvarnished room reeking of beer and testosterone? But what is any sacred space but a plot of ground where birds have shat and animals chewed bloody carcasses and buried bones? Draw a circle in the sand with ash, say a prayer, honor those who've walked before you, sit in the center, and voila! The space is blessed.

Going to the Jacks was certainly a ritual. It required intention and commitment. It required ritual attire (or lack of it). It occurred inside a safe container. Other nights of the week, J's Hangout (where the New York Jacks met after the Mine Shaft closed) was a typical dark, funky gay bar smelling of old beer, disinfectant, and cigarette smoke. On Monday nights, though, the door opened only between 9 and 9:30. After that, the front door was locked, and no one else could come in. People could leave whenever they wanted. Lots of workaday daddies arrived promptly at 9:00, stripped down, got off by 9:45, and were home in bed not long after 10. But at 9:30 when the doors closed, you could look around see who was here and know that whatever took place in the next hour or two would happen among these men and no others.

The bar supplied the pool table (no cues or 8-balls in sight), the pinball machines, the free cans of soda, the porn loops on a couple of crummy monitors with the sound turned off, and the endless tapes of jaunty, far-from-Top-40 music. With dues collected each year as regularly as taxes, the New York Jacks supplied rolls of paper towels and tubs of greasy Albolene cream, placed at convenient intervals or passed from hand to friendly hand. The members themselves supplied their own beer, fetish wear (ball-stretchers and hydraulic pumps), and camaraderie. After periodic, unplanned and unplannable peaks of activity, a whole group of playmates would repair to the toilet to piss and wash up, like a softball team piling in from practice.

Then, too, there were off nights at the Jacks. One minute I'd be having a good time, and the next minute the spell was broken, or it never got cast at all. Suddenly, I'd look around and find myself among a bunch of sad sacks in droopy drawers, with glazed eyes and grabby hands. *Old bonds are broken down/Love is gone.* Dionysus had left the building. That's the way it goes. You can never predict or control what happens in ritual space.

CHAPTER TWENTY-TWO

Sexual Healing

Whatever I might have imagined a sexual revolutionary would look like, Joe Kramer was not it. I pictured him as a dark, mystic, radiant sex guru. A wild-haired Krishna, perhaps, or a bald gnomic monk with a deep voice and a thick mustache. He turned out to be more Middle-American than that, which was both disappointing and intriguing. He was tall, big-bellied and pink-cheeked, with reddish brown hair and mustache trimmed in a proper Chamber of Commerce style. He had clearwater-blue eyes that he hid behind a pair of tortoise-shell eyeglasses. He looked like a grownup version of the president of the Catholic Youth Organization, the kind of fresh-scrubbed apple-cheeked guy who got a varsity letter in basketball and played guitar for folk Masses and wound up working as an elementary school principal. Which, considering his background, wasn't that far from the truth.

Born and raised in St. Louis, Kramer grew up in a devoutly Catholic family. His parents went to Mass every day, and Joseph himself, the oldest of six children, went to Catholic schools from first grade through university. He pursued post-graduate studies as a Jesuit and nearly became ordained as a priest. Still, he was a sexual radical from early on. "Even though I had this repressive, guilt-ridden, mortal-sin mentality thrown at me in Catholic schools, I loved to masturbate," Kramer told me once, when I quizzed him about his origins as a Middle American sex guru. "I think the Catholic church helped me there because it was a mortal sin to masturbate. I didn't want to go to confession and tell the priest I masturbated six times yesterday or 25 times last week. I figured if it's a mortal sin, maybe even after coming I would just keep stroking, keep going, so it would only be one mortal sin. That's how I learned multiple orgasms.

"The other thing that repressiveness of Catholicism did was it brought God and sex together in my mind. God cared every time I had sex. It made sex not just some paltry thing, but God of heaven and earth was concerned about me touching my little penis from the time I was five on. Later, once I got rid of the guilt, I realized that the God space, the religious space in me was intimately tied up with sex. This was part of what spirituality meant to me."

It dazzled and delighted me to hear Joe say these things. I'd never heard anyone speak so joyfully about sex in a Catholic context. And I found his personal history compelling both because it paralleled my own and because he'd pursued the kind of sexual self-exploration I'd barely begun to dream of.

He attended an all-boys Jesuit high school where he said he learned about male bonding. "There wasn't a hint of homosexuality, but there was tremendous male intimacy. The Jesuits taught me to love myself and to love boys. Part of it was making the homophobia extremely low, so touching was okay. I felt weird with my body and my orientation until I was 14. That homoerotic high school experience made me want to be a Jesuit. This was 1965, four years before Stonewall. The only other option I knew about homosexuals was there were homosexuals in prison. If I could just get into prison! But I was too good a boy to do anything bad. So I joined the Jesuits and trained toward being a priest for 11 years."

For seven years he studied mathematics, philosophy, and theology while maintaining his celibacy. Then in 1972, while taking classes at Berkeley's Graduate Theological Union, he found himself sitting for hours a day in Sproul Plaza, the headquarters for the free speech movement in the '60s, watching the students, the street singers, the preachers, the politicos, the Hare Krishnas and the Moonies. "In New York I think there's toleration of diversity, but in Berkeley there was celebration of diversity. And I realized I was diverse, I was a gay man, and I was not celebrating my diversity." He continued his theological studies for a few years until it became clear that he didn't want to be a Jesuit. "Vatican II had just happened, and Pope John XXIII's whole thing was 'Open the windows of the Catholic church.' There was a lot of emphasis on love and following your heart. So that's what I did."

His heart took him to New York in 1976, a time when gay liberation had met the sexual revolution head-on. "I moved from a monastic tradition in seminary life to a sex monastery," Kramer recalled fondly. "Everybody was having sex everywhere. And when I went into sex, I wanted to drink life to the lees. Later, when I studied Reich, I realized I was doing Reichian therapy. It wasn't compulsive, addictive acting out. I was vibrating out all the dead spots in myself. And everybody else was, too. This is where I learned tantra. Because it wasn't about cumming, it was about being in the erotic vibration and staying there."

One of Freud's star pupils, Wilhelm Reich became a true revolutionary through his insistence, in works like *The Function of the Orgasm* (published in 1926!), that "those who are psychically ill need but one thing — complete and repeated genital gratification." Even more threatening than his championing of sex as therapy was Reich's political perspective: that authoritarian societies intentionally suppress the natural sexuality of children to paralyze rebellion and to inhibit critical thinking. The American government considered him a dangerous quack and arrested him for shipping an "orgone box" across state lines. Reich claimed the device (no more than a tin-lined wooden box big enough to sit in) could, among other things, cure cancer by containing and concentrating healing energy. His books were pulled from libraries and burned, and Reich was sentenced to two years in jail, where he died in 1957.

Not overlooking the political parable in Reich's story, Kramer saw that Reich was one of the first Westerners to share the Eastern view of health as energy. Steeped in these teachings, Kramer began to explore a massage practice, then a school, that would specifically connect conscious breathing with eroticism.

"Most Western sex is necrophilia — one dead body having sex with another dead body," he told a lecture audience at UC Berkeley one night. In contrast to the Chinese concept of sex as energy — a life force that through continual charging can take you to high erotic states and keep you there for hours at a time — most Western men's erotic experience, he said, is "balloon sex: you tense your legs, squeeze your chest, and blow up the middle 'til it pops."

Then someone in the audience called out, "This is a great lecture. When's the lab period?"

A sex lab period! He'd never thought about it. He quickly invited any interested men to come to his house the following night for a session that would involve nude oil massage. Twelve showed up. "We had just three hours. It was tribal. We had a fire going. Everything was structured — breathing, genital touching. Sometimes six people stood in a circle and the other six knelt before them touching their heart and genitals, and then the men in the middle would move to the next man. Nobody came the whole evening. But at the end four of the men said this was the highest erotic experience of their lives.

"This, surprisingly, did not make me feel good," he added. "It made me feel sad because I started to realize how paltry sex was in most people's lives. All that happened was they got out of their rut, and it was, like, 'Wow!' I started to understand how easy it is just to set up environments that can pull people out of wherever they are and let them play in another realm. I said, 'This is what I want to do.'"

Inspired by that first sex lab period, Kramer created the Body Electric School for massage in 1984 and began his life as a sexual healer.

He understood that the sex negativity of the culture creates its own damage and alienation. For some people, their sexuality — their juiciness, their comfort with their bodies, their talent for intimacy — is a gift they're not asked to share often enough. When they act on it, they run the risk of being viewed as pathologically compulsive, promiscuous, or somehow perverted. How often do we encounter public discourse that treats sex as something other than a sin or a joke?

Kramer embarked on a mission to change all that. Originally, the Body Electric School was set up to offer California state-approved professional massage certification courses at its center in Oakland. But what put Body Electric on the map was a two-day, all-nude, hands-on workshop called "Celebrating the Body Erotic" for "pioneering gay, bisexual and non-gay men." In 1987, a close-knit group of gay men in New Mexico invited him to teach them to have sex with their friends in an epidemic. Kramer created the blueprint for this course that promised participants, "You will relearn sex as sacred, playful, non-addictive, non-compulsive, and non-stop." In 1988 Kramer taught the course himself 15 times, mostly in New Mexico and Oakland. By 1992, he and a faculty of five gave almost 40 workshops in 17 cities across the country and abroad (including Amsterdam and Berlin).

I noticed that many people recoiled from the merest description of Kramer's workshop. It brought up all kinds of body shame, religious guilt, intimidation. "I don't like even my doctor looking at me naked," wrote a young reporter who interviewed Kramer for *Au Courant*, Philadelphia's gay weekly. "I couldn't imagine getting naked in a well-lit room in front of a group of equally naked men...It wouldn't be worth the stress." Others sniggered and dismissed the workshop as some kind of two-day circle jerk.

Personally, I was hoping it would be a two-day circle jerk. I somehow managed to get through eight years in the Boy Scouts without ever encountering that boyhood ritual. And when I showed up for "Celebrating the Body Erotic," I couldn't wait to get naked.

To my surprise, Kramer's workshop turned out to be less of an erotic experience than a spiritual awakening. By introducing tantric, Taoist, and Native American ritual practices — including conscious breathing, shamanic drumming, continuous eye contact, simultaneous heart-and-genital connection, and building ecstatic sexual energy without ejaculation — Kramer placed within a spiritual tradition the discussion of exchanging body fluids usually confined to safer-sex manuals.

Not that he would characterize his work as AIDS-prevention education per se. That makes it sound too much like those bland, sexually squeamish but eminently fundable seminars in "negotiating social skills" that organizations like GMHC offered. Nonetheless, if AIDS brought a shift in consciousness about sex, pleasure, life, death, and the spirit within all these things, Kramer's workshop permanently altered the way I have sex — motivated not by fear of AIDS but by desire for change. It made me realize that not just my aging body but my soul wanted more from sex than just getting it up and getting it off as quickly as possible.

On the other hand, Kramer didn't let his unabashed spiritual approach to eroticism settle into cant or New Age mumbo-jumbo. At the end of the first day of the workshop, he introduced an exercise that he said was inspired by listening to one of Marianne Williamson's lectures on *A Course in Miracles* while driving. "I wasn't paying too much attention until suddenly she said, 'God is but love.' Only this is the way my mind works: I heard her say 'God is Butt Love.' And I thought, 'Yes!'" And he proceeded to give instructions for the most popular ritual of the day: two men covered with oil stood with their backs to a third man and massaged him all over with their rear ends. God's Butt Love, We Deliver.

CHAPTER TWENTY-THREE

Celebrating the Body Erotic

When I first met Joseph Kramer, I was on a quest of my own. I had spent the previous couple of years working as an editor for a high-powered weekly magazine in New York. I was operating at the peak of my capacity as a journalist, calling on all the skills as a writer, reporter, editor, and administrator that I'd been accumulating for 15 years. I had published three books and established a national reputation for myself. And I was more than ten years into my marriage to Hardy. We had created a glamorous and exciting life for ourselves that combined cozy domesticity with a rich diet of culture-vulturing: theater, concerts, film screenings. For romantic gay aesthetes like us, this was New York living at its finest.

Then something changed for me. In 1989 my friend Bob, a quick-witted Irish butterball of an actor, died of AIDS. I wrote his obituary, which was published in *Variety*. It ran to three paragraphs, listing his major appearances on Broadway and in touring companies. Bob was 39 when he died, and I knew he hadn't accomplished everything he'd dreamed of doing. I was 35 at the time, and although I didn't feel in danger of dying any time soon, I looked at his obituary and thought: when I die, perhaps I'll be lucky enough to get a three-paragraph obituary. What do I want it to say? And if I'm not doing now the things I want people to remember me for when I'm dead, then what am I doing? One thing immediately became clear. I didn't want to spend the rest of my life as an editor, worrying about other people's headlines and deadlines.

I wanted to write more books and articles, it's true, but I also felt a deeper yearning. I wanted to know myself. I felt that I didn't know myself well at all. When I turned 35, I began the inevitable reevaluation that happens when the carefree glow of young adulthood starts morphing into mortality-minded midlife, hastened for me by the premature deaths of friends from AIDS. As I started to wake up, I realized that I'd spent most of my adult life living up to other people's expectations — to the point where I scarcely knew who I was beyond those expectations. Suddenly and passionately, I needed to know. Yet I felt ill-equipped for self-exploration, strictly forbidden for so long. I felt like a baby. I needed to learn. So I did what so many baby boomers did in the 1990s: I hit the workshop circuit. I avoided all the offspring of Werner Erhard's est seminars — the Forum, Lifespring, the Advocate Experience — because they sounded too corny and cliched for me. I gravitated toward paths less well-trodden: ACT UP, men's gatherings, the Radical Faeries, Siddha Yoga. I did a week-long vision quest that included a three-day solo fast in the high desert of Wyoming. So when I took "Celebrating the Body Erotic" in the summer of 1990, at the time it felt like just one more step toward my graduate degree in Know Thyself.

The workshop attracted such a wild mix of characters that it looked like one of those World War

II submarine movies. The class I took included a physician's assistant who worked as an HIV counselor for drug addicts at Harlem Hospital and a man with AIDS who'd recently been through a scary bout of toxoplasmosis; a Canadian conceptual artist and a Broadway stage manager; a half-Filipino, half-Mexican restaurateur and a daily newspaper journalist (that was Hardy). When we formed a circle the first morning — still in our street clothes — I felt all those junior-high-dance emotions: shyness, anticipation, sweaty palms. Like everybody else, I'd come in off 14th Street through the grim lobby, climbed the stairs to this funky second-floor dance studio, and shed my coat and shoes. We all stood uneasily looking around the room, rehearsing our mantras of body imperfection (I'm too fat, I'm too sweaty, my dick isn't big enough) and counting the cuties and the trolls (I hope I get to be with him, I don't want him anywhere near me).

Joe Kramer immediately got us breathing together, for relaxation and bonding. He cast a spell with language, clearly stating intentions, naming fears, and drawing guidelines: don't worry if you have an erection or not; the goal for the class is to build erotic energy without ejaculation; buttplay is off-limits for hygienic reasons. Prefacing his directions with a beguiling "I invite you...," he encouraged us to honor our ancestors, our parents and loved ones, our guides and teachers with the Native American term "all my relations" (which I thought would be a great name for a New Age soap opera). And he introduced the ritual designation "Sacred Brother" to use with one another. Some grumbled privately about the ickiness of Joe's language. He had cutesy names for massage strokes (Twist and Shout, Hairy Palm Sunday), said "magic wand" in place of dick or cock, and referred to the asshole as "the Land Down Under." Considering some of the historical alternatives (Bitch, Faggot, Miss Thing), though, "Sacred Brother" sounded rather sweet.

Finally, what Joe did best was weave people together. To my slutty, horny sex-radical mind, the main question was: how soon are we going to be naked and touching each other's cocks? Joe took a few giant steps backwards. In his workshop we spent hours together before we even took off our clothes. The first thing we did was form two circles, an inner circle and an outer circle, facing each other. For the first hour we moved around the circle, connecting one on one with each man, according to a set of structured exercises set up by Joe. Some were simply social: say hello, exchange names, talk about how you got here today. Some were physical warmups: stretching, shaking, bouncing together. Some were exercises in verbal communication: practice saying out loud "That feels good" and "Please stop." The most important ones were the most simple: look in this man's eyes, put your hand over his heart, breathe.

Making eye contact brought up a lot of stuff for me. Growing up, I got the message that it was either intrusive or dangerous to look people in the eye, or both. I wanted to look in people's eyes. I was afraid, though, of seeing my father's belligerent, angry, bloodshot eyes glaring at me fiercely. Right behind that look was a raised voice that chilled my blood or a painful slap or punch. If I didn't look in people's eyes, I could avoid those awful feelings. Reich always began his therapy working on people's eyes and wouldn't go any further until he could get them to release the blocks held there. Laurie Anderson said it best: *Your eyes/It's a day's work just looking into them.*

In the Body Electric circle, I felt like a newborn infant, parting my eyelids for the first time. I felt vulnerable, defensive, curious, nervous, giggly, judged, unexpectedly compassionate. I saw myself. Looking back at me were 35 variations on my own surprise, curiosity, sadness, and excitement. To put my hand on another man's chest and feel his heartbeat while I looked into his eyes, I had to be awake and alert. To allow someone to see me and touch me, I had to trust. I had to open the door and invite someone in. When I bowed to one man, took a step to the left, and repeated the whole exchange with another man, I started to realize that whatever was happening inside me was going on all over the room. In such a room, things can happen that wouldn't happen elsewhere.

Breathing was also new to me. I'd been inhaling oxygen all my life, of course, and I was starting to practice deep three-part yogic breathing as part of my daily meditation. But Joe talked about conscious, vigorous breathing as a device to raise energy in the body. "We are a nation of sub-ventilators," he said. "We breathe just enough to stay alive but not enough to really feel."

After a trial run of 10 minutes of conscious breathing, I felt different in my body. It wasn't 100% wonderful. I felt my emotions heightened, and at the same time I felt my defense mechanisms kick in, the ones that resist feeling powerful emotions, willing to sacrifice feeling good if it meant avoiding feeling bad.

Joe said a lot of stuff about breathing (which he sometimes called "rebirthing") that I didn't understand. One image that stuck with me, though, was when he talked about the Chinese concept of the body as a triple-heater system. He said there were three ways to bring heat (or fire or energy) into the body — through the lungs, by breathing; through the belly, by eating; and through the genitals, by sexual stimulation. In this workshop we would be focusing on the connection between the breath and erotic energy. (We'd have to take care of feeding our bellies on our own.)

In tantric and Taoist practice, Joe said, conscious breathing was a way to charge the body with a lot of energy. Later, erotic energy could be added on top of that. The important thing to do first was to wake up the body with vigorous breathing. As an introduction to the power of breath, he led us through a ritual in which we spent an hour breathing under his instructions. The idea was to take in as much oxygen as possible on the in-breath and let the exhalation simply fall out without pushing it. We wanted to avoid hyperventilation, the unpleasant lightheadedness and cramping that could happen if you blew out more breath than you were taking in. The idea was to suck in breath and then let it fall out. When Joe exaggerated to demonstrate, it sounded something like, *Foo-ahh, foo-ahh.*

I found this ritual strenuous and boring. I didn't like the feelings it created. My jaws got tired of sucking in breath. It seemed stupid to me. I wanted to quit and go to sleep. But I was raised a good Catholic boy, trained to obey my strict military father, so I tried to follow all instructions to the letter. Joe pounded out rhythms on a big resonant frame drum. Eventually, he invited us to lie down on the floor and breathe more vigorously. On cue, he had us take three deep breaths and hold the third one while squeezing every muscle in our bodies tight — butts, bellies, hands, feet, face — and lifting our heads and feet in a slight jackknife position. This was an exercise that contemporary Taoist master Mantak Chia called "The Big Draw." After holding the breath as long as we could, we let go, relaxed all our muscles, and fell back onto the floor lying flat.

What happened next was unexpected and difficult to describe. I'd been pumping oxygen into my body for an hour. When I held my breath, squeezed the oxygen into every last extremity, and then let go, I felt a wave of sensations flood my body. It literally felt like a torrent washing over me. At the same time, Joe's assistant, a red-haired pixie named Matthew Simmons, unleashed a piece of music at high volume that combined tribal drums, solo oboe, an orchestra, and a chanting chorus that steadily built to an intense crescendo that conjured images of the heavens opening up and bands of angels beaming shafts of golden sunlight down — a scene from some corny Hollywood Biblical epic.

The sensations I felt in my body were unusual, intense, not painful but a vibrating, buzzing hyperawareness, especially of my hands and my head. They seemed to expand to several times their size. A bigger part of the experience was what was happening elsewhere in the room. Some people came out of the Big Draw into convulsive spasms, their bodies flopping and writhing like fish out of water. The music ignited a volcano of emotion just below the surface. First one person started sniffling, then another sobbed, and soon the room filled with the kind of uninhibited wailing you'd expect to hear in a maternity ward at feeding time. That kind of emotion is contagious. I burst into tears. Wave after wave of sadness, grief, and free-floating emotion stormed across the room, sweeping everyone in its path.

The music changed to something quieter and cooler. Joe let us drift for ten minutes or so in this newborn feeling. After an hour of arduous effort, it felt peaceful to be still and do nothing. I fell into an almost disembodied state. For a minute or two I gave up my usual need to figure out what everybody else in the room was doing and to find words for it. Joe later explained that in Tibetan Buddhism, the Big Draw is a way of dying, "the ejection of consciousness." The way I understood it was that when you clench and squeeze and hold your breath, it's as if you're casting a giant net out into the universe of consciousness — some state of being that is beyond the brain, beyond the body, beyond the self — and then when you inhale again you're pulling in the net to see what you have caught. The period of time after the Big Draw is an opportunity for deep meditation on whatever you've caught in the net — images, memories, words, faces, messages from beyond.

I was impressed to discover that it was possible to have such an unusual experience simply by breathing. I didn't get the whole picture of the Big Draw until the next day when the workshop culminated in a Taoist erotic massage ritual. We took turns lying on massage tables for about an hour and a half while seven different men came along and touched us for 10 to 15 minutes apiece. This ritual gave concrete practice in extending orgasmic sexual pleasure, using the 20-some strokes that Joe and Matthew had taught us the day before. Joe kept a running commentary encouraging us to focus on continuous breathing and nonstop cock massage without ejaculating. If the man on the table seemed close to squirting, we were to immediately release the cock and touch him other places, slapping and patting his belly or the soles of his feet or tugging his hair to pull the energy around the body.

What an extraordinary scene this made. The room looked like a makeshift hospital ward near a battlefield with naked men lying on tables arranged end to end and covered with sheets. Each one was attended by another naked male angel-nurse. As with the breathing ritual, this extended exercise produced a variety of responses. Some men wept, others howled with joy, some lay limp as dishrags, others bucked and writhed as if undergoing electroshock therapy. Matthew played music that started slowly and sweetly and then built to an increasingly intense rhythmic peak.

At the end of the seventh massage, Joe led the men on the table into a Big Draw. The combined flooding of breath and erotic energies had some profound effects. Some people hallucinated, wept, or had physical contractions that looked for all the world like grand mal seizures. Some reported making contact with otherworldly realms, receiving communications from deceased loved ones, or being visited by powerful dreamlike images. Others just felt a pleasant tingling in their hands.

This vigorous breathwork also brought up long-buried emotions, which again didn't necessarily mean total joy. For me, it was quite the opposite. The Big Draw produced no big physical effects but only made me realize how in-my-head I'd been for the whole massage: remembering the sequence of strokes, listening to the instructions, judging each masseur on his technique, my critical nature compounding my good-Catholic-boy follow-the-rules upbringing. No, you're doing it wrong, hands *off* the body when you breathe on me, slower circles, not *that* leg, the *other* one, etc. Then I felt sad and depressed and angry because I'd screwed myself out of the experience. As my final masseur wrapped my sheet around me and some seraphic music began to play, I felt like I was experiencing my own death. I began to cry, grieving over my lack of generosity to myself. That inevitably connected with a seemingly bottomless pool of grief over friends who've died of AIDS. I found myself sobbing uncontrollably long after other people were starting to exclaim about having out-of-body experiences and seeing heavenly lights. I discovered, quite unexpectedly, that by trying to cultivate only positive emotions I had created a logjam of grief that blocked me from feeling almost anything, including sexual arousal. And once I let it out, suddenly the spectrum of emotions spread out like a peacock's tail, and I felt cleansed, exorcised, light enough to levitate.

Besides blowing participants into another dimension, the Taoist erotic massage ritual also served another, more down-to-earth purpose that went to the heart of Kramer's work on erotic spirituality. It broke down the tyranny of types — men (especially the gay tribe) are just as susceptible as women to what Naomi Wolf called "The Beauty Myth" — by allowing each of us to look, as if in a mirror, at the multitude of answers to the question, *What is a man?*

During the Taoist erotic massage, the varieties of manhood were laid out before me like specimens on the table. Each one was different, and I learned each particularity: the hair pattern, the size and shape of the balls, the belly button, which dicks are spotted or red or thick or stiffen fast or not at all. And I observed how they worked, how they received sensation in the form of pleasure, pain, or pressure (sometimes hard to distinguish). This one loved to have fingernails scrape his nipples; for others, nipples were a waste of time. One man asked to have his balls fondled, rubbed, tugged away from his body; another preferred I never touch them at all. Brisk? Slow? Concentrate on the "magic wand" and all else follows? Open the chest and emotion flows? I saw each man's history in his body — the layers of fat, the hours at the gym, the surgical scars, the intentional piercings and curious, dainty tattoos. What made them laugh, moan, shout with pleasure, sob like a baby.

By the end of the day, I looked around the closing circle and saw not cuties-and-trolls — and certainly not necrophiliacs — but a sea of shining eyes, differently shaped candles burning with the same flame. This landscape of bodies couldn't help reflecting my own divine possibilities, calling to mind Walt Whitman's refrain: "I am large, I contain multitudes."

CHAPTER TWENTY-FOUR

Midwife to the Dying

Of all the psycho-spiritual adventures I pursued, why did Body Electric grab me the most? Virtually all the healing I'd sought in my life — through years of therapy and my varieties of inner work — centered on my Daddy wound, the mile-wide gap in my heart aching for the love and approval I didn't get from my own father. I needed love, and I had received it abundantly from men who loved me. I needed to be seen as smart, and I had gotten plenty of attention and admiration for my intelligence and my ability as a writer. The thing my father neglected that I still craved was approval for my sexuality, my homosexuality. In the Body Electric work, it was not only seen but celebrated. I was invited to shine.

Joe Kramer knew about gay men and their Daddy wounds. He had a stormy relationship with his father, who once broke his own arm during an altercation with Joe. And he understood how painful it was to hide your gay light under a bushel. At a conference in Toronto, I heard him deliver the keynote address called

"Making Love for the Whole World to See," in which he provocatively insisted on the global implications of sexual healing. "Queer Nation's slogan is *We're here, we're queer, get used to it*. I don't know, that doesn't sound very evolved to me," he told the audience. "We don't just exist. We have gifts to give the world. Our talents are needed. Our gifts are essential. And it's self-indulgent to deny our gifts."

Those gifts, he suggested, could be a beautiful smile, an ability to write — or a cock that gives joy to those who suck it. He went on to proclaim that gay liberation should be about more than passing laws to protect homosexuals but about "sexual liberation of all beings and the idea that your special way of loving is okay." Enough with dwelling on childhood sexual abuse: "Look at the abuse we experience today with our jobs, our breathing, our diet, the sex we have." And with the alluring fervor of any man of the cloth, he pounded home the importance of sex as service to the community. "The Catholic church sets aside millions of dollars to take in young men and women to train them to be of service. I'm interested in convening a sex temple in Amsterdam within two years. I'm not talking about a brothel with candles and incense. I'm interested in erotic pioneers who are willing to be of service."

My reaction to hearing Joe Kramer speak was a mixture of fear and excitement. Any frank public acknowledgement of the joys of sex scared me, initially anyway. To extol the virtues of sucking cock without euphemisms or code or pretty words was ... I don't know, rude or sleazy or at least politically inadvisable — wasn't it? Or was it? Another part of me rejoiced to hear physical pleasure and desire spoken of so freely and delightfully, the way I frequently experienced my own sexuality. The gym coach who taught my seventh-grade health class didn't talk that way. My father, sitting me down for a leaving-home heart-to-heart, didn't know how to say anything remotely like that to me. Joe Kramer talked about sex in a way I'd waited my whole life to hear.

In the first lengthy conversation I had with him, Joe elaborated on the idea of erotic pioneers doing community service. He called them "sacred intimates."

"It comes from what was called the sacred prostitute. And the sacred prostitute is the greatest challenge of all to this culture. It weaves together spirituality and sexuality. In the Old Testament, when they talk about sacred temple prostitutes, the translation was 'the holy ones.' Even the Jewish interpretation of it was, 'These are the people you have sex with to have sex with God.' In New York in the '70s there were times when I had sex, and I had sex with God. Everything became white light, and it was clear that that's why I did it. If it was just about getting off, some sordid encounter in an abandoned pier, why would you commit your whole life to this? But it was about a connection with wholeness, with the divine, with god/goddess, whatever names you want to say."

Somehow we'd skipped quickly from Old Testament temples to the sex piers of the 1970s, as if the continuum between them was common knowledge. Or had Joe discovered the missing link? I'd certainly never heard the expression "sacred prostitute" before. It heated up my curiosity in the same primal way that the mere word "naked" did when I was a child. As an adult and especially as a journalist, though, I'd learned to conceal both my emotions and my ignorance. When I interviewed someone, I wanted to go deep into the interior of the person's mental processes, and I found that an attitude of sympathetic knowingness got me there faster than playing dumb (even if I was). So I nodded my head and pretended I knew what Joe was talking about.

It didn't take much to encourage him to go on. "In the last few years, I've done 100 weekend workshops and six-day workshops, where the risk-takers, the pioneers show up who know they're going to take their clothes off and have tribal sexuality. I look around at all these risk-takers, and I see that some men are so gifted sexually they glow in a special way. They shine. It comes out not just in their cock but their heart, their eyes, everything. Just by being around them, other people shudder. Sometimes they're old, sometimes they're fat, sometimes they're ugly, and sometimes they're *Blueboy* centerfolds. It doesn't matter what they look like, it's an energy. What I see is they belong to the sacred intimate.

"I don't like to use the word 'prostitute,'" he added, "because it's an ugly word that we as a culture have put on that phenomenon to denigrate it.

"In my work, I see all kinds of gay men who are sacred intimates. When they're intimate with you, a transformation takes place. You feel your wholeness. There are plenty of prostitutes around, so you can go and get off with a prostitute. And the next day you have exactly the same craving."

I was reminded of the scene in Luis Bunuel's film *Belle du Jour* where Catherine Deneuve asks her husband to explain the concept of brothels to her. He says, "You find a beautiful woman, you spend half an hour with her, and you're depressed for the rest of the day."

"A sacred intimate is different," Joe Kramer explained. "This is about being around someone who you're transformed by. You either model him — that is, you see that vibrational energy and you bring it into yourself — or maybe there's an energy that comes from higher places through this person into you. Or you have the experience of being with an unconditional lover, just for a while, that changes you and you learn what unconditional love can be.

"This is what's important: these are the teachers, but there's no place for them to teach. So what happens to a lot of them is they end up in Sex and Love Addicts Anonymous and Sexual Compulsives. I've gone to these meetings, and I went to a national convention in Oakland last year, and I think half the people there are sacred intimates. These are people who've been given special gifts. If you believe in lifetime after lifetime, they've brought this gift into this lifetime. And our sick, dysfunctional society has no place for them. So when they feel a desire to act this out, to be in that space, it ends up being in a bookstore tricking, or paltry sex. I've been thinking about how to activate this profession. Because we need sexual healers.

"There are all kinds of sacred intimates," he said. "The place where the sacred intimate is most activated in the gay culture right now is as midwives to the dying. This is one of those sacred intimate roles. People were brought to the temple, and as they died they were there with the divine, with the god/ goddess person. I think lots of people who sit with people while they're dying or do hospice work have moments where all of a sudden they recognize that they are living out an ancient profession: midwife to the dying. Tending to someone's erotic energy is about the departure of that energy, too, leaving the body and going on."

As a profession, "sacred prostitute" sounded alien and exotic to me. But Joe's comments about midwives to the dying brought it closer to home. I flashed on my experience taking care of Bob. We'd met as volunteers for Gay Men's Health Crisis about six months before he was hospitalized with the pneumonia that was synonymous with an AIDS diagnosis. We became friends and then, vacationing together in California, we became lovers. I remembered the ecstasy of our feverishly passionate and conscientiously safe lovemaking, heightened by the strict secrecy of our affair, which lasted until his death. After all, I was "married" to Hardy, and Bob was harboring what we kept being told was a deadly virus primarily transmitted between sex partners.

He started acting funny on his birthday. He had a headache. He couldn't remember things. He forgot words. He slurred when he spoke. Within a week he'd lost most of his ability to walk, talk, write his name, and feed himself. His doctor lined him up for radiation, but the brain tumor grew fast. Lymphoma. Bad news.

His parents drove in from their small town in western Pennsylvania. I accompanied them to a conference with Bob's doctor, a thin man with glasses and a trim black beard who always made it a point to be as cheerful as he possibly could. Today he was sober. His gaze was direct, and he kept his voice level as he explained to the three of us the race between the treatment and the disease, complicated by the gaps in Bob's depleted immune system. While we were sitting in his office, a call came in from the hospital. It was clear on the doctor's face that the news was not good. Bob's temperature was dangerously high. The doctor didn't say it in so many words, but the sense was that he could go anytime.

I walked back to the hospital with Bob's parents. The day was gray, damp, and chilly. We said nothing until we got to the hospital, when I volunteered to call a priest I knew. The three of us rode the crowded elevator with tears burning our cheeks. Bob looked bad. His skin was dry and ashen. His lunch sat on the rolling tray table untouched. His eyelids occasionally parted with a sluggish underwater motion, but he looked comatose. His mother stayed in the lobby. His father kept walking into the room, looking at Bob, bursting into tears, and rushing out again. I sat next to him holding his swollen, inoperative hand.

I searched Bob's face for a sign of my friend, but he was sunk deep in some pain or chemical trance or fever dream I could scarcely imagine. I noticed the ridge of flaky skin on both his lips. His mouth opened slightly, and he touched his top lip with the tip of his tongue. Then his mouth stuck shut. A few minutes later I watched this maneuver again, the stirring of the mouth, the tentative emergence of the tongue like a shy turtle.

"Do you want a drink of water, Bob?"

No answer.

I saw a covered plastic cup with a flexible straw poking out of the lid. I lifted it to his mouth and nudged his lips with the straw. His eyes rolled open and looked at me hazily, then closed again. Did that mean he was sleeping? That he wasn't thirsty? That he'd forgotten how to use a straw?

I took the top off the cup and removed the straw. I held the cup up to his mouth and tilted it so that a splash of moisture met his lips. His tongue shot out and met the water. I put one hand behind his head to bring it upright and tilted the cup more so he could take a sip of water in his mouth. Then another sip. Then another. Then he nodded once, and I let his head rest back on the pillow.

For the rest of the afternoon, I sat next to the bed watching him like a hawk overlooking a henyard. I waited for the tongue to emerge and flick the dry lips, the gesture I read as thirst. He never drank more than a sip at a time, but he was taking in fluid. I stayed as long as I could. Then I left him in the care of his parents, who were gradually able to sit in the room and speak to Bob in comforting tones without breaking down.

The next morning I stopped by Bob's room on my way to work. He was sitting up in bed, his big blue eyes alert and shining. His parents were jovial and smiling,

grateful to see the fever had broken. He'd made it through the night.
 I knew I could never provide for Bob the deep consoling support of his loving parents. I didn't know enough about medicine to take his vital signs, read his chart, and design a course of treatment like the many doctors who attended him could. But I did know this much: I could stay close and keep my eyes open and, with the mind of a loving friend, try to guess what he needed minute by minute. I knew how to love him.
 Bob died a few weeks later. I spent the summer blown apart. By the loss of my friend, yes, but that might have been the easier part. I'd also gained something from taking care of him: an awareness of a reservoir of love inside previously unknown to me. Now that he was gone, I didn't know what to do with all this emotion. I had a big love for Hardy that was passionate and erotic and intellectual. But Hardy didn't need me to notice that his lips were parched when he couldn't ask for a drink of water. Hardy didn't need me to figure out that when he said "underwear" it meant "I'd like to have some of the vanilla Häagen-Dasz in the freezer." Hardy didn't need me to organize 24-hour nursing care for him, monitor his medications, translate his complaints to his doctor and then the doctor's instructions to his nurses and his parents.
 From taking care of Bob, I learned how fulfilling it was to tap this reservoir of love. After he died, I felt a persistent, perplexing ache like a mother whose infant dies leaving her breasts full of milk, or a traveler who returns home after years in a foreign country and has no one to speak to in his new language.
 I could have done more volunteer work with GMHC, I suppose. I could have pursued nursing or counselling. But I had loved Bob sexually, and our sexual passion had enriched my ability to care for him above and beyond

our erotic relationship. I wanted to know more about that. I thought about the last time we had sex, the day he had a catheter surgically inserted above his heart for easier administration of his intravenous medications, and how triumphant we felt demolishing the myth that his illness made him untouchable. I recalled lying in his bed at home with my arms around him near the end, when he could barely speak yet with a child's pleading voice begged me to stay with him all night. I remembered watching the tiny nurse lift his swollen, unconscious body from one hospital bed to another and hearing the shocked gasp of his last breath. Oh, how I wish I'd been able to ease that transition with a touch of erotic energy!

Joe Kramer was still enumerating the various manifestations of this sacred intimate archetype. "The main role of the sacred intimate is to clear out one's body totally of toxins and just to bring in light and wholeness and holiness and God. By seeing that, other people are transformed. It's a very personal path. In the old days it was done in the temple, so there were many people together. And there were teachers. They taught each other, and they had teachers. That's what I'm calling a sex monastery. I am interested in temples, where people come together and do this. Clear themselves out." Establishing a full-time sex monastery was a cherished but distant dream. As a preliminary experiment in creating such an erotic community, Joe told me that the Body Electric School would be offering a ten-day training for sacred intimates the following summer at a retreat center called Wildwood in the Russian River resort area north of San Francisco.

As I heard him spin out his fantasy of a vocation called "sacred intimate," I felt myself falling under a spell. I heard in his words a description of myself that I had never heard before. It pulled together my childhood as an altar boy — some kind of temple slave operating behind the scenes of the Catholic worship service by carrying props for the ritual priest — with my experience taking care of Bob and my long history of committed domestic partnerships with lovers, not to mention my enthusiastic career as an exhibitionistic connoisseur of communal revelry in sex clubs. Suddenly, Joe had connected the dots, and I got a picture of my destiny.

CHAPTER TWENTY-FIVE

Wildwood

When I first got there, Wildwood had been operating for almost 20 years as a retreat center owned and operated by gay men, mainly serving San Francisco's gay community, for whom the Russian River area was a popular vacation enclave — the West Coast version of Fire Island. It had sponsored notorious gatherings of leather aficionados as well as training sessions for the Shanti Project, San Francisco's original AIDS service organization. Its secluded, gay-friendly, physically beautiful setting met the needs of the Body Electric School perfectly.

A winding twenty-minute drive up the steep and very narrow Old Cazadero Road from the town of Guerneville, Wildwood sat at the top of a 1200-foot hill behind gates that could be closed and locked when a gathering was underway. From an unpaved parking lot ringed by skyscraping pines, visitors climbed stone steps to arrive at the heart of the place. To the left was the swimming pool and the indoor hot tub. To the right was the lodge where the caretakers served three delicious healthy meals a day (sprinkled, for some reason, with more sliced olives than any cuisine outside the Peloponnesus). Surrounding the lodge were an array of flower gardens, stands of eucalyptus, a sun porch, and the outdoor hot tub. Nine tents were pitched on wooden platforms under the trees, and dormitory space was built onto the back of the lodge and above the garage at the end of the parking lot. But most guests at Wildwood stayed in a baker's dozen of rooms built back-to-back in a separate building commonly known as "Motel Row." At the farthest end of the grounds from the parking lot stood a large, sunny, wood-beamed meeting room that became headquarters for all Body Electric trainings. This was known to everyone as "The Temple."

I first visited Wildwood in June of 1991, when I attended a week-long intensive called "The Dear Love of Comrades," which further developed the erotic massage rituals that Joe Kramer introduced in "Celebrating the Body Erotic." Later that summer I took part in the first Sacred Intimate Training, a nine-day workshop focused on sexual healing. The following year and then again in 1994 I took additional Sacred Intimate Trainings. I spent two more weeks doing workshops at Wildwood along the way – the one called "Advanced Anal Massage" (also known as "Historic Butt Love" or "Butt Camp") and another called "Dark Eros," which was about BDSM as spiritual practice. Over a period of four years, I spent a total of 53 days at Wildwood. Yet each workshop was such an intense experience of temporary community, dense with information exchange, that it felt much longer. "Time moves so strangely in this place," someone once remarked about Wildwood. We joked that we were living at the speed of 500 years a day.

Men came from all over the country and as far afield as Australia, New Zealand, England, and Germany for these Body Electric intensives. Probably half of them worked in the healing professions as doctors, nurses, therapists, bodyworkers, priests, and artists, but there were also bankers, hairdressers, businessmen, court reporters, and flight attendants. We had in common only that we'd all taken the "Celebrating the Body Erotic" workshop and were sufficiently jazzed by the fusion of sexuality and spirituality to travel to a mountaintop in California to study it — no, embody it — more fully.

Joe Kramer assembled a peculiar and charismatic team of teachers for these trainings. Virtually all Wildwood intensives involved some exploration of anal eroticism; these rituals, and of course the weeklong anal massage class, were conducted by Chester Mainard, "the Avatar of Assholes." For Sacred Intimate Training, Joe enlisted as teachers John Pasqualetti, a choreographer and Reiki master, and Keith Hennessy, a Canadian-born performance artist and community activist in San Francisco. When I first got involved with Body Electric, Joe's right-hand man was Collin Brown, who was quiet, thoughtful, and meticulously practical in all the areas where Joe was tempestuous, emotional, and recklessly visionary. Collin, who identified as bisexual and who'd given up an East Coast career in publishing to pursue self-realization in California, eventually bought the Body Electric School from Joe and became its director. Though each of these men would become an important figure for me over the next few years, I'd already encountered and begun a relationship with them before we all converged at Wildwood for the first Sacred Intimate Training.

That first morning after breakfast, we gathered in the temple. Morning sun tumbled down the hill into the greenhouse windows along the south wall, which was built into the hillside so rocks and earth protruded into the room. We sat in a circle in the cool mountaintop daylight. I looked around the room full of emotions: little-kid excitement and critical-parent skepticism, good-student attentiveness, and a certain nervousness. It felt like the first day of school, Sacred Prostitute school. Mentally I had my pencils all sharpened.

I scanned the circle, registering with some surprise how many people in the room I already knew from New York or from other Body Electric activities. It was a good group. A big age range, from Philip and Kerry, the youngest and cutest, to a few elders who looked to be around 60. Lots of facial hair and natural bodies. On one level, it looked like a room full of regular friendly gay men, but I reminded himself that each of these men in some way accepted for himself the identity of sacred intimate, temple whore, erotic shaman. The number of circles like this that have ever been assembled on the planet is small.

"The sacred intimate is the most open and generous of individuals," Joe was saying. "The work is about being present multidimensionally."

I figured I wasn't the only person in the room who longed to hear more definitions of this thing called a sacred intimate. I wondered if I was the only one wondering what the fuck "multidimensionally" meant.

"Ask yourself, 'How generous am I? How stingy?' Keep in mind that even though you may be generous with time, you can still be stingy with heart."

One of the other teachers, John Pasqualetti, interrupted to say, "Energetically, think about moving not just to generosity but to abundance."

Multidimensionally .... energetically ... abundance... I knew this was New Age-speak, and I had mixed feelings about it. Part of me thrilled to the concepts and saw each word as a new road opening up, a scenic detour from the mundane commuter highway of everyday life. The writer part of me reared up on its hind legs and whinnied at any manifestation of jargon. Jargon is either competitive (I'm in because I know what this means and you're out because you don't) or willfully stupid (I actually believe what I'm saying makes sense) unless it's downright snake-charming. It made me impatient and suspicious.

"My commitment," Joe said, "is that at the end of nine days you be visibly shaken. I want you to be in a state you didn't think was accessible to you. This is the same commitment that you as a sacred intimate make to your clients, to bring them to a place where they say, *I didn't expect this much.*"

Talk about intimidating. I already felt inept.

The conversation turned to the more practical matter of hygiene. "Brush your teeth a lot," Joe suggested. "In the work we're in, it's permissible to tell people if their breath is bad. And bathe in salt crystals to remove unpleasant body odor."

"Salt is the oldest cleanser in the world," Keith Hennessy interjected as the resident anarchist pagan. Sporting tattoos of wiccan symbols on his upper arms and back with silver rings through his nipples, his nose, and the entire edges of both ears, he was naturally opposed to anything as bourgeois as deodorant or breath mints. "Gargle with salt water," he urged.

"It's important to be impeccable, to get rid of smells, body odor, bad breath. I offer this teaching in honor of Ron Gable, whose clients pay for the most expensive showers," Joe said, smiling at a tall sexy man sprawled on a pillow in the corner of the temple. Ron Gable had pride of place at this gathering, being the only self-identified "sex worker" in the group. I noticed that Joe Kramer was both awed and titillated by Ron's professional practice: for $150, he would put men in the shower and personally bathe them, then have sex with them, then give them another shower.

I admired Ron's audacity in publicly identifying himself as a sex worker, and I especially liked using the Marxist designation for "prostitute." But that sounded like way too much water for me.

"We all have major gifts," John Pasqualetti was saying. "Let's spend time to find out what they are." Although this morning circle felt like a rambling discourse, I saw that the staff had planned to take turns dispensing some introductory thoughts.

"I want you to look into yourself and find out what you need to wake up!" John Pasqualetti continued. "Experience the bliss of the joybody!"

The main theme of Pasqualetti's talk this morning was "energetic speaking," a concept that both intrigued and puzzled me.

"I request that you begin by speaking the conversation inside yourself," he said. "By naming the energy, you are presencing The God." He said The God as if we were supposed to know which God he meant. Dionysus? Pan? The Green Man? Cernunnos? I'm the kind of reader who likes footnotes and who stops to look up unfamiliar words in the dictionary. Apparently, Pasqualetti couldn't be bothered with obsessive notions of perfect clarity.

"There are ways to induce energetic speaking," he said. "Through breathing, through the cock, through trance, you can increase the energy charge and practice dancing with the energy, listening and speaking it. When you're with a client, you need to be able to read the energy. Hear what they say, and also take them somewhere else beyond massage to transformation in the presence of a sacred intimate. Use sacred hot chat to intoxicate and seduce them. Use the names of the cock strokes and the information you know about them to turn people on more. When they look at you, they see eyes full of compassion. When they hit a dead spot, change something quickly. Say 'Breathe this way,' and breathe right into their ears. Touch taboo places. Give a jolt of electricity. What you're aiming for is to leave them irreparably transformed. Nothing less."

Visibly shaken and irreparably transformed? My sacred intimate performance anxiety increased another notch.

CHAPTER TWENTY-SIX

The Food of Love

In the afternoon, talking gave way to touching. I felt more in my element. Everybody in the room had done Taoist erotic massage rituals before, so by now we knew the drill.

I had to hand it to Joe Kramer. He created a beautiful thing with this ritual. Half the men were lying on tables, and the other half moved down the rows, spending 15 to 20 minutes apiece massaging seven different men. The ritual leaders cast a spell with language and with music. The talk was all about making connections between heart and cock, opening up to feeling, conjuring the Native prayer "All my relations" to invite the participation of each man's loved ones in this world and the unseen world. The music started slow and sweet, with violin music to tug on the heartstrings. Of course, as soon as warm hands started touching naked bodies, boners began sprouting around the room, and the energy snowballed from there. The music became more rhythmic as the erotic energy built, and the flames crackling on one table would spread in concentric circles until the room became a pulsating mass of sighs, moans, and concentrated loving touch.

I chose to be a masseur first and felt surprisingly unself-conscious. It was fun. For the first time ever, though, it was even more fun being massaged. Hyper-conscientious about following all the instructions and doing the massage correctly, I was accustomed to receiving clumsy touch from well-meaning, untrained amateurs in workshops. This group was different. These were, after all, the holy whores of the global gay community. They gave great touch.

My first masseur was Philip, the beautiful blue-eyed shaved-headed Canadian muscle-boy. As he tenderly stroked my face, I wept. Oddly, I thought about my parents and missed them. During the first segment of the seven-part ritual, Joe Kramer invited those of us on the table to state an intention, something we wanted to get out of this massage. I whispered to Philip, "I want to be the food of love."

I decided to surrender to the pleasure of skilled touch and not rate my masseurs every minute. I felt hot oil slide across my skin, my hair, my sensitive dickhead, and I breathed along to the music. I let myself go. It wasn't until the fifth man, though, that I found myself getting turned on. It was Kerry, the bedroom-eyed male model from LA, who wasn't standoffish at all. He got right into shaking and rocking my body, working my cock into a state of frenzy. "Go crazy," John Pasqualetti called out, "go crazy on the table!" And I did. As Kerry leaned over me, rubbing his smooth tanned muscular body over my chest and torso, I pulled him on top of me, so we writhed around together on the table. I had the ecstatic sensation that I was the beach and Kerry was the ocean washing over me, rolling and sliding and laughing. It brought new meaning to the term "body-surfing."

During the climactic final sequence, my masseur was Woody Draper, a tall and loving ex-Jesuit from Southern California. As the sound system poured out the tribal rhythms of Babatunde Olatunji, Woody started slapping my chest and belly and thighs to the beat, playing me as if I were the Drums of Passion. When Joe led the group into a Big Draw after an hour and a half of continuous breathing, I clenched my butt, tightened my fists and belly, and held my breath as long as I could. When I finally let go and gasped for air, I felt myself almost drowning in the intake of oxygen. As I floated in the sensations rushing through my suddenly still body, I felt my mouth open wide to receive a supply of divine grace pouring like liquor from a golden goblet suspended in midair with a single unblinking eye hovering over it.

That evening, sitting in a circle after dinner in the nightly ritual of council, Woody began speaking with unusual eloquence, putting in words some of the perceptions that many people in the room were experiencing. "The message that a sacred intimate conveys to his client," Woody said, "is this: I would rather be here with you right now than anywhere else with anyone else."

Anxious in the morning, ecstatic in the afternoon, by bedtime I was feeling downright cranky, more angry than sexual. Partly I was in a bad mood because I called Hardy after dinner, and he'd been weird and distant. I had to drag out of him the information that he'd gone to the theater with a friend of ours, and they'd just finished having sex. It didn't bother me that he would have sex with someone else, but why couldn't he be more upfront about it? I was running a lot of nervous sexual energy myself. I always did the first night I went to one of these things and met a whole bunch of new guys. I felt stirred up with lust for Philip and Kerry. I wanted to fuck and get fucked.

Plus, I felt critical of everything, especially John Pasqualetti's way of talking. "We will create a new language here. There's no space for complaints or whining. Speak in terms of presencing the language you be." The language you be? What kind of talk is that? I suspected that John had been to a few too many New Age workshops and didn't know how jargon-clotted his speech had become.

Mostly I felt self-conscious, like I had set myself on an obstacle course, or I was about to take a difficult test for which I hadn't crammed. I understood, but only vaguely, that I was undergoing an identity shift. For years I had worked as a journalist, for whom others had always been the subject of inquiry and the authority of the situation. I didn't want to be the passive observer anymore. I wanted to be the authority; I wanted to be the hero of my own story. But that felt unusual, unfamiliar. It was hard. I saw how easy and comfortable it was to let other people take risks and weather the anxiety that arises from seizing the spotlight. The shift from watching on the sidelines to playing in the field terrified me. It kicked my ass. I was accustomed to giving my power away. Here I was invited to exercise my power, which was something else altogether.

John Pasqualetti talked a lot about the concept of "energetic speaking." What did that mean? I didn't feel like speaking. Where is my center? Where is my power? What am I here for? What do I seek? I thought I knew what this sacred intimate stuff was about. I thought I was spiritually centered and sexually alive and therefore had gifts to offer the world. But now that I was here, my mind went blank. I felt stupid and punished for not having as much clarity as John Pasqualetti had.

I wrote in my diary, "I just hate it when I don't know everything."

CHAPTER TWENTY-SEVEN

Stations of Priapus

Nobody ever got to Wildwood without hearing Joe Kramer's vision of starting a sex monastery. I took to it right away. I wanted to be a sex monk. Whenever I visited any spiritual community — whether it was the San Marco monastery in Florence crawling with tourists inspecting the frescos drawn in the monks' tiny cells, or the Lama Foundation in the mountains high above Taos — I felt the desire to live there. I wanted to pray and chant and meditate and not have to keep up with the trivia of the entertainment world or take some shitty job to pay exorbitant rent on a minuscule apartment.

Sitting in the temple at Wildwood, I looked around the room and wondered how many others were living out their monk fantasies. If I remembered correctly, eight or ten of them already had some experience of living as seminarians; Joe had taken a show of hands. Two-thirds had been raised Catholic, and about one-third had taken some steps toward the priesthood. It's a function of how thoroughly Catholic the Body Electric gang was that when Joe put on the schedule "Stations of Priapus" — the first opportunity in the training to practice being temple dancers and spirit vessels — no one bothered to explain what that meant. Nor did anybody ask. Apparently they had all understood the reference to Stations of the Cross.

Any practicing Catholic knows well those Easter Week services in which the priest ritually leads the congregation through a recreation of Jesus's agonizing journey from his arrest to his crucifixion, a drama in 12 scenes. Older churches commemorated these stations permanently in stained glass. At the bland chapels I remembered from Air Force bases, banners bearing key images (the Crown of Thorns, Mary Magdalene washing the feet of Jesus with her long Barbara Hershey hair) represented the Stations. Father Pigface and his minion of altar boys in rayon blouses would troop from one banner to the next, reciting the oft-told tale in a dread-inducing drone. It was one of the most boring ceremonies of the Catholic calendar, in my recollection, made all the more excruciating by the countdown. ("Five down, seven to go.") How wicked and wonderful of Joe Kramer to merge this Catholic solemnity with the myth of the ever-hard Priapus, to promise a boner behind every banner, to put a little kick in this 12-step program!

The idea of Stations of Priapus was: half the group would stay in their rooms or tents, and the other half would travel from room to room for six different healing sessions. The roles would switch after every session. The first time, the hosts would be "sacred intimates" and the visitors would be clients who could ask for whatever healing they wanted. In the next session, the travelling group would be "sacred intimates" making out-calls to the clients in their rooms. Each session would last 30 minutes with five minutes between.

Keith Hennessy would be the timekeeper and circle the perimeter of camp in his black mesh tutu banging a gong when it was time to change.

I was absolutely terrified at the prospect of giving someone a "healing session." I assumed that the people who were doctors and shrinks and masseurs and sex workers already knew what it was like to greet a new client, ascertain his needs, plan a course of action, and complete a session. I didn't know any of those things. I could feel failure looming in front of me. I would be exposed as a hopelessly inept sacred prostitute and be paraded through camp wearing a conical cap with a big red F on it.

When I was assigned to be a stay-at-home whore, I was grateful. A true Taurus, I feel more secure at home. I had one of the best rooms at Wildwood, a large corner room overlooking the garden. It was relatively quiet because it was on the opposite end of the building from the communal bathrooms. I shared it with Kenny Jay, a tall funny guy from San Diego whose life had been changed by swimming with dolphins in Florida yet who maintained an earthy pragmatism instilled from his occupation as a hairdresser. His motto in life was "Next!"

Preparing my private temple to meet my clients, I lit a stick of champa and waved the incense into each corner of the room. I cleaned off the top of the bureau except for my altar with pictures of my spiritual teachers. I set up my portable stereo speakers and put on a tape of Enya with the sound turned down low. [MFF: Now it seems so corny, but once upon a time Enya's schmoopy Celtic music was considered hip, piped into boutiques and spas.] The day was warm, and I wasn't wearing anything at all.

The bell rang. Practice began. The first client to knock on my screen door was Tom Hammond. That was a relief. We'd gotten all hot and bothered doing energy-reading exercises together in the temple, and it wouldn't be any trouble at all spending half an hour together. Tom came in dangling a strip of rawhide, and we quickly fell into a leathery mode of tying up cocks and balls. But after a few minutes, I felt like I was putting on an act pretending to be some kind of stud raring to go. We dropped the act and hung out together talking for a while, resting on my bed with our legs intertwined. Tom had hooked up the second day of camp with my roommate Kenny, and he filled me in on the progress of their whirlwind romance. Before he got far into the story, we heard a gong sound, the signal to wrap things up and move on. This didn't feel like a temple prostitute session to me. I felt like I'd played hooky and smoked cigarettes in the bathroom with another bad boy during social studies.

Lesson #1: Sacred intimate work wasn't as hard as I thought it would be.

Woody Draper had joked about having the nipples of God, so when he came in, I chose to curl up in his lap and nurse at his nipples. I closed my eyes and let myself drift into the infantile contentment of suckling. Suddenly an image flashed into my brain that made me gasp. It was brief and intense, like something from a dream: I was indeed an infant nursing at my mother's breast. My mother and father observed that my baby penis was erect from the pleasure of sucking. They were laughing about it at first, and then my father got turned on. He moved me away from my mother's breast and took my place. They proceeded to make love while I lay next to them on the bed, still hungry. Was this a long-buried memory bubbling to the surface? An archetypal Oedipal fantasy? A poetic distillation of my lifelong feeling of being undernourished by my parents? All of the above? Whatever it was, I found it to be powerful and disturbing chunk of psychic product.

Lesson #2: Sexual healing work didn't have to mean having genital sex. The body could simply be a doorway to the realm of the soul.

In another session, I found myself alone with Freddy, a friendly psychotherapist from Seattle. I'd hardly spoken to him, but I'd been fixated on him because he had the most unusual face in the group. He had some of the most extreme acne scars I'd ever seen. His face wasn't red and scabby — the pimples were all healed — but it was so covered with pockmarks that it looked like a topographical map. Far from repulsing me, it intrigued me. Like receding hairlines and speech impediments (especially stammers), acne scars attract me. They represent vulnerability and I like being near them; it brings out my protective nature. With his permission, I traced Freddy's pockmarks with my fingers, admired their texture and how they made his face special among faces, and rubbed both my lips and my stiff dick across the moonscape of his countenance. He told me that he'd been with his lover 14 years, and they'd never once had a conversation about his acne scars.

Freddy told me that he'd been scared to approach me because, he said, "I'm afraid of your power." He turned his fear into an accusatory faux-affirmation: "You take your power at my expense." I asked him to repeat that statement. He said, "You take your power at my expense," and then he added in a small pathetic voice, "Please?" We both caught our breaths and then burst out laughing. Truth had been spoken! Seeing others as powerful and himself as weak was a collaboration between his imagination and his desire.

Lesson #3: The distinction between "sacred intimate" and "client" is not always easy to discern. Who's healing? Who heals?

After we'd completed the "Stations of Priapus" exercise, we were encouraged to spend our free time the rest of the week scheduling practice sessions with anybody we wanted to. If you wanted to get a real massage from one of the bodyworkers in the group, you could do that. If you wanted to sit in the hot tub with someone gazing into one another's eyes, you could do that. Or if you'd been flirting with someone for a couple of days and just wanted to get together and fuck, you could do that.

That's how I ended up in bed at lunchtime with Neville Rowe. He was a tall, handsome New Zealander in his fifties with salt-and-pepper hair, a shaggy mustache, and big soulful dark eyes who gave up his career as an electrical engineer in the oil business to become a past-life regression therapist. In certain New Age circles, he was famous for appearing onstage in rented halls to channel dolphins. I doubt if I could have gone to bed with him if I'd ever witnessed one of those performances. The main thing about Neville, though, is that he was notorious for fixating on the youngest men at Body Electric gatherings, in that tragic Aschenbach way that many people considered pathetic and laughable. I was hardly a boy, yet something about my way of frisking around at Wildwood triggered his boy-trance, just as he pushed my Daddy buttons.

Enchanted by my wild boyishness, he wanted to make love with me. I wasn't especially attracted to him physically, though I was flattered by his attention. Still, something about him stirred my soul. As we kissed and made love in my room, with the California sun streaming through the screen door and the birds piping in the eucalyptus trees, time seemed to slow down and stop. In his sad, ancient, searching eyes, eternity opened up for me, and in those few endless moments I felt I was acting out with him the love I wanted to give my father, and to God, that I would have given to Hardy had he been with me. In that moment I was able to have the experience I wanted by having it with Neville. There was something mysterious and healing about it.

I think that's when I understood that for me sex is not reserved for the people I love or think are cute or attractive. My desire to have sex with someone is often profoundly transpersonal. Not impersonal. Impersonal would mean it didn't matter who the person was — I'm just using them like a Kleenex to shoot my wad into. But transpersonal means actually having the experience of ... sounds so corny to say, but MAKING LOVE TO GOD through having sex with a person. Sexiness is close to godliness. In other words, when I have sex with someone who's not my intimate partner, if I have any consciousness about it, I'm choosing to have sex with the spark of divinity that he is. In that sense, sex is a form of prayer, no less precious for being abundant.

I know that this concept became part of my experience through Body Electric work. It started with my first Taoist erotic massage ritual, when I understood that I was touching each of the seven men on my route not because I thought they were cute and I hoped to marry them and have a share on Fire Island with them, but because I wanted to add to the amount of pleasure experienced in the universe. I wanted to make love, with my hands — literally, like making a loaf of bread. I wanted to pitch in to the communal ocean of love and in doing so receive what I needed, exactly like the Christian concept of communion. The exchange was not personal and quid-pro-quo but symbolic and transpersonal. The feelings were no less real for being generated by a symbolic action. I wanted to be a sexual Good Samaritan — make love unto others as you would have them make love unto you.

And that's what I act out with my clients daily,

a symbolic act of communion. Body Electric made me a sex priest, and since I began I don't feel entirely complete unless I've said my daily Mass, performed my daily ceremony of anointing a man's body on the altar of my massage table and receiving the blessing of flesh and blood made holy — made whole — by the ritual of touch and prayer. Give us this day our daily bread.

CHAPTER TWENTY-EIGHT

Scared Inmate

I'm tempted to detail every ritual, every awakening, every conversation that took place at Wildwood. But that could fill another book, and, frankly, I think you had to be there. Suffice it to say that Sacred Intimate Training fed my burning passion for erotic-spiritual community. After that, the wildfire spread.

In the summer of 1992, an old friend of Hardy's offered me the free use of his house, a two-room cabin without electricity back in the hills of Mendocino County, three and a half hours north of San Francisco. This house-sitting gig was meant to be a writer's retreat, but in the six months I spent there I ended up doing very little writing and a whole lot of soul-searching. My residency in Laytonville launched the definitive separation from Hardy and the beginning of my truly terrifying drift as a writer removed from theater and New York journalism, which had been my professional home for 12 years.

Six months of solo self-observation and existential

contemplation led, upon my return to New York, to the trauma of divorce and relocation. It was the end of an era that had lasted almost half my life. In the despair of being single for the first time as an adult at the advanced age of 39, disillusioned and somehow pained by my profession as a journalist, I found myself in 1993 unable to resist the call to act on my archetypally remembered identity as temple whore, erotic midwife, sacred intimate.

When the practice became concrete, the conversation changed. The ideals suddenly confronted the reality. I struggled to keep my balance, morally, ethically, idealistically. I scrambled to find a way to accept as right, correct, and acceptable the unpredictable human reality that erupted as one stranger after another took his naked place on the phallic altar of my massage table.

What I wanted from Joe Kramer and Wildwood and Body Electric was permission: to see and touch and be seen and be touched by many naked men; to connect this desire to my experience of spirituality. ("Spirituality" meaning what, exactly? Union with God? Being myself-and-more-than-myself? Yes.) This is what Joe Kramer held out in the context of Sacred Intimate Training. In the circle it seemed possible, perhaps because in the circle it has always been possible. The circle has historical memory. Back in New York City, in my funky home temple, there was no liturgy, no culture of erotic spirituality shared with my clients. Instead, there was The Real World, a culture with strong traces of sex-negativity, anti-spirituality, and homophobia. At Wildwood, I saw my calling as religious, and I felt I was accepted into a priesthood. We were an assembly of like-minded men. I was dancing with wizards. At home in the big city, I was like a missionary, fighting an uphill battle that at times felt surpassingly foolish.

Caught in a massive identity shift for which "midlife transition" is a grotesquely mild euphemism, I cycled through self-definitions. Dutiful student and keeper of the Body Electric faith. Single man craving contact. Ever-curious writer willing to keep the tape rolling, the eyes open, the notebooks filling with scribbles. The kid in the candy store, releasing into sexual indulgence, physical triumph, daily joy, vanity, wish-fulfillment, long-held inhibitions set aside, a period of self-knowledge through copious sexuality.

Full of questions, I felt a nagging sense of insecurity and self-judgment. Overwhelmed by difficult-to-articulate emotions, I staggered from the weight of taking on the sexual issues of my clients (wounded by shame and sadness and scarcity) and the projections which I clearly invited. The good boy, the dutiful student, the humble devotee wanted to Do It Right, and I felt something was amiss. After working continuously from August 1993 to the fall of 1994, I took a break for a couple of months.

When I began again, my practice changed. I got more self-conscious about my work, less free sexually, more concerned about my responsibilities as a healer. I began to understand my own wounds: my quest for daddy approval (especially of my sexuality); my little-child hurt; my deep need to receive kindness, tenderness, and intimacy without having to perform sexually to get it.

The first time I heard Joe Kramer talk about sacred prostitutes, I recognized some part of myself that had never been seen. The changes I made in 1994-95, the second year of my practice, induced a new flavor of melancholy: I missed the part of myself that felt fulfilled by being a sacred prostitute and channeling God's energy. Was it God, though, or was it ego? I had so many questions, and instinctively I knew that I wasn't going to be able to answer any of them if I continued the way I was going, trying to fulfill any sexual need my clients brought in the door. It's so easy to forget yourself. I needed to remember why I wanted to do this work in the first place. I needed to remember the difference between sheer sexual indulgence for the fun of it and sexual healing as a doorway to self-knowledge.

To do that, I knew that eventually I would need to redraw my boundaries and learn a different way of being with my clients. But I wasn't ready to do that. I didn't even know how to do it, and it would take me a long time to figure it out. I had what seemed like a giant task ahead of me. I felt afraid and in the dark. Suspending my sex work felt like a big move. Backwards or forwards? I couldn't tell.

PART THREE
Course Correction
(1995-2002)

Eugene (Part 1)

Yesterday I had a session that I worried about in advance. This was with my client-husband Eugene, the affluent black businessman who's going through a divorce. Since our second session, he's been nudging me about "going all the way." I've resisted that mentality and tried to convey to him that erotic massage/bodywork/sex can be lots of different things besides penetrative-intercourse-to-ejaculation. But in our last session we found ourselves in a place of experimenting. He was feeling especially aggressive and horny, and we were lying around in bed in the afternoon, rather than on the massage table.

There's a particular moment that I love. It's when a guy is sprawled invitingly on my densely patterned Australian comforter in front of my architecturally splendid bay window, either in his underpants or completely naked with a healing boner pointing up toward his navel. I love walking slowly toward him and draping myself over his body, as our arms and legs find just the right position to interlock like jaws. That coming together feels great. I like to wrap my arms all the way around his back and bury my face in his neck. I like it when he stretches his legs around my hips and we lie there, a happy clam. The thing about Eugene, too, is that he loves to kiss. He has big fleshy lips that are fun to chew and suck. His mouth tastes good. He knows how to use his tongue. He's sweet and warm and never uptight about his body. He has an open curiosity about his body and mine and a taste for affection that seems neither desperate nor chary.

In our last session, he quickly slid me onto my stomach and lay on my back with his knob resting in my crack, the way I usually do with him. He nibbled on my neck and the top of my back. I took a couple of his fingers in my mouth and sucked them deep into my throat. He leaned back and put some spit on the end of his dick and then lay back on top of me. We were heading into the danger zone. He seemed intent on sliding into me without benefit of either lube or loveglove. Uh-unhhh baby. I rolled onto my side, and we had a little chat. He was happy to have that chat, happy to agree to using rubbers, happy to go slow — but mainly happy that I seemed to have consented to letting him, you know, put it in me.

Eventually I did roll him over onto his back, put a rubber on him, lube myself up, and slowly lower myself onto him. It took a while, and it went slowly because his dick is extra-large. We never got to the point where he could let go and fuck me the way a guy likes to fuck, long strokes, bang bang bang, with abandon. I hovered on the threshold between pain and surrender. I kept trying to relax, which generally made my erection wilt. Then I'd work myself up to full hardness again. I know that's a way to override the sensations in my butt, to go a little numb and avoid the feelings, which I'd rather not do. But it does keep me interested in prolonging the process.

Every time I would start jerking myself fast, Eugene would say, "Don't cum yet! Don't cum yet!" Finally I had to stop and dismount. It wasn't pleasurable anymore. I took off the rubber. We switched positions, him on top butt-surfing me, and I introduced some sacred hot chat. I imagined him entering me and fucking me and cumming inside me, and blam! He shot til he was wobbly in the knees.

It's funny, you know — during that session I found myself feeling a little like a jaded hooker, wondering what time it was, wondering when he would cum and we could stop. I wasn't getting much pleasure out of this interaction the way that I do sometimes when I'm sucking cock or simply holding someone, lying around cuddling and being close without moving. Afterwards I felt like it was time to have a conversation with Eugene and try to steer him away from the straight-guy mentality that all our sessions were building up to some version of fuck-the-pussy-til-you-squirt. That's why I was nervous.

When he came in yesterday, we spent 45 minutes fully dressed talking. He told me that our last session was enormously meaningful to him. Fucking with a man was something that he'd thought about doing since he was a teenager and had always suppressed the desire. To act on that desire at last, in a slow and conscious way with someone who's intelligent and able to talk about the experience together, showed him a piece of himself that he was grateful to have.

So we weren't as far away in our thinking as I imagined we were.

Nevertheless, I made it a point to talk about my interest in interrupting the pattern of upping the ante with every session: progressing toward intercourse, or defining our sessions as checking off a list of sex acts to perform. He admitted that he's a linear thinker, but that he truly didn't have that agenda in mind.

I did have an agenda for the day. I didn't want to launch right into erotic play with him. But I knew that Just a Massage wouldn't do today. We only had 45 minutes left, too. So I decided I would introduce some classic Taoist erotic massage with conscious breathing, which I'd never done with Eugene before. At first he didn't like the idea of a session predicated on not ejaculating. "I'd be lying if I didn't say that I do like a sense of completion" was how he put it. But I reframed it this way: Taoist erotic massage is not about denying pleasure but about expanding your capacity for sensation and making contact with spirit.

It's hard work breathing vigorously for 25 minutes nonstop, especially the first time you do it, before you know that there is an ecstatic experience on the other side of your initial resistance and discomfort. I worried the whole time that I wasn't allowing enough time for this experience. Trying to cram it all into half an hour might give Eugene a bad impression of this kind of energy work. But he was erect throughout the massage and kept going with the breathing. I led him into a Big Draw, even played the corniest Body Electric post-Big Draw music (from the soundtrack to *The Mission*) and gave him a few minutes to simply luxuriate in that feeling. When I asked how it was for him, he liked it. It did feel like a spiritual experience to him, more so than an erotic experience, which surprised him. "I think I needed this today."

After he got dressed, I gave him a copy of my article about Joe Kramer that was published in the *Voice*. He called me this morning to say he'd read the article and wanted to take me to dinner to discuss some of the ideas in the article, which he found exciting.

All of which is to say, I guess I'm doing good work. It feels scary to me because I'm making it up as I'm going along, this combination of holy whore and hot hairy horny priest.

CHAPTER THIRTY

Eugene (Part 2)

I want to stop and register all the things I'm not saying about my relationship with Eugene. How do I feel about being with him?

I am, among other things, intrigued with getting to know a black man who is upper-middle-class, who's a successful businessman. I have met entertainers or people in show business who meet that description, but I've never had any friends who did. Although I never show it or talk about it to him, I'm fascinated to hear about his "lifestyle" — taking his two sons on a skiing trip to New Mexico, flying to Washington for a date with a woman, living in a townhouse on the East Side. His (soon to be ex) wife is black, and his friends fix him up with black women. I suspect that most of his business colleagues are white, but I don't know. Aside from comments about his dates and that everyone thought he and his wife (who works at the New York Public Library on Fifth Avenue) were a good match, he has never talked about his life in terms of race. And yet it's always in the forefront of my mind that Eugene is a wealthy black married man exploring his bisexuality. I am mystified by my role in his life. I'm a slender, muscular, masculine white guy with a handsome face, a hairy body, and the slightly olive complexion that comes from my Portuguese heritage. Plus I have a brain and a good heart. I'm a pleasure to be with, not to mention look at. I'm youthful but clearly not a kid. I consider my maturity a plus; it means I have more to offer as a person. I'm open and friendly, and I'm inclined to see the best side of people. That makes me a little naïve, I guess. I take people at face value, which means I will listen to miles and miles of bullshit before challenging someone. Anyway, if I were a married man in his forties looking to experiment with homosex, I'd be thrilled to encounter a handsome smart guy who's willing to give me the experience I want for $100 a pop.

So the money. What do I feel about this? I know that Eugene has money, he knows how to tip, he appreciates me. Does it make me more willing to go along with things he wants to do that I don't especially enjoy? No, that's not it. But I do go out of my way to expand his desire-body. I do feel like a geisha with him – not just a pleasure-provider but a curator of an aesthetic experience.

Here's one thing that I accept about him: his closetiness around his bisexuality. I'm willing to bet that he has never told anyone that he goes to see a male masseur for erotic touch. I wonder if he has told anyone that he has experimented with cocksucking and buttfucking. I have refrained from pushing him toward "coming out." I try not to let egregious assumptions about gay culture go unchallenged, but I haven't said to him, "Eugene, instead of going out with women, why don't you try going out with men and having a relationship with a male peer?"

Oh my God — I guess I'm it. I guess by agreeing to

have dinner with him, we're having some version of a date. This will be his experiment with being in public with a handsome (slightly) younger man that he knows is gay. What should I wear? Should I be real swishy and obvious? Wear my pink fuzzy sweater? Or should I butch it up and be obvious that way? Leave my three-day stubble on my face and wear my motorcycle jacket with a long dangly human-skull earring? Or should I go straight and mainsteam, in khaki trousers and a button-down shirt?

What do I like about Eugene sexually? Well, for one thing, I do find him physically attractive. I like his body. In some ways, I acquiesce to erotic-play sessions because it's easy. Rolling around in bed is more fun and less work for the money than giving a massage, that's for sure. Eugene has a giant dick that gets hard easily and stays up. It's delicious to slurp, and I've managed to take it all the way down my throat, which excites both of us. The fact that he's never had any experience with men makes me extremely tempted to drain his balljuice, to get my long-desired forbidden jolt of male protein. I do like kissing him. He has a great butt that responds to touch wonderfully. It makes me hot to butt-surf him. I would love to just slide my dick in his ass and fuck his butt good sometime until I deliver my squirtage deep inside him.

As the kid asks in Bill Finn's musical March of the Falsettos, "Is this therapy?"

Yeah, I have to say, this is clearly an invaluable initiatory experience for him. He gets to explore forbidden desires, and so far nothing has happened to say, "Stop! Bad! Danger! You shouldn't do this or have this!"

What am I getting out of working with Eugene? The pleasure of intimate touch with a handsome man isn't new or urgent to me. What is new and valuable and challenging is the opportunity to improvise each session. I don't know exactly what we're going to do or what's going to work.

CHAPTER THIRTY-ONE

Eugene (Part 3)

When I saw the restaurant where Eugene suggested we meet for dinner, I was tickled. It was on the first floor of the Lipstick Building, where I'd never been. "It's a little flashy," he said on the phone and again as we were being seated by the haughty mocha-colored maitresse d'.

"What do you mean by flashy?" I asked. To me flashy meant neon chasers, loud music, and patrons in shades.

He corrected his description to "theatrical," and that it was — pastel lighting from multilayered sconces, the floor plan of a Japanese water garden, strange chairs with low wooden backs. Eugene clearly had been to this restaurant before and was conversant with its relationship to others run by the same owner. I got the feeling that he followed these things not out of his own passion but because he felt a social obligation to keep up with them.

I arrived at the corner of 54th and 3rd as he was walking into the restaurant, and I got a glimpse of him from a different perspective than I usually do. I saw that he hunches his back and pitches his head forward slightly, a look that reminds me of turtles. He looked more beaten-down than usual. His hair seemed grayer from this distance.

He was amusingly formal to begin with. "Thank you for coming out this evening," he said. "What have you been up to?"

What have I been up to? You mean in the two days since we last saw each other? I'm not good with that kind of small talk. But I know the feeling. It says, *I'm nervous, and I want to talk about something inconsequential for a few minutes until my heart rate stabilizes and I stop sweating.*

The waiter inquired if we wanted drinks. We both thought we'd have a glass of wine. Eugene asked what the house choices were. "Red or white?"

"Red for me," I said.

Eugene said, "White."

Okay, I went into male-competitive judgment mode here and thought, *Real wine drinkers drink red wine.* As if I'm an expert, right? The waiter rattled off the choices — a merlot and a Cotes du Rhone, and a sauvignon blanc and a chardonnay. Eugene nixed the idea of a sauvignon blanc. I don't know why. That's the choice I would have made. He went with the chardonnay, which made me think, *Faux wine drinker.* I had the merlot. The waiter brought a spicy peanut sauce and rice cakes, which we dug into.

A question about my writing led gracefully into the conversation Eugene seemed most eager to have, about the article I gave him about the Body Electric school and the concept of sex as spiritual practice.

"I enjoyed the experience I had the other day," he said, referring to the Taoist erotic massage with a Big Draw. "But I didn't know what to do with the experience or the images that came to me."

"It helps to have a daily spiritual practice, so that

your meditations deepen and accumulate. Another way to do that is to practice these meditations with a partner," I suggested. "What's your experience with spiritual practice?"

"Basically, it goes back to black Baptist churches," he said. "I have a lot of memories of people in the throes of spiritual ecstasy. You know, holy rollers. The thought of losing control that way scares me. I guess I worry that if allow my sexual energy to connect with my spirituality, I might go into a trance and not be able to come out."

"Spiritual experiences usually happen inside a strong container," I pointed out, "and it takes conscious effort to create that container. Even though that teenage girl rolling on the floor in the aisle of the church may seem to be out of control, she's held by a safe container — the congregation, the music, the minister. She couldn't have the same experience on the street corner. The same goes with erotic spirituality. The ancient practices of tantra have a different goal than the climax-oriented experience of sex. They offer people a way to create a structure within which to have a direct experience of God or the divine or whatever you want to call the powerful energy that sexuality arouses in your body."

"I almost had a breakthrough the other day in our session," Eugene said, "but not quite. I felt somewhat isolated. I wanted a more active participation in the experience."

I spelled out in more detail two different tracks of where to go with this erotic-spiritual experimentation. "You could practice solo and make it an inner journey, or you could practice with a partner. Either way, the idea of tantra is to move sexual energy — or kundalini — through the chakras from the base of the spine to the top of the head."

He didn't know anything about tantra and didn't know what chakras were. "I'm a businessman," he said.

I declined to give the whole lecture about chakras on the spot. Perhaps later.

I realized that when you're getting into this whole realm of sacred sex or conscious sex, there is a lot of groundwork that you need to know. That's how the conversation started, I guess. Eugene was intrigued to learn from my article that there is a whole intellectual underpinning to this work, a scholarship and tradition. It wasn't just about flailing around in a bunch of feelings. One of the things that I like about Eugene is that he's interested in understanding things on an intellectual level in addition to experiencing them physically. He's not afraid to have the experience, but a little bit of verbal or intellectual information allows him to go much farther. I'm like that, too.

"How did you learn all this stuff?" he marveled.

His rapt attention was starting to stir up my grandiose fantasies of being a sex guru. Was I getting too preachy? Or was I performing for Daddy's approval, and then turning skittish when I got what I wanted? In any case, I felt exposed and a little embarrassed suddenly, talking to a man of the world like Eugene. He had a lot more to teach me about making a fortune in the publishing business than I could tell him about tantra.

"Oh, I'm still a baby at this," I said. "I'm still a student." I was grateful when the line of questions shifted more toward biography.

We traded life stories. He grew up in a poor family in New Jersey. His father was a construction worker. Eugene himself was slated to go into industrial work rather than to college. In his junior year he took an elective course in ancient history and became the best student in the class. That changed everything for him. His family, strangely, wasn't thrilled at the idea of his going to college. "It was out of ignorance," he said. "I think my dad felt threatened because he hadn't gone to college." He spent a lot of his undergraduate years travelling beyond the small college he first enrolled at in New Jersey. He went to Georgetown for a year and then London. When it came time to go to graduate school, Harvard accepted him, but he chose the University of Michigan at Ann Arbor instead. He felt unworthy of Harvard. We talked about how easy it is to adopt the intellectual insecurity of an undereducated father.

So blah blah blah, we found out a lot about each other. We finished dinner and left the restaurant. At the corner he said, "I don't feel like ending the evening now. Would you like to continue?"

This took me by surprise. "What did you have in mind?" I said.

"I don't know, maybe touch, physical contact," he said.

I didn't say anything. "I've put you on the spot," he said. "I'm sorry."

"You have put me on the spot," I admitted. "I'm just checking inside myself to see what my body feels like doing." And inside I felt torn. I didn't know what I was going to do the rest of the evening except putter around at home longing for contact. Why not loll about with Eugene? But do I want to do that? What about boundaries with clients? I tried once before dating a client, and we discovered that we both had a better time within the context of a massage session. Would it be any different with Eugene?

Since I couldn't decide on the spot, I suggested we walk for a while. Inevitably, we walked toward my house. I had to admit that I had a big hard-on walking down the street. He said he did, too. We were at the corner of 56th and Park, stopped at the light. Cabs raced uptown past us. I took a step back to see if I could spy the big bulge in his pants. It was early evening in mid-spring, getting dark, and he was standing there in his charcoal pinstriped suit, with his briefcase slung over one shoulder. "It's easier for me to disguise it," he said. His left hand was in the pocket of his trousers, covering the tree root rising inside his pants. I looked down at my own crotch. I had dressed mainstream for this date, black trousers, gray shirt, Chinese silk windbreaker. But I was wearing my fanny-pack (ubiquitous accessory at the time), which often looks like a codpiece anyway. It rested strategically over the boner poking out of my crotch. It felt fun and exciting to walk down the street with another man, both of us aroused at the thought of being naked together and touching.

By the time we got to my house, our erections had wilted. I had second thoughts about the prospects of spending the rest of the evening in bed with Eugene. Wouldn't it be merely a continuation of our working sessions, me showing him the ropes and giving him space to get experience at being sexual with men? What's the difference between that and the sessions he pays me for? He was saying that he felt our sessions were one-sided, defined by him, that he called when he felt needy. There wasn't an option for me to propose getting together with him.

Suddenly I felt all the professional ethics I'd ever thought about coming to the forefront. "This may seem so obvious that it goes without saying," I said, looking in his eyes, "but the sessions we have together are work for me. It's what I do professionally, it's how I earn my living, and I've been trained to do this work. I offer you a service by creating the space where you can have the experience of being who you are, and in exchange you pay me money. It's value for value."

That did the trick with Eugene. He got what I was saying. I was reluctant to say that, because it sounded a little callous: "I spend time with you because you pay me money for it." Somehow, though, with Eugene it relieved the guilt he had that he was taking something from me that he found valuable and didn't think it was fair unless he gave something back in kind.

Instead of going up to my apartment, getting naked and using each other's faces for sausage garages, I steered us toward the park where we sat on a bench in the dark holding hands and talking.

"I want to kiss you," he said, and "I want to learn to manage my horniness."

As gently as I could, I pointed out to him that he hadn't told anyone else in his life that he was attracted to men and that he was wanting me to take on the entire burden of his secret sexuality. I kept dancing around saying bluntly, "What's in it for me?" But I did say, "I am not your destination. Sooner or later, you'll have to take the next step in meeting other men to explore your attraction to them. Sooner or later, you'll have to tell someone in your life. Your friends love you and care about you and only want you to be happy. They think they're doing you a favor by introducing you to available women. They might be delighted to introduce you to available men."

He agreed that was true, but he doesn't feel ready for it. Of course, what he wasn't saying was it would be so easy if I would do it all for him. I specifically declined to do that. I'm glad I did. The last thing I need is to start getting emotionally wrapped up with a closet-case boyfriend.

As it dawned on him that we weren't going to go back to my place and touch each other naked, I could feel Eugene slump with sadness. He didn't feel like ending the evening yet, and he didn't want to go home to an empty house. I suddenly got the inspiration that I should take him to the Townhouse Bar, which is an East Side bar for discreet homosexual gentlemen. This would be probably the least intimidating introduction to gay bars for Eugene. I'd never been there myself, and I ended up taking him to the restaurant rather than the bar.

It was crowded, but a drunk queen with bizarre pointy black-framed glasses gave up his barstool for us. We sat and had another glass of wine apiece. He had two, come to think of it, while telling me his wife's amazing family background. Her grandfather was a Yoruba chief in Nigeria with many wives, one of whom was Michelle's grandmother, whom he met in Port-au-Prince on a brief business expedition. He eventually had something like 75 children, the oldest of whom was Michelle's mother. It was an oppressive situation, though, and on a pretext of going shopping Michelle and her mother flew to Paris and never went back. Her mother returned to Haiti and married a local man, which scandalized the clan back in Nigeria. But there it was. Michelle grew up the daughter of a Yoruba princess, and that gave her the self-possession to go to the Sorbonne and eventually get her MBA at Harvard. Eugene said his wife had never told their children this story. I was dazzled. Her background also explained to me her high-strung nature and her habit of slashing Eugene's shirts down the back in fits of jilted-female rage.

We parted at the corner. We hugged and he got in a cab to go uptown. I felt a little guilty in that people-pleasing way because I didn't give Eugene exactly what he wanted. I wondered if I denied myself some pleasure by spending the evening cerebrating and drinking wine rather than touching. Mostly, though, I felt like I did the right thing.

CHAPTER THIRTY-TWO

The Nether Eye Opens

When Jerry called, I knew from his name and his tense, timid voice that I'd given him a massage once before. I found him in my client log, but the entry didn't churn up any detailed memories. The creature who arrived at my door might as well have been a total stranger. He was short and nearly bald on top, an out-of-shape blob of a middle-aged man with reptilian slits for eyes. My notes reminded me that he was "overweight and ashamed of it."

He didn't seem to recognize me or remember that he'd seen me in the past. So I pretended I didn't know him, either. We had the standard first-time preliminary chat. Did he have any injuries I should know about, or sensitive spots, or places he didn't like to be touched? He told me he'd just gotten a bunch of shots to go overseas, therefore I should avoid working on his arms.

"Did you get your shots earlier today?"

He said, "No, yesterday, but they're still a little sore."

I didn't point out that yesterday was Sunday, an unusual day for inoculations.

He went to the bathroom and came back wearing only his white button-down shirt. He slipped off the shirt and wanted to hop right onto the table. I said, "I'd like to have you do some stretching before we put you on the table, to loosen you up." He looked at me like I was crazy. Reluctantly, he took a step away from the table. As I directed him to close his eyes, take some breaths, and become aware of his body, he followed my instructions, but he acted like a little kid annoyed at having an adult make him do stupid things, like walk downstairs one step at a time.

When I had him stretch him arms up to the ceiling, I noticed he was holding something in his right hand.

"What's that in your hand, Jerry?"

He showed me the white plastic inhaler.

"No," I said, feeling shaky. "I don't use poppers."

He said, "You don't have to."

I said, "I don't mix poppers with massage."

He said, "They help me relax."

I said, "I'm a good masseur. You'll be plenty relaxed."

He dutifully deposited the tiny bottle on top of his clothes, which he'd left on the chair next to the massage table. As he lay on his back and I stretched out his arms and legs more, I tried to lighten the atmosphere. I mentioned that I lived in Japan when I was young and the shots we had to get before moving there. He didn't respond. He kept his lips pressed together tightly. He seemed to be pouting about having his poppers confiscated. It made me nervous. I felt guilty for shaming him about using poppers.

He resisted a lot of the massage. He seemed restless and impatient with my slow tempo, scratching himself and coughing. He never sighed and sank into the pleasure of being touched. I got the picture that he's someone who's used to going to masseurs for a half-assed backrub and a handjob, no questions asked. Perhaps at the beginning I could have broached the subject of his real desire and made some accommodation. Often I do say something like, "What's the experience you'd like to have today?" Not that anyone ever says, "A half-assed backrub and a handjob, please."

Guys like Jerry who crawl around in a snail-shell of sex-shame rarely have much experience at asking for what they want. They either expect you to read their minds, or they're masochistically resigned to whatever you want to dish out. In my desire to be conscious about sexual touch, you'd think I'd have developed a smooth routine by now of letting shy, sexually undernourished guys like this know what they're in for with me. For instance, I could say, "I'll get around to focusing on your erotic body, but first I'm going to spend about 40 minutes massaging the muscle tension out of your back and your legs and your feet." I refrain from being that direct because I want to avoid sounding too much like one of those wholesome Danish sex-education films. Rather than tease clients up to my level, I suppose I tend to sink down to their level of inarticulateness.

In any case, now I was launched into my usual massage routine, and there was no way of stopping it gracefully. I knew giving him a thorough massage had value. I also suspected that he couldn't give a shit.

Everything changed when I got around to his butt. My notes told me I had done buttwork on him before, so I felt confident in moving in for close butt touch. When I spread his cheeks and lightly brushed the coarse black hairs and the shiny pink skin around his stretched-out butthole, he twitched as if shocked by an electric current. When I rested the palm of my hand against his pelvic floor and rocked him back and forth, his erection swelled out from under his ballbag, the snail poking its head out of its shell, antennae first. Even if I'm fairly certain that someone wants butt massage, I like to check. Sometimes people have hemorrhoids or loose bowels or some other condition they'd prefer to conceal. I leaned in close to his ear and said, "If you like, Jerry, I could put on gloves and do some more massage around your butt."

"Okay," he said.

I reached back to my supply cabinet and grabbed a pair of gloves and a tube of K-Y. When I turned around, he was reaching for the inhaler he'd left on top of his shirt.

I was on him in a flash. "If you insist on using poppers, Jerry, I can't continue with the massage."

"What?" he said. I couldn't tell if he was hard of hearing or just selectively so.

I retreated from my ultimatum. "I'd rather you not use poppers during the massage."

"Okay," he said again. He returned his head to the face plate like a child scolded.

"I want to invite you to keep breathing and taking in all the sensations you're feeling, Jerry. Does that sound okay to you?"

He shook his head yes, face down, buried in his shame.

I climbed up on the table and knelt between his spread legs. The sight in front of me — the hairy back and flabby butt of a middle-aged man — wasn't the most appetizing I'd ever encountered. I wasn't turned on but I wasn't turned off either. Some people can't imagine touching let alone giving an erotic massage to somebody they're not attracted to. For a lot of young gay men, the idea of having anything to do with a guy like Jerry would be unthinkable. I don't mind. In fact, I like it. I like the feeling of control, of being entrusted with another human being's vulnerability. I have a hard time only when clients assume that, because I'm touching them erotically, that we've suddenly moved into reciprocal sex mode and they're free to grope me.

I guess that sounds awful. *Don't kid yourself. I'm the attractive one around here. I'm the one who gets to touch and have power.* Well, it's true. I want it to be clear that I'm in control. I want them to behave. There's arrogance on my part. But no contempt. Anyone who presents his tender butt for loving touch gets a big gold star in my book. He can rest assured I'm going to take good care of him.

With Jerry, I felt like a spelunker ready to hunt for treasures in the secret cave. I pulled on first one white vinyl glove, then the other. The latest box of surgical gloves I bought were the smallest size, and they're skintight on my hands. They make me look like Mickey Mouse in evening wear.

In contrast to his lassitude during the back massage, the man on the table now began to respond to my every move — the cool breath on his tight butthole, the firm pressure of three fingers over the opening, the cool slipperiness of lubricant being rubbed rhythmically over the folds of skin covering his sphincter. He jerked and twitched whenever I hit an especially sensitive spot. I knew I wasn't hurting him. I knew he was flinching because he wasn't breathing smoothly enough to distribute the intense sensations. I coached him to breathe all the way down to his toes.

I went into him easily, one finger then two. I brought him up onto his knees with his head resting on the table, his butt in the air. He wrapped his feet around my calves. When I slid the length of my middle finger across his swollen prostate, he groaned with pleasure. "Deeper," he requested. I adjusted my posture so I was a little higher and slid a third finger into his ass all the way up to the last knuckle, held it there, and vibrated it. With the other hand (whose glove I'd peeled off), I stroked his inner thighs, circled his balls, and tugged on his hard cock. Then I reached around and put my left hand on his lower belly just above his pubic bone and pressed inward, so his prostate received pressure from both sides.

To be this deep inside a man is about as physically intimate as you can get. The quality is so different from fucking, in some ways much more intense. Articulate, multi-jointed fingers can reach places inside the body that a hard cock cannot. They can increase or modify pressure on the sphincter or the prostate at will. And while someone who's fucking often has to keep sliding in and out to receive pleasure and to stay hard enough, a hand can stay put when it hits a spot that produces moans. I know when I'm fucking, I can get mental about the state of my erection, wanting to please my partner and prolong my own pleasure at the risk of losing it altogether. Doing butt massage, I'm liberated from that anxiety.

Touching Jerry, fiddling with his erotic knobs like an engineer tuning up a delicate machine, I felt detached, distant, powerfully in control. Like the most beneficent of gods, at once servant and master, giving exquisite pleasure and requiring nothing in return.

Once he was accustomed to being penetrated, I picked up the pace. Now I was fucking him — with my hand, anyway — in and out, pumping his butt. Inarticulate murmurs issued from his throat. He raised his butt higher. With my free hand I slapped his big rump hard, first one cheek then the other, again and again. He jerked and cried out with each slap. His cry did not say "Stop." The sound of bare hand against bare butt excited me. I escalated the strength of my slaps. Then I paused and ran my fingertips lightly over the reddening skin. I reached down and wrapped my fist around the base of his bulging cock and balls and pulled them toward me.

"Do you have your whole fist in me?" he suddenly asked.

"No, not quite," I said. "Three fingers."

"Can you fist me?" His voice was quiet, not timid but hopeful.

"Have you ever been fisted?"

"No. But I'd like to try."

"Let's see how it goes," I said. I put some more lube on my hand and slid all four fingers inside him. He groaned with satisfaction. I could feel his belly, his bowels, his rectum, his insides breathing with me, letting go. When I slid my hand back, a few bubbles of air pressed their way out, relieving the interior pressure. Without clenching or clamping, his ass wrapped itself around my hand, like a starfish on a rock.

I got off the table and stood next to him. I ran my free hand up his back and stroked his shoulders, his neck, the scaly top of his bald head. I leaned into his butt, which opened slightly wider. He sighed. Now I slid my thumb into his manhole, so my hand formed a wedge that pushed all the way in until my knuckles rested against his sitz bones.

I noticed that he was no longer hard. It occurred to me that he might be hurting. He might have had enough. But the gurgles he released whenever I bore down on his prostate told me he had entered a deeper zone, that altered state of erotic experience that is beyond erection-and-ejaculation. It's a mystical place, akin to dreaming or nearly dying, where the membrane that separates matter from spirit becomes vanishingly thin. Memories and emotions slither up from the murky depths. The nether eye opens to what's usually hidden. The roof of the planetarium slides open, and the infinite beckons. I knew he was travelling through space, like those scenes in *2001 — A Space Odyssey* where suddenly the spaceship would be hurtling through a blur of stars. Only this was inner space, a tunnel of quiet dark. Vaulted ceilings. Echoey stairwell. A horse's eye. I hung out there with him.

Almost an hour and a half had passed since he got on the table. "I'm going to slow down now and start coming out of you, Jerry," I told him. One finger at a time, I brought my hand out, cupping my palm over his hole before releasing it entirely. Then I laid him flat on the table again and cleaned his butt with a Baby Wipe and toweled off his back before turning him over.

"How are you doing?" I asked him.

He looked up through his slit-eyes and said, "Good."

I knelt at the end of the table looking at his face upside down. I saw his stubbly chin, his thin lips (relaxed now), his fleshy ears.

"You've been on a little trip I think."

"Uh huh," he said.

"Uh huh," I confirmed. I rested my hands on his shoulders and looked down into his steely green eyeballs. They were the eyes of someone on a trip, who has seen something from the other world and not averted his gaze. He didn't seem confused or shy or embarrassed.

"Did any images or memories occur to you during this session?" I asked.

"Yes," he said immediately. I was surprised. I like asking the question but usually people don't relate to it.

"Tell me," I said.

"I remembered that my father used to take me over his knee," he said slowly. "He would pull down my pants ... and pull down my underwear ... and spank me."

"And that was exciting to you?"

He nodded.

"Did your father know it excited you?"
"No."
"Did you get a hard-on?"
"No, not at the time."
"But later when you thought about it ... ?"
"Uh huh."

I let that memory sink in. Inside me something large and dangerous moved, like a giant octopus tentacle flopping across the room. When I started slapping his big hairy butt, little did I know that I was stirring up his oldest erotic fantasies. Or mine: the forbidden-Daddy-love-touch.

"There's something about an older man, your father, taking an interest in your naked butt that's exciting and forbidden, isn't there?"

"More forbidden," he said.

"Ah," I said. "Many things that are forbidden are exciting."

He was quiet for a minute.

"Anything else?" I inquired.

"Yes," he said.

I was overjoyed. More!

"I was in Morocco once," he began. "Have you ever been to Morocco?"

"No," I said. "I'd like to go." [MFF: A few years later I did travel to Morocco to attend a festival of world sacred music. Sadly, I did not have the bathhouse experience that Jerry had.]

"This was many years ago," he said. He spoke slowly, as if in a trance. "I was there with some other people on business ... and we were all taken to this bathhouse ... There were men and women there ... I got separated from the people I was with ... I saw some stairs ... I went up there ... It was a little room ... I met a Moroccan guy ... He was big ... well, not big. Stocky."

He paused.

"Then what happened?" I said, barely controlling my impatience to hear the whole story.

"There was a bench there ... He pulled it over to the middle of the room ... He had me get up on it ... the same way you had me do ... with my butt up."

Aha.

"And then he ... you know, he fucked me ... And there were two other guys ... Moroccans ... Three of them all together."

"They all three fucked you?"

"Uh huh."

"One right after the other?"

"Uh huh."

"That sounds hot," I said. My dick grew in my pants. To tell the truth, I was jealous.

"It was," he said immediately. "The other guys were walking around the place ... I didn't know where they were ... Men and women..."

"Oh," I said, "it was a place where everybody was there having sex, men and women?"

"Yes," he said.

"But they could have walked in at any time and seen you?"

"Yes."

We both quietly took in the thrill of that scenario.

This guy had more going on inside him than I ever would have suspected by looking at him. I got up and sat on the table next to him. I picked up his arm and let it rest against my chest as we continued talking.

He wanted to know more about fisting. "Do you think you could get your whole hand inside me next time?"

"I don't know," I said. "For fisting it's a lot easier if you're in a sling, because your whole body is able to relax. When you're on a table, your muscles unavoidably maintain a certain tension."

"Do you have a sling?" he asked eagerly.

"No," I said. "Some people have them in their private playrooms, and some sex clubs have them."

"I couldn't see myself doing it in a sex club with just anybody. But I could do it with you. What if I lay on my back?"

"That might be easier," I conceded. I started feeling slightly apprehensive. I've never fisted anybody. This session was as far as I'd ever gone in that direction. I didn't want to set myself up as an expert. [MFF: Later I did acquire more experience and expertise in this extremely intimate form of erotic play.] But his eagerness to explore touched me. He didn't seem like a numbed-out thrill seeker. From the stories he told, I understood that intense bodyplay connected him to his deepest erotic fantasies and memories. What else can you call these things but experiences of God, memories of heaven? In those moments, brief and eternal, you feel most alive in your body and most spiritually connected to the tempestuous energy of the universe, that mystery at once so physical and so invisible. How many saints and monks, meditating days at a time on their dusty mats, have dwelt on just this, remembered or wished-for episodes of ecstatic buttfucking?

"We need to stop for today, Jerry," I said.

"Can you help me get off?" he asked.

"You want to squirt?" I asked, a little dubiously. I thought he'd gone way beyond it. I thought he'd had a sacred-sex breakthrough and realized that you don't always have to ejaculate to have a powerful erotic experience.

"Sure," he said. I looked at his dick, which he'd been idly toying with during our conversation, and I saw that it was stiff and dark pink. I oiled him up and stroked him. He had a medium-sized dick, maybe five inches long erect, circumcised, with a big split down the middle, a thick frenum. Pressed flat against his belly, his cock looked like an arrowhead — or a devil's tail. As I worked on his cock, he started running his hands over my body. I found myself tensing up, afraid that he was going to start invading me and grabbing my cock. I didn't invite him to touch me, and I wasn't at all turned on. I wanted to finish up the session. Sacred sex is sacred sex, but after an hour and a half your time is up.

I pumped his cock with one hand and reached my other arm under his neck and around his shoulders. He lifted his arm to pull me down to his face. I resisted, but eventually I allowed him to press some stubbly kisses against my face.

As I pressed my hairy chest against his, his thin lips smacking against mine pressed closed, I became for a moment that angry daddy pulling down his underpants, that stocky Moroccan towering over him and swallowing him up, the horned god appearing by magic in the forest clearing where the chubby boy lay on mossy grass pleasuring himself. The world turned upside down with a lurching sound like a train pulling out of the station. Blossoming flowers erupted from the earth. Waves of air pressed into his lungs until he burst.

How do I want you to touch me, Daddy? I like having power over you. I want to be somewhere you can't hurt me. I like it when I can see you and you can't see me. I can see every part of your big hairy body. I see your scar under your shoulder blade. I see the razor line of your barbershop haircut. I see the curled callous on the edge of your big toe. I see your pink balls peeping out from under your thighs. You're face down so I can spread your cheeks and look right into your wrinkled butthole.

I can see where your sallow skin turns rosier, the color of the inside of a velvet cape lined in silk. Whorehouse pink — not garish but muted. I could write on your butthole with a Magic Marker. Little hieroglyphics. Sportina Cheese.

Marco Wuz Here. Close Cover Before Striking. Bad Advice. Liar. I could slide the Magic Marker in and out of you, like Midwestern boys caught fucking themselves with pencils. I've turned the tables on you, Daddy. I'm fucking you.

I don't want you to notice or say anything. Not right now anyway. Later I want you to tell me I'm wonderful and give me some money. Right now I want to squeeze a pile of slippery goo onto my rubbery fingers and slide them into your butt, so you feel me fucking you, you feel me naked and towering over you, planting a seed, mowing your lawn, making you pregnant, making you moan. You reach out and grab my leg. Suddenly I feel like Don Giovanni in danger of being dragged to hell. What do you want? Let me go. Let me go! You want something from me, something more, and I don't want to give anything more. I want to say no without saying no. I turn you over and you look at me with your slanted reptile eyes, dark green, from just under the surface of the water, you alligator with the crooked smile (no lips) and hairy belly. You reach up to touch my cheek. I lean in to your ear, you turn your head to kiss me. I open my mouth and our tongues press together like cheese and burger. We fry. I'm kissing you, Daddy. I always wanted this.

We're both hard. I'm running my hands through your hair. Now I've given up shame. I have no restraint. I strip down to my jockstrap and take that off too. I wrap it around your neck. I climb on top and slide into you without stopping. I pump into you and pull the jockstrap tighter around your neck. Your eyes bulge. Your dick swells. It's unbelievably huge. It's like a big balloon. It's a baby lying between us. It's a baby boy growing out of your crotch, and the longer I fuck you, the bigger he grows. Now he's sucking on your tit and I'm fucking you and your face is getting redder, like fire around your watery eyes and I flood you, I flood you, your banks overflow, blood trickles from the corner of your mouth. I take the baby and wrap it in your T-shirt and run. I run through the snow looking for a taxi. There's no one on the street but me. We get to the airport in no time. I don't have any luggage. They let me walk on board with the baby, both of us naked and crusty. I sit in first class, order a beer, and toast you, Daddy, love of my life.

CHAPTER THIRTY-THREE

Second Thoughts

I went to see my psychic reader, Nino, the other day to see if he could tell me why I feel so exhausted these days. I know he sells vitamins and handles crystals and makes necklaces from stones that have particular properties — all that arcane New Age scholarship that I don't have and I don't exactly trust, but hey. Maybe he could tell me how to change my diet or sleep better or figure out something I'm not seeing about myself.

Well, he did give me some good advice, but it wasn't exactly easy to hear. He suggested I keep my clothes on for a couple of months when I'm doing sessions with clients.

"I know, you worry that if you don't give clients what they want, they won't come back to you," he said.

Bingo.

"Don't worry," he said. "If they don't want to receive what you have to give, they won't come back, but other people will show up who do want it."

"Right," I said dubiously. And when the rent comes

due, maybe Nino can imagine a thousand dollars materializing in front of me.

I know what he was saying, though. He said that my clients drain my batteries, and that's what's exhausting me. And the reason they do that is I let them do it. Because I want something from them. Because I want physical contact. I like their admiration. I'm turned on by their bodies. I'm exhilarated by the opportunity to have intimate touch every day. So they tap into this level of primitive need, and that allows them to clamp their jumper cables onto my ecstatic energy and drain it dry. I'm running their vehicles on my own energy. They may walk away refreshed because their reserves haven't been touched. And even if I've gotten touch or sex or something else that feels good temporarily, it doesn't fulfill me.

"Your job for the next couple of months," Nino said, "is to go on observation mode. You're not in touch with your feelings. You have to interrogate yourself constantly. Ask yourself: is this serving me? and is this serving my client? Or is it simply maintaining some old pattern? Is it possible to shift that old pattern or do something differently? Remember, you're not working to keep people stuck in old ways of being. You're here to facilitate the evolution of higher consciousness."

I am? I mean, right! That's what I'm here for. Whew! I almost forgot.

Armed with this challenge, I watched my bodywork sessions for the next couple of days. I had a session with Jake, a client who figures prominently in my private masturbation fantasies. When I give him erotic massage, he twitches and jumps. His cock thickens before it gets hard, which fascinates me to observe, like watching a Polaroid develop. His cock has a beautiful shape and length when it's fully erect, which doesn't take much doing on my part. It's so beautiful that at some point I couldn't help asking permission to taste it. He agreed without hesitation. This experience enflamed me, and so the next couple of sessions were all about anticipating the moment when I could slide his perfect-sized phallus into my hungry throat.

Yesterday I took Nino's advice and conducted the session differently. Instead of stroking him lightly to erection and playing for a long time in that condition, I oiled up the front of his body and had him breathe vigorously, raising and circulating the energy without going for a climax. And wouldn't you know? If I didn't supply the intention and the heat, he was dead in his body. He barely breathed. He seemed laggard and sleepy — a dead battery. Damned if I was going to let him suck all the energy out of me. I held back my own energy while still giving him a vigorous erotic massage, working his magic wand with several different delicious strokes and sliding a finger behind his balls into the crack of his ass. He groaned and twitched. I had him breathe continuously. He almost came, and I slapped his chest and his thighs and ran my hand in a big U all the way up one leg, across his chest, and down the other side of his body. When I got back to his cock, it had drooped. The sensation had peaked, so I slowed him down and brought him in for a landing. He had the same camel-like languor getting off the table as he usually did, even when he'd cum or we'd 69'd.

That tells me something I need to know: that what I sometimes perceive as the clients' needs or desires come from me, not them. Or we're both thinking, "Well, I don't care if we have sex, but if that's what he wants, I'll go along with it." When the truth is that they're perfectly satisfied with whatever I give them. Because I always give them good loving touch, no matter what.

When I think about the place of sex in a healing practice, there are so many strands to separate. What's the difference between offering massage, and offering erotic massage? What's the difference between giving an erotic massage and having sex with someone, or getting someone off? What's the difference between having sex and making love? Where is the connection to spirit in all these things?

Relief of pain caused by muscle tension: there's no doubt that's a healing result of massage. Getting someone to breathe fully until he feels his body's capacity for sensation puts him in touch with something larger than himself. But when a man is lying face-down, his butt up in the air, and he's blindly groping for my cock in my pants — what's going on there? When I crawl on top of a favorite client and take his cock all the way down my throat, what's going on there? There's a shift from erotic massage into sexplay. Does that automatically imply that one is a healing practice, therefore "good," and the other is merely recreation, and therefore "not-as-good" or (dare I say it) "bad"?

Sorry, hon, you're not going to get me to say sex is bad. And I'm not willing to say that Just Having Sex can't be a healing practice, either. I have a big emotional investment in not putting down sex. Puritanical American society is full of negative messages about sex. Religious guilt cripples enough people. But what does it take for sex to be sacred?

Uh-oh. Stop! Wrong question. "Sacred" is such an icky word. "Sacred sex" doesn't sound fun. It sounds like sex with the fun sucked out of it. No place for good old-fashioned energetic butt-licking in "sacred sex." What's another word for it? "Conscious sex"? Whatever you call it, it's when both parties are awake in their bodies and minds. Words pass between them. They've looked in each other's eyes. They've shared breaths. They not only respect but celebrate their bodies (each other's and their own), their desires, and their feelings.

They agree that they're being sexual together, and they're on the same wavelength.

That doesn't always happen in my practice. Sometimes a guy is turned on but there's some shame or guilt going on that prevents him from being able to talk. Literally, he can't speak. A guy like Al, for instance. He wants the good feelings in his body, but he's afraid to say anything — afraid to bring consciousness to what's going on — because that will also bring the consciousness that he's having sex, and that's bad. You know, all the rules and voices in his head.

Is this guy someone who's pent-up, who gets no touch and no love in his life, for whom this is a moment out of time, a precious experience, a drop of water in the desert? Is this someone who jerks off five times a day and can never get enough? Is this someone who has been sexually violated as a kid and has no boundaries? Did he grow up physically neglected and starved for affection, so he thinks he has to endure sexual invasion just to get someone to touch him tenderly? Is this someone whose emotions are totally shut down, in whom grief or anger or sadness have been building up and getting shoved down, for whom getting sexually aroused can bust the logjam of emotions and give him a reward for feeling something, anything?

Who is "this guy" I'm talking about now — my client or myself?

CHAPTER THIRTY-FOUR

Mandatory Sex

Logically, it makes sense to me to operate on one of two assumptions: either erotic massage and sex are both healing practices, worthwhile pursuits, good things to do, or they're both not. Yet in my everyday practice, I'm constantly trying to shove them apart. When I first started doing bodywork professionally, all my Sacred Intimate training was still ringing in my ears loud and clear. The way I remembered it, Joe Kramer's teaching didn't make fine distinctions. "Sacred intimate work" or "sexual healing" included a continuum of services including but not limited to loving touch, erotic massage without ejaculation, and full-tilt boogie-down.

Or maybe that's what I wanted to hear. There was a time when I accepted that my bodywork practice gave me an opportunity to have sex with a different person every day if I wanted to. And there was a time when that's exactly what I wanted. It was fun; I was hungry for the contact; I felt liberated. Was I being skillful as a masseur? Absolutely. Was I doing erotic massage, or was I doing prostitution? That was a moot point. I imagined I was embodying Joe Kramer's vision of the sacred intimate — someone who is skilled at touching people and honoring the body as the manifestation of spirit, and someone who expresses respect for sexuality by including genital touch rather than pronouncing it off limits.

That's the theory. But in practice I eventually discovered an urgent need inside myself to make distinctions, to say "I will do this" and "I won't do that." Having no boundaries was making me crazy. I was falling into codependency. Someone wanted sex from me; I wanted him to like me, approve of me, pay me money; therefore I would have sex with him, even if I didn't want to. I believe this is what therapists who treat sex addiction would call "acting out." This is the epitome of what's called sexual compulsiveness.

I have a lot of resistance to the diagnosis of "sexually compulsive" because the social discourse around it seems to reinforce the sex-negativity of American culture. I understand there are many ways to look at it, though. No one has the single right answer, including me. What I can say for myself is that I did have an epiphany about where sex goes wrong for me.

I went to a sex party at an apartment on the Upper West Side. It was exactly the kind of orgy I dreamed of attending in my untouched adolescence. Unlike a New York Jacks event, there were no restrictions. Guys were sucking and fucking, with and without rubbers, right and left. The men were attractive, and the atmosphere was sexy, though not particularly joyful. In this situation, I found myself strangely unable to choose whether or not to have sex with other partygoers. If there was a hard cock in my immediate vicinity, I would put it in my mouth at the first opportunity.

I didn't enjoy that party. I didn't enjoy the

encounters that I had. But I learned an important lesson. I realized I'd crossed over a line. I realized at that party my tendency to behave according to this principle: "When sex is possible, sex is mandatory." That defined sexual compulsion to me. Fortunately, as soon as I made that recognition, I regained my ability to choose. I'm smart enough and self-controlled enough — maybe I should say, I'm enough of a trained Catholic schoolboy — that once I've determined the right thing to do, I'm not happy unless I'm doing that right thing. Unfortunately, I was still in the midst of a bodywork practice where men came to me ostensibly for massage but often I would get naked, too, and we would end up having some version of sex. I had choices to make every day, and now I faced the challenge of making different choices than I had in the recent past.

Partly, I realized, it was a control issue. I wanted to control if sexual interaction happened and what it was called. If I was attracted to my client and wanted to interact with him, then it was erotic massage and that was okay. If he was attracted to me and I didn't want to interact with him, then that would be sex and it wasn't okay. What if there were other possibilities? Erotic massage is fine, and sex is fine, if both parties agree. If I want to have sex with a client and he doesn't want to, it would be wrong for me to proceed to have sex with him. That would be rape, wouldn't it? That's easy. If a client wants to have sex with me and I don't want to, it's wrong for him to proceed to touch me sexually, right? Not so easy.

It's difficult for me under any circumstances (at the baths, at home with a boyfriend) to acknowledge that I don't want to have sex, but especially in my bodywork practice. I'm afraid of hurting the client's feelings, which will then have economic consequences: he won't come back. My default position is to tell myself, "Well,

I don't want to have sex, but I'll tell myself that this is a healing session in ritual space, and that will make it okay for me to override my own feelings."

Then the pendulum swings. I've decided categorically I'm not having sex with clients. Then someone shows up who turns me on. Now I'm having to pretend all over again, this time giving the opposite impression, that I don't want to have sex when I do. If we're both attracted to each other, what's the problem with having sex? Then it becomes a matter of integrity, not consent. Am I offering a service? Am I teaching people about erotic energy? Am I working for the evolution of higher consciousness? Or am I simply making myself available for sex?

Whether I'm concerned about integrity or I'm simply not interested, I still feel reluctant to say no to sex. I'm afraid that by doing so I'm saying "Sex is bad" or "Sex is inappropriate" or some other shaming message. Why can't it be a matter-of-fact statement, like "Thanks but no thanks"? Maybe because we don't all have the same facts. This resistance to saying no may also be partly a liability of identifying too strongly as a sex radical.

I've been thinking a lot lately about Annie Sprinkle. Annie is a legendary champion of sexual freedom, a former prostitute and porn star who toured the world with a performance art piece in which she had five-minute orgasms onstage and invited members of the audience to inspect her vagina with a speculum. She's always been wonderfully outspoken about sex in a way that's both outrageous and innocently heartfelt. Once, after she'd turned her 2,100th trick at an East Side massage parlor, she realized that she had never gotten the praise and social acceptance for her work that she craved. First, she wept. Then, being a practical-minded artist, she decided to create an award for herself. She called it the Aphrodite Award, "for sexual service to the community."

"All over you see monuments in memory of those who 'served' in war," she said. "I wanted to see monuments for those who serve in pleasure."

Annie was a close friend of Joe Kramer's and immensely supportive of the Body Electric work. At the last Sacred Intimate Training that Joe taught (in 1992), each of us received an Annie Sprinkle Aphrodite Award. The certificate features the logo for Prostitutes of New York (PONY): a heart with a vulva down the middle flanked by two rearing ponies, all resting on a pedestal emblazoned with the legend "Look for the union labia." In the letter that was read aloud at the ceremony bestowing the awards, Annie said, "You don't need to be a prostitute to have one. You only need to have given sexual pleasure to many people." It was the most wonderful honor I'd ever received. I still display it proudly in my temple, though I sometimes wonder what people think when they see I've gotten the Good Housekeeping seal of approval from Prostitutes of New York.

What's the difference between what I do and what a prostitute does? It's easy to say what's similar. We're both willing to touch strangers for the sake of their sexual gratification, and we accept payment for this service. I, however, do not accept Visa or MasterCard. Some boys with beepers do. It's a California thing. [MFF: I would eventually accept credit cards, Venmo, Zelle, PayPal, and CashApp. I draw the line at cryptocurrency.]

When I focus on the differences, I guess my definition of "prostitute" shrinks from "goddess" or "sex therapist" to common streetwalker, who has mainly one thing to sell — the willingness to engage sexually with a stranger. That's no small thing. Not everyone can do it. Prostitutes aren't expected to do anything but provide sexual service, which can mean a handjob, a blowjob, or fucking. God knows those things take skill to perform, and it's not easy to have sex with a stranger who doesn't attract you and still make him feel like he's having a good time. But there's the first distinction between what I do and what a prostitute does. I set up my appointments so there's no expectation of interaction. I would never agree to take someone's dick in my mouth or my ass, nor do I feel comfortable agreeing sight unseen to suck or fuck someone.

Of course, I have done all those things with clients. But the circumstances in which they took place define the difference between a prostitute's job and my work as a sacred intimate. For one thing, I'm a trained masseur. I have a state-certified skill. Many prostitutes have had some version of massage training. It's a good skill to have. Anything that creates some space around a genital transaction makes it a better experience for both parties. I think that's the essence of my work. Before there's any genital contact, usually I have had a conversation with someone. There's been talking, negotiating, stretching, breathing, guided visualization, often there's been toning, and there's been massage aimed at waking up the whole body, creating a stew of sensations into which erotic energy gets stirred, little by little, so that the result is a delicious and integrated meal.

Maybe I'm flattering myself. Maybe I'm underestimating the self-awareness of prostitutes. In James Ridgeway and Sylvia Plachy's book about the sex industry called *Red Light*, I came across an interview with Cynthia Connors, who now runs a computer business and volunteers for PONY. She described her experiences as a teenaged prostitute. "I was a bad prostitute. See, I believed that prostitution involved exchanging sex for money. Wrong. It involves exchanging perfunctory sex followed by a great deal of psychological hand-holding, and a kind of psychology and nursing care. Basically, you're a social worker," she said. "What I've come to decide is that in this society men are not allowed to say they have problems, and not allowed to go to social workers, not allowed to go to psychiatrists. It is manly, however, to go to the peeps, to go to visit a prostitute, and so those people are forced to become their educators in sex and become their marriage counselors, and also become their psychologists.

"To this day I still am in shock," she added. "I was too young to understand how ridiculous this was. I would love to find some of these men who used to be my regular clients and say, 'I was a 13-year-old heroin-addicted little street kid. Why did you think I should be your marriage counselor? Why did you try to impress me so?'"

Obviously, I'm not a teenage junkie. I rather like playing amateur psychologist with my clients. And sex work is not the same experience for women and men; the balance of power and the range of choices are vastly different. All the same, I'm not ashamed to declare solidarity with prostitutes and sex workers. Strippers, lap dancers, dominatrixes, go-go boys, society walkers: I believe we're doing God's work.

Self-definition is the key, and it always comes down to the words you use to describe yourself. Sometimes when I'm talking to other veterans of Sacred Intimate Training, they'll casually refer to all of us as "hookers" or "whores." For some people, it's liberating to embrace those tags. Even Annie Sprinkle, who has been a major role model in claiming "prostitute" as an identity akin to "priestess," refers to her work at the massage parlor as "turning tricks." I guess I feel like Richard Pryor, who returned from his first visit to Africa no longer willing to refer to himself and other blacks using the n-word. If I call myself a hooker or a whore, it has a definite impact on the way I feel about myself. I can smile and laugh and go along with this street-smart gallantry, but in my heart I'm clear that what I do can't be reduced to the expression "turning tricks." To me that sounds like the kind of lowest level sex work that street hustlers have to put up with, handjobs in cars and doorways for $20. I consider myself a counselor, a meditation instructor, an intimacy coach, an energy worker as well as an erotic masseur. When my client named my occupation as "pleasure activist," that designation made me as proud as getting my Annie Sprinkle Aphrodite Award.

The reason I've been thinking about Annie recently is that Keith Hennessy solicited an article from her for a small-press book about sex, art, and community. She submitted an open letter that had some surprising things to say.

"I have noticed that there is a lot of blind faith, even fanaticism, among sex radicals in the belief that all consensual sex is a totally positive thing. (I was once one myself.) Until recently, it seemed important to be wholeheartedly 'sex positive,' to defend and encourage all promiscuity, all kinks and fetishes, all getting paid for sex, all group sex, etc. There were so many forces against our sexual choices, including our own inner voices. But my sense is that now lots of those battles have been won. We've reached a critical mass, and as Betty Dodson said recently, 'We've changed the world.' Perhaps there's no need to keep fighting for or defending something that we largely have and know to be true. I think this modus operandi has become obsolete.

"For the past six months I have had the great luxury of taking some time to look back, to reflect, analyze and critique my personal sexual journey. Yes, I had a lot of fun, gave and received a lot of pleasure, and had a lot of great orgasms, but I have also come to see that I was also quite naïve, very immature, and in denial about a lot of things. I'm realizing that much of the porn, prostitution, S/M and group sex I had 'in the name of love and sex positivism' wasn't necessarily all 'healing and enlightening' but [was], on occasion, abusive to myself and others and often perpetuating a totally dysfunctional, destructive, patriarchal model of sexuality. I now realize that I was often motivated more by a low self-image, the need for money, a desire for power, fear of intimacy, the need for attention, an addiction to intensity, etc., than I was aware of or cared to admit."

Reading Annie's words melted something in me. I identified with a lot of what she said. It's true that I'd had some intense and joyful experiences in the radical sex world of Body Electric connecting sexual ecstasy with spiritual bliss, two deep cravings that had previously occupied separate and parallel tracks through my soul. I realized, though, that somehow I believed that I would be "letting down the team" — the Body Electric/sacred intimate team — if I questioned for a moment the mantra "Sex Heals."

CHAPTER THIRTY-FIVE

Geisha in the Pigpen

Chris called. He said he'd seen me once before, at my old place. He wanted to come over right away. He couldn't stay more than an hour because he had to get back to Connecticut. I gave him the address. When I got off the phone, I looked him up in my client log and my heart sank: "Chris 'from Connecticut'/ PIG/could only spare an hour/grabby/buttwork/ wanted to be jerked off, but only half-hard/used poppers." That creep! I wished I'd remembered him when we were on the phone. I didn't remember what he looked like, but I remember how offended I was when he wanted to use poppers. They were in his pants pocket, and he asked me to get them for him. I didn't want to, but he kept wheedling until I did it. I indulged him during the session and acted like I've seen it all and done it all but I was outraged after he left. I'm a sacred prostitute! I thought. How dare he desecrate my temple!

The fact is that I don't get poppers. They've never been a big part of sex for me. They seem like a sinister accessory, a symbol of sheer oblivious decadence, or at least a crutch. No, crutch is the wrong image. A crutch is something to lean on when you're injured, but it's on the way to healing. Poppers are more like a short cut that keep the wound open. Like people who have to get drunk or they're too uptight to have sex. I guess it's not just poppers. I'm afraid of chemical substances, too much booze, recreational drugs. I'm afraid to lose that much control myself, and I don't like how it makes other people's behavior unpredictable. [MFF: Since then, my perspective on substances has evolved tremendously, to the point where I married a happy stoner who introduced me to the many pleasures of cannabis and I spent many years in a deep exploration of "teacher plants and master molecules," including doing a year-long training in psychedelics-assisted psychotherapy. I have come to appreciate poppers as a sexual enhancement, but I still observe how people use them unwisely. The alkyl nitrites that you see guys huffing from little brown bottles are vasodilators, meaning that they expand the blood vessels, which creates a quick rush of sensation to the body. But it takes a while for the blood vessels to constrict again, so if you're constantly huffing, you're not going to get the same rush you get at first, and you might end up with a terrible headache from ingesting a lot of toxic chemicals. A seasoned aficionado gave me his ideal scenario: you wait until you're fully turned on to take the first hit of poppers, and for best results wait until you're ready to get off before hitting them again. And it's not a good idea to combine poppers with Viagra or other medications for erectile dysfunction because they are also vasodilators, and the combination can lower your blood pressure so much you can pass out, fall, and hurt yourself. Just saying!]

    I got into a slight tizzy. What to do with Chris today? Should I just not answer the buzzer? Should I lay down the law beforehand? What would Joe Kramer do? Then I thought about my conversation last week with Dominic, whom I met through the Body Electric School's sacred intimate training. We were walking to a leather bar in the West Village, and Dominic was answering my nosy questions about his fee schedule, and he said he charges $100 an hour for all-night sessions. Dubious that anyone I know has all-night clients, I pressed him for details. He told me about a client he's seen a couple of times who basically likes to play with Dominic's wiener for a little while and then take ketamine (aka Special K, or just K). After a while, he goes into K-holes, and Dominic makes sure he doesn't fall and hurt himself.

I said, somewhat condescendingly, "So you're sort of the babysitter."

"I'm the sacred intimate!" Dominic insisted, grabbing my shoulders and shaking me. "I'm present with wherever the client happens to be. I don't just do that mommy-daddy-waaaah stuff," he said, mock-cuddling me and rubbing his hand in a circle over my heart. I had to laugh.

So today I thought: well, what would Dominic do? He wouldn't give a shit if Chris wanted to snort poppers on his table. He's one of wild young queer boys who propel themselves through disco marathons on a pharmaceutical choo-choo train: ecstasy, acid, crystal meth, Special K. But then we don't have the same lifestyle. He's 28, independently wealthy, HIV-positive. What does he have to lose?

I decided I would meet Chris where he's at and not do anything I didn't want to do.

He was older than I remembered, white-haired and barrel-chested. He was probably around 60 and hadn't seen the inside of a gym for a few decades. He immediately started undressing. While making friendly conversation, he took a little brown bottle and put it on the table next to my oils and lotions. I stifled the urge to say anything about it. I could barely contain my anger.

"Maybe you'd better tell me what the experience is that you'd like to have this afternoon, Chris," I said as evenly as I could.

He scrunched up his face and looked at the ceiling. "I'd just like a good massage, especially my lower back and, uh, you know, the groin area," he said. I could tell we were in shame territory because although he was looking at me he wasn't meeting my eyes. He's the kind of guy who says "lower back" when he means "butthole" and "groin" when he means "dick." He lay down on the table on his belly. "Oh, and I have to be done at 20 to 2."

I looked at the clock. It was 1:00. He'd booked a one-hour session at 1:00, and now he was telling me he only had 40 minutes. Okay. Easy $100, right?

Still, I couldn't let the poppers go unnoticed. I walked over to the bureau and picked them up. "What's this for?" I asked.

"It's poppers," he said.

"I know it's poppers. It's not customary for people to use poppers on the massage table."

"It's for during the release."

"What makes you think you're going to need something other than what I'm doing?"

"I just want to enjoy it more."

Ugh. This guy is everything I hate in massage clients. His assumption is that a massage ad is a front for hustling, and his expectation coming in the door is the goal of the session is for me to jerk him off. He doesn't take care of his body at all, yet he expects me to interact with him as if he's a potential sex partner. He's already decided that he's not going to get enough sensation from the massage, and he needs a chemical boost. I felt like a refined geisha faced with the typical Ugly American.

I put the poppers down on the chair near the head of the massage table. "Can I make a suggestion?" I said.

"Sure," he said.

"I want to invite you to feel what you're feeling throughout the whole session."

"I promise."

That was my lame way of playing schoolteacher (Boy Scout?) and suggesting that he didn't need to snort poppers to have a good time. I didn't feel any better after I said it.

I gave him a truncated version of a back massage. As I suspected he didn't respond verbally until I oiled up his inner thighs and ran the side of my hand up the crack of his butt.

"Ooh, you're so good," he said, reaching out with his hand. I moved so he couldn't touch me.

Seeing that I had about 20 minutes left, I went to work on his butt, doing my usual Land Down Under routine. He loved it. I put on gloves, lubricated his butthole, and slowly opened him up. Then I invited him to get up on his knees while I eased in one finger, then two, and swirled them over his prostate. "Ohh, that feels so good," he moaned.

He reached back between his legs and grabbed my soft cock through my shorts.

"That doesn't feel good to me, Chris," I said.

He withdrew his hand. I kept sliding a wedge of three fingers in and out until he said, "I want to turn over onto my back."

"Would you like me to keep working on your butt?" I asked. Sometimes I do sound like a Boy Scout, I guess.

"Yeah, baby, keep going. You're good at it," he said.

He seemed to be holding his breath and sucking his belly in, so I coached him to let go and breathe. His dick was tiny, a limp baby penis wrapped in a shriveled red-brown sheath with a drop of viscous liquid at the end.

I got up on the table and knelt between his legs, with his right leg resting over my thigh. In this position it felt like a fisting situation. Undoubtedly, he'd been in the sling before. He got more excited and kept calling me "Baby."

"You're so hot, baby. You know just what to do."

While I perched over him working on his butt and sweating like crazy, he reached up into my armpit with two fingers, rubbed them against my skin, and then drew them back to his nose.

"You like my man scent?"

"Unnhhh."

He started pulling the hair on my legs. At first it didn't bother me. But he was so grabby and oblivious that it got on my nerves. "Ow," I said, when he plucked too hard, "watch the hair, okay, Chris?"

"I love your fur, baby. I want to see more of it. I wanna see that hairy chest. Take off your shirt, baby."

I looked at the clock. It was 1:32. "We need to stop in a few minutes, Chris."

"I can't stop now," he said.

I paused. Shit. Does he expect me to keep this up for another hour? "What do you mean?"

"You've got me too hot, baby. You've got to keep going."

"Okay, Chris. But you said you needed to stop at 20 to 2. I need to know what time you have to stop in order for you to have a good time."

"I have to stop and get dressed at quarter to 2."

Oh, right. I'm not dealing with Mr. Ecstatic Sex God here. We're just talking another five minutes in the pigpen. I can deal with that.

"Take off your shirt, baby. I want to see more of that hairy body."

"I have to take my hand out of your butt to get my T-shirt off."

"That's okay ... Your shorts, too."
"No, I need to leave my shorts on."
"Why?"
"Because that's what I need to do to have a good time," I said firmly.
"I want to see that hairy asshole of yours," he whined.
"Feel it," I said. "Feel your desire."
He didn't know what I was talking about. His response was to lean back and grab the bottle of poppers off the chair. He unscrewed the black top and held the bottle first to one nostril then the other. I vibrated my whole hand against his butt. His face flushed as the poppers kicked in. I fucked him hard with my hand.
"Oh, yeah, baby. Oh, yeah, baby. Ow, not too hard."
I slowed down.
"Don't stop." He snorted more poppers.
The next few minutes were a comedy. Poppers every 30 seconds, him begging me to kiss him, touch him, let him taste my asshole. "Next time I want to see that asshole. Next time I want to taste it."
"Feel what you're feeling right now," I suggested.
"Oh, yeah, baby. You're so good. I could really pig out with you."
"Yeah," I said, "you're quite a pig, aren't you?"
"Uh huh!"
While I worked on his butt, I squeezed his dick a few times. It never got any harder. After a few minutes, he said, "Okay, it's time for my release."
"What do you want me to do?"
"Just what you're doing."
I rubbed his baby penis between my thumb and forefinger. It felt like a rubber band.
"Oh, oh, oh!" he cried. A single drop spit out the end of his dick and landed near his bellybutton. "Oh, you have perfect timing," he said.

I cleaned him up and toweled him off. He got off the table perfectly happy with his experience. He said I was the equal of a masseur he'd seen in the South of France. "I'll call you again," he said. "Remember, Chris from Connecticut."

CHAPTER THIRTY-SIX

Hitting Bottom

Last night I had my first Whore Job. I asked for $150 to get naked and have mutual touch. It was a bad experience.

The client was Roger Whitlock, whom I'd seen four times before, with three or four months between sessions. He's a former actor who works as an account executive at a world-famous ad agency. He has a teenaged daughter who lives in Texas and a lover with whom he shares a house in New Jersey. Physically, he's a type that turns me on — a Big Beefy Bottom Boy. He's tall, fleshy, and redheaded (although most of his hair is expensively custom-made) with a bland, Midwestern corporate demeanor. He always came in oozing excessive politeness to mask his horniness. We always began with a thorough massage and ended with some version of having sex. Yet his indirection drove me up the wall. When I'd ask him, "What's the experience you'd like to have this evening?" — he always arranged to have the last session of the day — he liked to turn the question back on me. "What do you feel like doing?"

Sometimes he would play head games with me and try to psychoanalyze me as a way of deflecting attention from himself. "Don't be defensive," he'd say. Or "Don't be so serious." I found these maneuvers annoying, tedious, and somewhat sadistic. At the same time, I knew he was attracted to me physically, and I suspected that his desire made him feel vulnerable, needy, child-like. I learned that he was never happier than when he was flat on his back with his legs in the air watching me hump his slippery butt with my hard cock. I guess I put up with his penchant for pulling power-trips because I felt flattered by his attraction, and attending to his little-kid neediness made me feel powerful.

I decided that Roger would be an ideal client to try out a new strategy in my bodywork. When he called this time, I said, "I've changed the way I'm working these days. I'm offering two different kinds of sessions. I can give you an erotic massage for $100. For that session, I keep my clothes on and there's no interaction. Or I can give you what I'm calling a 'fully intimate' session, where we both get naked and touch each other, for $150." I'd cooked up this scheme in an attempt to be a) clearer about my services and b) better paid for sex work.

Roger prided himself on being a cool customer, but he clearly was taken aback by this turn of events. He said he'd have to think about it and call me back. I considered it a good sign that I felt no anxiety about his deliberation. If he booked the session, fine. If he didn't call back, that was fine, too. It had become so important for me to be clear and conscious about my bodywork practice that I would rather Roger not come to see me than to go through the charade of pretending that the session was about massage when it was actually about sex.

He called back to say yes, let's do it, the — ahem — "fully intimate" session. Okay, I rejoiced. We're naming it and claiming it instead of shaming it. A step forward for

DADDY LOVER GOD

clarity! That's not how it turned out, though. Not at first, anyway.

When he arrived, he asked for a glass of wine. We sat in my reception area chit-chatting for quite a long time about nothing in particular. He made several trips to the bathroom to pee, which indicated he was nervous. When I asked what he wanted from this session, he was his usual evasive and manipulative self. Eventually, though, we both got naked and reclined on my bed. His body was warm. We wriggled like puppies. We started fooling around, but it felt disconnected. For a change, he didn't seem especially horny. His erection came and went. I toyed with his butt, usually a prime pleasure center for him, but he didn't seem to be into it. Sheepishly, he admitted that he'd had insomnia the night before. Wide awake at 3 a.m., he'd put on a porn video and jerked off. He told me, "I thought about refraining, thinking I'm seeing Don tomorrow night. Maybe I should save it up for him. But I didn't."

He got up to pee again. When he came back from the bathroom, he walked over to his briefcase and rummaged through it. He came back to bed holding a little brown bottle of poppers. Trying out a new attitude of acceptance, I didn't object. He unscrewed the lid and held the bottle up to his nose, inhaling through one nostril, then the other. He offered me some. Well, maybe this once ... . I lay back on the futon, resting my head against a pillow. Roger got busy between my legs, licking my balls. His shoulders brushed the inside of my right thigh. My head swam with fumes, a sharp, acrid attack on my sinuses, a smell strong as lighter fluid, ammonia, model-airplane glue. It conjured memories of being at the baths, dark corridors, crummy disco music. My face heated up. It felt like it was swelling up. Blood pulsed in my ears. I closed my eyes and let go. I let go of trying to hold the space for Roger's experience and released into the pleasure of having his wet tongue lapping my tender skin. For a split second I felt myself merge. We were one body, a delightful body that could lick its own dick, that could cover it with sloppy spit and lavish it with swirling motions. The thermometer rose suddenly. The strong man pounded the platform, and the weight on its pulley headed straight for the bell.

"Whoa," I said, pulling Roger's head away. I grabbed my cock with my hand and held it away from his face. Too late. Point of no return. I gave it a few quick strokes. After a tiny pause, a jet of semen spurted onto my belly, then another, then a stream of thick droplets dribbled down the shaft.

He spun open the bottle and snuffled some more. Frantically, he pushed his face between my hairy legs. I noticed he had his own legs twisted together, his ankles locked around each other.

I felt like I'd cat-napped for two minutes and now I was wide awake. Communion was over. I stared at the pale body lying across my legs, tensed and rigid except for the blurry hand working his cock, the contorted face with its eyes squeezed shut, the mouth frozen open. *One thousand one, one thousand two, one thousand three, one thousand four ....*

Immediately he was up looking for a hand towel. When he came out of the shower, I sat in a chair at my dining table and made small talk while he tucked his white Hanes undershirt into his white jockey shorts and reassembled his impeccable Madison Avenue workday outfit, complete with knotted necktie. Then he took out his wallet and paid me in a pointedly resentful way — counting out $100 in one pile on the table, then stacking five more tens in another pile next to the first. I didn't say anything. I sensed that there was something on his mind.

There was. "May I give you some marketing advice,

from a business professional?"

"Please," I said.

He let me know, in his mild corporate-PR way, that he was offended that I raised my rate so steeply for a mutual erotic session. He would prefer that I had said something like, "For new clients I charge $150. For you, $120." That made sense to me, the good-customer discount to encourage repeat patronage, and I felt a pang of shame for not having thought about this in advance. Roger's suggestion that he was entitled to a special rate, however, was only part of a larger picture of wounded vanity. He wanted to believe that I had sex with him because he turned me on. He told me in no uncertain terms that most guys operate on this fantasy: "I went to get a massage. The masseur liked me. So we had sex." I think he went so far as to say, "Everybody feels this way." For me to spell out the terms of my services in such fine detail made the session less attractive to him. It became a situation where I get naked not because I'm turned on but because he's paying me to.

I was completely fascinated to hear him say all this. Hardly anyone had ever complained to me about a session, and no one had spoken so clearly about his expectations and how they weren't met. But it also made my heart sink. It was exactly what I dreaded hearing. It confirmed my worst suspicions. How could I be so naïve? I keep trying to move in the direction of more conscious, more direct, more straightforward communication about sex and desire. Meanwhile, guys like Roger — I doubt if "everybody" felt the same way, but he surely wasn't alone — prefer less. I knew that some clients who came to me for massage acted as if we were on a date, as if we were having a mutual reciprocal relationship and we both just happened to have that hour free. But I thought it was an unconscious scenario going through their heads. Here was Roger telling me that was what he actively wanted. It's the classic falling-in-love-with-a-hooker story, wanting to believe you're the only one. Shades of Richard Gere and Julia Roberts, although no one yet had offered to "take me away from all this."

I could understand it when someone wanted to engage in BDSM role-playing. I'm the cop and you're the driver I've stopped for speeding on a secluded highway after dark. I'm camping without a permit and you're the park ranger with handcuffs dangling from your wide leather belt. Show Daddy your butthole. That's not what Roger was saying, though. He wanted to believe that when I touched his cock or got naked and rolled around with him, I was departing from my usual routine because he was special. He wanted me to flatter his ego by convincing him that he was uniquely attractive to me. The truth is, I did find Roger attractive and sexy. Otherwise I couldn't have engaged with him sexually as much as I did. But I didn't think it was a good idea to verbalize my attraction to my clients. Partly that came from my own need to control — I was afraid that if I expressed my desire, I would lose some of my power — and partly it seemed simply inappropriate. After all, I made it clear: we weren't on a date. This is my work. This is what I do.

Besides, Roger had a habit of putting himself down: he was too old, too fat, too this, too that. It's called "fishing for compliments." You're supposed to respond with "No, honey, you're not fat. Honest, you're not. You're gorgeous. No, I'm not telling you that because I know it's what you want to hear. I swear it's true!" Most people who need someone else to tell them they're okay can never get enough. I admit it – I'm not good at playing that game.

"You're so cold and businesslike on the phone," he complained. "Every time I call you, I feel like I'm back at square one, like you've never seen me before."

This struck me as a classic example of the pot calling

the kettle black — or what psychotherapists would call blatant projection.

"Roger," I said, getting exasperated. "you've come to see me several times. You know how I work. You know the range of possibilities. Yet every time I ask you what you want, you're never willing to say."

"Well, I have a lot of control issues," he said. "I need to exert control."

Okay, I thought to myself, that makes two of us.

"What's the payoff, though?" I said to him, trying to keep my voice from rising to an angry whine, not completely successfully. "You come here and pay me to give you pleasure. Then you spend the whole time trying to control me. How does that serve you?"

He paused for a moment and swallowed. "I don't have an answer for that."

Despite the unpleasant feelings that came up, the conversation was remarkably frank, revealing, and quite cordial. Rather than contest his assertions, I treated them as information that was good for me to collect. He seemed grateful to be heard. We talked for at least half an hour. Finally, before he walked out the door, he said, "What I want from you is an hour of massage and half an hour of sex. And I'd rather pay you $120 and leave sex optional, depending on how we feel at the moment." I was amazed. It was the clearest request I ever heard from him. I felt relieved that he'd cleared the air enough to envision future sessions with me, although my own opinion about that was: Never again. Life's too short.

The session with Roger disturbed me, but I learned a lot from it. I came face-to-face with my denial. I'm in denial about my clients' lack of interest in making distinctions between massage, erotic massage, and sex. As Mitchell says — Mitchell is this guy I've started dating — "Most guys call you because they're horny and they want to get their rocks off." I'm in denial about how much guys want to have not just their dicks but their egos stroked as well. I'm in denial about how I make clients fall in love with me and then I feel uncomfortable when they do. And Roger's deviousness — his refusal to answer when I ask "What's your pleasure?" except to say "What do you feel like doing?" — tells me I must be doing something wrong. When it comes to offering sexual bodywork, I'm fooling myself or fooling my clients with what I tell them on the phone.

If I want to do healing work, I have to tell people that. If I want to offer bodywork that integrates touch, breath, meditation, yoga, a healthy diet, and erotic energy, I can't assume that everybody else makes those associations when they see an ad for "massage." If I leave things unspoken, other people will fill in the blanks with their own needs, their fears, their shame, their ignorance. It would be like going to the baths and expecting to practice tantra with people who are desperate to get off. I need to put the word out to people who know they want to do something different with their sexual energy.

CHAPTER THIRTY-SEVEN

Where Is The Love?

Sometimes when I review my notes about sessions, I'm taken aback. What am I doing here? What am I doing with my life? What am I doing in my supposed healing practice? I'm giving people perfectly good massages while keeping one eye on their state of erection, fantasizing the whole time about what I want to do with it — that's if I'm attracted. Otherwise I spend the whole time dodging their hands. I sit in meditation practicing how to ask for more money on the phone. I go back and forth about whether I want to continue seeing Lester and running through my repertoire of soft-core BDSM scenes with him. I think about referring him to Dominic, but then I remember that Dominic charges $150 a session, which Lester may not be able to afford. Then I think why should I charge $100 for a session Dominic would do for $150??

As Roberta Flack and Donny Hathaway sang, *Where is the love?*

I was taught better. I know better. I want being

with people to be an experience of love and affection and safety and spiritual expansion. I don't want to be someone's guilty pleasure. But when I feel a tiny tender warm spot under my rib, I know there's something missing here.

Where did I get these notions that it should be any different? Where did I get the idea that I could have a profession touching people and talking to them and encouraging them to expand their idea of sexuality to include breathing and energy and God?

Blame it on tantra.

Blame it on Mantak Chia.

Blame it on fucking Joe Kramer, that Pied Piper of tribal tantra. Whenever I come to a crossroads and I don't know what to do in my healing practice, I come back to principles that Joe espoused and that got accepted as gospel those weeks on the mountaintop at Wildwood in Sacred Intimate Training.

Then I look at days like Wednesday, when I had three clients who had healing experiences that went in different directions. Drew, my GMHC client, came for his weekly free massage. He's getting tired, bless his heart. Who knows how long he will continue this fight. Considering that, as he puts it, "I'm too evil to die," he could go on for years, dragging himself to his appointments and otherwise holing up in his room, making doll dresses, listening to Maria Callas and smoking joints. I know, though, that one of the pleasures he lives for is having my hands touch every inch of his body (well, almost every inch — his is one cock I've never stroked, by my choice), stretching him gently, coaxing all the tight contracted spots into letting go.

After him, I saw Rick, a new client who's adopted a battery of spiritual practices to keep his T-cells high and his spirits sailing. As soon as I put my hands on him, he started to weep. All the anger and grief he's been pushing down to maintain that facade of New Age cheer came rushing to the surface. His lower back radiated such heat that I kept my hand there while he bucked and sobbed. After a while, I turned him over and lay down with him and let him cry on my shoulder for the rest of the session.

Right after Rick, Gerald arrived bursting to relate his sexploits in the last couple of weeks. His confusion of desire and guilt and denial about the problems in his relationship with his lover Dwight seemed to demand my full attention, so we processed for the entire 90 minutes with clothes on, no touching. Stuff got stirred up, most of it painful for Gerald to acknowledge. He was visibly shaken when he left, and it wasn't with the erotic buzz he usually gets from a session with me. Still, it felt like good work.

Afterwards I sat quietly for an hour reflecting on a day of healing work that went outside the boundaries of my massage-cum-sexwork routine. How did I come to do this work? It seems miraculous to me. It feels like it just happened, that it's beyond my control. But I have to stop myself and remember that I willed this practice into being. It didn't come from nowhere. Watching Bob die taught me about being present and listening. Irene Smith taught me practical skills for being with people who are seriously ill and touching them with love. From Sacred Intimate Training I learned to abandon my preconceptions and go with whatever healing needs to be done in the moment. From Chester Mainard — the Avatar of Assholes — I learned to sit still and face my shadow, my dark emotions: rage, anger, fear. I owe something to Joe Kramer for starting me on this path, and I owe a lot to Hardy for co-creating with me the container of a 14-year relationship in which many things could happen. All these people and lessons brought me to this place I am at today.

CHAPTER THIRTY-EIGHT

The Higher Octave

I stopped doing sex work with my clients, but I didn't stop being a sacred intimate. I didn't stop doing erotic massage or honoring erotic energy as a part of bodywork. I did stop using my sexual body as a tool in my practice. Not because I think it's bad to have sex, or bad for me to have sex with my clients, or bad for them to want sex with me. I stopped because I saw that having sex with my clients wasn't having the healing effect on them or on me that I wanted. I saw that I wanted things in my life that couldn't be gotten from having sex with my clients — a freedom to be needy as a child, to be held and cared for, and to surrender responsibility to a loved and trusted partner. I was giving away what I needed to get. It wasn't good for me. And if it wasn't good for me, it wasn't good.

I stopped because I saw that I was inevitably promising something I couldn't deliver. I wanted with my abundant sexuality to repair people's low self-esteem, their shame, their internalized homophobia, their codependence, their alienation from God — things that require hard, brave, self-compassionate inner work. I can be a guide, and I'm struggling to be that with clients. But I can't do it for them. I stopped doing sexwork because I realized my fantasy of making a difference in the world by doing one-on-one sexual healing was too hard. Both my clients and I are so overwhelmingly at the mercy of culturally inflicted sexual wounds.

I instigated some other changes, too. I undertook some preliminary training as a gestalt therapist. I embarked on a serious study of holistic medicine. I began to find and experiment with and fail at and struggle further with efforts to work consciously, safely, and skillfully with sexuality. I know so much more now about myself and my work than I did when I began my bodywork practice. I know so much more now, at the end of writing this book, than I did when I started.

When I first hung out my shingle and began touching people in exchange for cash, the only model I had for sacred intimate work was being at Wildwood with other sexual-healers-in-training. They weren't necessarily the most enlightened beings in the world. But they were loving, soulful, articulate, respectful, gifted individuals who brought a lifetime of thought and experience to the exploration of erotic self-realization. I guess I naïvely thought my massage clients would be something like my Wildwood companions. I assumed they'd want to have the same experience of sexual-spiritual integration I had gotten from the Body Electric work. I guess I imagined they'd be just like me. They'd be in relationships, in therapy, in a spiritual practice. They would come to lay their burdens down and walk away refreshed. I suppose I was prepared to be as sexually free with them as I was with other would-be sacred intimates. Somehow, I didn't foresee that I would be handling clients for whom getting a massage was their primary sexual outlet. After all, no one went to Wildwood just to have sex.

Alarmed by the sexual expectations of my clientele, I was also excited by the challenge of fulfilling them. However, sex outside a ritual context — where breathing and eye contact and verbal processing of desires were key elements — was alien to my impression of sacred intimate work. I cycled back and forth between anxiety and excitement, increasingly overwhelmed at being thrown back on my own resources. I wondered, "What am I doing here?"

One thing I know now is that my temptation to have sex with my massage clients had a lot to do with the fact that after two long domestic partnerships I found myself, at the age of 40, single for the first time in my life. From the time I came out, I was always oriented toward relationships. I never had the sowing-your-wild-oats period of rampant sexual experimentation that I thought young men were supposed to go through. In a sense I was making up for lost time by exploring sexual opportunities with my clients.

That wasn't the primary thing, though. I was suffering intensely from intimacy deprivation. I loved being married. I missed daily contact with a loving companion. In my loneliness and desperation, I often let myself believe I could get that from massage clients. I merged my need for sex with my need for simple contact — affection, kindness, tenderness.

When I started out, I was unaware of my own neediness, so I judged it harshly in others. I'm thinking especially about Al, the guy who couldn't bring himself to leave his 26-year marriage and so acted out his closeted homosexuality with phone sex, visits to porno theaters, and sessions with guys like me. My ability to perceive Al's wounds so clearly and even to identify with his struggles ought to evoke compassion in someone who considers himself a healer, you might think. So why did I write about him with such impatience, anger, and contempt?

What I know now that I didn't know then is that I was hurt by my interactions with Al. I didn't want to have sex with him but I did it anyway. Partly I allowed him to manipulate me into giving him what he wanted. Partly I felt I was doing my job as a Sacred Intimate, which I mistakenly believed meant healing people by having sex with them. Instinctively I recognized that he was dishonest and untrustworthy, which was alarming to the little kid inside me who wants to be protected from harm. Instead of valuing my instincts, I set them aside. Both Al and I were playing a kind of charade, not admitting what was going on between us. It didn't hurt me in any physical way to be sexual with him, but it caused considerable distress to my little kid, who depends on me to pay attention to my feelings. If I didn't have compassion for myself, how could I have any for Al?

I feel a little apologetic about lapsing into therapy language. I admit, though, that it helped me a lot to work this stuff out with a therapist whose background in transactional analysis helped me track the ever-shifting roles of Child, Parent, and Adult. Everybody has this population inside with varying degrees of good and bad, nurturing and abusive, sensible and crazy. The hurt kid in my clients brought out the hurt kid in me, the one who wanted his daddy. I would act as if my client were my daddy. When that didn't result in getting what I wanted from him — unconditional love and approval — I felt hurt, betrayed, and resentful. It took me a long time to realize that much.

That hurt child inside me was often terrified at the unpredictability of my bodywork sessions. What I know now is that my harsh judgment of the behavior and appearance of clients like Al, or the ones I referred to as the Massage Vampires, comes from overriding my internal alarm system. Inside I was furious at Barry-the-pediatrician's invasiveness or Al's indirection, yet I acted like it was okay. I can trace the source of this dilemma directly to my lack of clarity on the phone about the sexual parameters of my work. I wasn't laying down ground rules for my clients because I wasn't exactly sure what they were. How could I object when they went ahead and made up their own? During the sessions I got locked into impersonating some magnanimous, all-accepting goddess of love. Only afterwards did I realize what it cost me to play that role. And I didn't play it perfectly by any means. The mask would slip, revealing my impatience, my anger, and my manipulativeness.

I needed to be seen by older men. I wanted the love of my Daddy, and I wanted to love my Daddy. I was willing to audition every client who came to me, silently asking: *are you the Daddy I can love?* Not only was my hurt kid rearing up his head — demanding to be seen and held and loved — but so was my internal Daddy. I was at a time in my life when I needed to be teaching, leading, and parenting. I needed to practice those things with myself and others, rather than get over-identified with the needy child always wanting more. That's a wound that I forget to notice: the unfulfilled parent. It's easier to spot in other people than in myself. Maybe part of the reason I don't want to pay attention is that I don't like the parental style I observed in my own father — harsh, strict, dictatorial. I'm afraid to admit how much I'm like that myself. Now I recognize this: the kid is the one who for a time was happy to get naked and play. The daddy in me is the one who didn't find that to be fun, who was more interested in tools (therapy) than toys (sex).

In one sense, that's the struggle I've enacted in my bodywork practice, between these two underrecognized aspects of myself — the hurt child and the internal Daddy. They've been trying to communicate with one another, and I guess my clients provided the bridge. The more I'm able to let my inner child sit in my inner father's inner lap, the happier I am and the less I'm inclined to get tangled up in frustrated emotions with my clients. Then I'm not only Icarus, excitable and high-flying, but also Daddy Daedalus, tinkering in his workshop.

Probably the main thing I've learned about this is that I can't be all things to all people. For clients whose need is to reach out and touch or to have mutual touch, I'm going to be frustrating to work with. Being touched lovingly and intimately can churn up long-buried needs for dependency. I might be looking at a 62-year-old stockbroker or a 55-year-old garment manufacturer or a 33-year-old hairdresser, but suddenly I find myself dealing with the pre-verbal emotions of an infant or the narcissistic demands of a 4-year-old. It's possible that working with me will perpetuate or reopen an old wound of rejection or abandonment.

On the other hand, it's possible that frustration will bring awareness to the need in such a way that he can move to fulfillment. He might not be able to touch me, but he might finally recognize how deep his need is to touch and find someone who's a suitable partner. He might learn that he has a pattern of seeking out people who will only frustrate him. He may see the folly of seeking fulfillment from a total stranger. He may think he wants to touch, but he may in fact need to be held. [MFF: In 2003 Joe Kramer created another erotic service profession that he labeled Sexological Bodywork. Practitioners are required to wear clothes and to offer one-way touch only.]

What I know now is that sexual healing does not equal having sex with people. I can do powerful work with people that is genuinely helpful to them in dealing with their erotic bodies without getting naked and having sex with them. Sometimes sexual healing means addressing a concrete wound, such as rape or abuse or crippling shame. These conditions may require other kinds of therapy before touching: talking, drawing out grief and anger to a place where they can be felt and then released, writing and speaking affirmations. Sometimes sexual healing is a balancing act, providing in a ritual sexual arena what's missing in the rest of your life. Someone who lives a tame, bland existence may need intensity, challenge, even danger. Many high-powered businessmen need just the opposite, to surrender control and be passive, receptive, even submissive. Sometimes sexual healing isn't about treating damage or lack but simply unconsciousness — psychic numbness. When I touch each part of a person's body (including the parts usually hidden by underwear), it's a kind of meditation or blessing that says "Every part of you has value." Always, always, sexual healing is about seeking a reminder of wholeness, the experience that body and soul both seem to crave.

    I've learned a lot, too, about the continuum between prostitute and psychotherapist. I started off wanting to be the former and judging myself for being reluctant to go all the way, and I ended up wanting to be the latter and judging myself for not measuring up to the standards and values of therapy. I've often looked down my nose at the social distance therapists put between them and their clients and the prohibitions around physical contact. To me, those rules seemed to put therapists on a pedestal and overemphasize their power. I still believe that to some extent. And I still believe that people can experience enormous insights, transformations, and self-liberations from one or two bodywork sessions that it would take months or years of talk therapy to achieve. However, I have come to have more respect and admiration for traditional psychotherapeutic strategies for containment.

One liability of doing sex work is the invasiveness, literal and energetic. When you let someone penetrate you or even touch you with whom you feel no connection, you can't help splitting off, leaving your body. It's dangerous psychically, because if you split off from your body, where are you? Many prostitutes quickly start to view their customers with contempt. And then because they're still interacting with men they hate, they begin to have a hard attitude toward their own bodies. They drink and take drugs to block the suffering that comes from letting someone else use your body for their pleasure and not yours. "Okay, meter's running, go ahead and fiddle with me, it doesn't do a damn thing for me, just pay me when you're through." That's not the approach to the body I choose to encourage. You get one body in this life — the least you can do is be good to it. I guess this is a luxury I've given myself. Other people work in jobs or live in relationships that are toxic and stressful in ways that wear down their bodies and their spirits. That level of anxiety isn't worth it to me. I guess I've chosen to live with lower ambitions and higher serenity.

When someone comes for a massage, I'm committed to touching their whole bodies expertly and lovingly. I don't grab their dicks first thing. It's no fun and no pleasure for me if a client wants to touch me and the first thing he does is grab my dick. It's such an unequal body experience. Or at the least bad manners. Maybe that's what I'm doing: teaching sexual etiquette.

As an erotic masseur, I needed to learn to set boundaries in order to provide intimate touch. When I allowed mutual touch, I was always on the verge of splitting off. My heart was guarded and shut down. I don't think you can do healing work that way. Deep

healing happens in a container. The therapist creates the container. The client does the healing.
Prostitutes have to assume that every session is a one-shot. Therapists usually work on an ongoing basis. There's a big difference in the kind of healing that takes place in a one-shot vs. a commitment over time, defined by the investment of the client. Good stuff can happen in one session, but not everything can happen all at once. Ongoing therapy is a process of identifying an issue, dealing with emotional resistance, doing soul work, integrating it into your life — it's a process. In my practice, I'm frustrated because I can clearly see that some people could benefit from a process. Yet they come to me irregularly so there's no container for that work. So their issues around, let's say, shame or low self-esteem or negative body image remain intact. What I offer is a kind of Band-Aid, a momentary cessation of pain. It's not nothing. Sometimes it has to be enough.

Am I ashamed to think of myself as a prostitute? Yes. It damages my ego because there's no status attached to it. A modicum of tawdry glamour, perhaps, but mostly social opprobrium (disgrace). And apparently I require status. When I think about being a successful journalist for national publications, prostitute seems like a big step down into desperation. It's partly status and partly accuracy. I don't sell my body. I do sex work, in that I work with sexual energy. Politically, socially, and spiritually, I'm proud of that — it feels important and radical in our sex-negative culture — and I'm verbally articulate enough to defend it. Keith Hennessy helped me with this. When I moaned to him early on, "I was a successful writer and now I've stooped to being a masseur," he corrected me: "Stooped to being a healer!"

A few other things I know now:

The best advertising is word-of-mouth — but closet cases don't refer their friends.

I don't need the money badly enough to do anything I don't want to do.

Wash sheets and towels separately in hot water with liquid detergent and Clorox 2 bleach.

I used to think: if I feel horny, why go to the baths or some other venue looking for sex when I can stay home and have sex with clients and get paid for it? What I know now: I'm too conscientious (perfectionist) to fully release into having sex with clients — so it only ends up wounding me. I'd rather go to the baths and have sex if I'm horny for stranger sex. Then if I want to suck, I can suck. If I want to fuck or get fucked, I can do it at my discretion without feeling I have to service someone because he's a client.

Of course, what I've discovered is I'm most satisfied crawling into bed with my boyfriend whether we have sex or not. I used to think I could never get my fill of sucking strange cocks. What I know now: I can get my fill. What I want at the end of the day is mutual affection based on knowing each other well.

I'm not a saint or a monk. I'm frequently tempted to get naked and roll around with a client, and once in a while I give in to that craving. I feel a little guilty about it, like a vegetarian with an urge for the occasional hamburger and French fries, but I let myself have it. It's not a capital crime. Why beat myself up?

After a few years of doing bodywork, I wanted to get more skillful about handling the emotional issues that massage clients showed up with, and in 1996 I undertook a four-year clinical fellowship and got trained as a gestalt psychotherapist. With its intrinsic focus on body-awareness, tracking the breath, and concentrating on what's happening right here right now, gestalt work was perfectly compatible with my massage and sacred intimate training. So I've developed parallel practices as an erotic masseur and a psychotherapist. I don't call all the work that I do sacred intimate work, though I do approach all my clients with a sacred intimate perspective. There is a big overlap between therapy and erotic bodywork, and that's what I consider sacred intimate work.

I've come to understand that much of the healing that takes place in sacred intimate work happens on extremely simple levels. Simple, nurturing touch is so important. Touch that includes genital touch plus breath plus presence feels like acceptance. Giving permission is a big part of sacred intimate work. It's about giving permission to receive pleasure, to feel your whole body, to speak desires, to bring consciousness to sex and touch, to live your spirituality without blocking your sexuality and vice versa, to be seen naked, to see another man naked. All these are opportunities to heal shame, isolation, erotic malnutrition, and touch deprivation.

Sacred intimates can help people keep their erotic bodies alive in a long and loving but sexless marriage. I'm thinking of a man named Howard who came to see me who's been in a relationship with another man for 27 years. They've never had a sexual relationship because his partner is not into it. Now at the age of 51, Howard is starting to feel the deficit of not living out his sexuality. He took a Body Electric workshop and found it exhilarating, but he found that he ejaculated almost immediately, without even feeling it, as soon as someone touched his cock. His only sexual experience had been masturbating as quickly as possible to get it over with. I did a couple of sessions with him, working on his breathing, moving energy around his body, and he was able to hang out much longer in a high erotic state without squirting or squelching his erotic energy. He left transported with joy.

In my practice I see a lot of men whose stories are a variation on Howard's. They're getting to be middle-aged and they're looking for adult sex education, or erotic mentorship. This is an area sacred intimates are well-suited to address. Many guys, especially those who identify as heterosexual and/or are married to women, have strong desires to experiment sexually with men. Because these fantasies have been strongly repressed, they consume a huge amount of energy. In a sacred intimate session, a middle-aged married guy can try out his fantasy of sucking cock or getting fucked and often will discover that the fantasy plays better than the reality. And they can learn this not by having bad or painful sexual encounters with strangers but by exploring consciously with a sacred intimate, experimenting playfully with simulated butt-fucking or verbal fantasy or having the actual experience of being naked with another man and checking out the true extent of his desires. Would he rather suck a hard cock, or would he rather fantasize about sucking a hard cock? Sometimes the reality is physically unpleasant, and sometimes it simply triggers too many fears to be pleasurable - the two biggest being fear of disease and fear that if he likes sex with men, that means he's gay and he'll have to leave behind everything he cherishes in his life and get his nipples pierced.

I'm thinking of Perry, a twice-married man with grown children. He desperately wants physical contact with men, but he tends to go about it in a way that is guaranteed to be frustrating. He refuses to name desires, saying instead that he wants to surrender to another man. But what that means is surrendering consent — a recipe for violation. So then he can disown his desire and blame the other person: I didn't want it, he forced me. He told me that when he was in his thirties he was coerced into sex once with his uncle, a Catholic priest, and once with a friend of his uncle's. I was curious about this, since a man in his 30s is well past the age of consent. It turns out that he grew up in a traditional Italian family and his older brother tormented him from an early age — whenever he showed signs of being soft or sensitive, his brother would say, "Don't you be a faggot!"

This told me a couple of things. From an early age, Perry's permission to say yes to his gay desires was taken away from him, and that took away his no as well, leaving him vulnerable to coercion. It also got him to internalize his brother's homophobia, which manifests by disdaining gay men who aren't "straight-acting" and advising his gay son not to go around telling people he's gay. Some of the work we've done together has been about supporting him in naming desires in an inhabited, emotionally authentic way — "I'd like you to be naked" as opposed to "Nudity is appropriate." I've also worked with him to increase his ability to tolerate naming desires, postponing the need to attach identity to sexual feelings or behavior, and giving him permission to play in an erotic zone and experience it directly. When that happened, his need/desire for intensely sexual contact diminished, and he discovered that a big part of his yearning is simply for another man to be nice to him (which is what he didn't get from his father or his brother).

Exploring anal pleasure is another task for sacred intimates. Many heterosexually identified men are curious about anal pleasure and long for a safe playground to explore. Plenty of gay men, too, have apprehensions about butt-play, based on fear of disease or bad experiences with insensitive lovers. As one client said to me in an e-mail, "My first gay experiences were with my friend Steven who had a huge dick. He used to fuck me and rip me apart — no real lube, just a little saliva. It has taken me years to get over the pain association." My extensive training and experience as an erotic masseur has equipped me with the information and ability to bring men through their fears at their own pace to arrive at the place where pleasure is available.

So much of sacred intimate work has to do with adult sex education, sharing information and teaching. I am far from being any kind of expert in women's sexuality, but I do have female clients, and I enjoy working with them. I find it amazing sometimes how a little bit of information and permission goes a long way. I've worked with a married couple, I'll call them Ron and Eva. Ron is an Italian from Staten Island, a construction contractor, hard-working and high-strung. He comes to me for massage to relax and to indulge his deep craving to be touched by a man. When Eva would come with him, they would often end up fucking on my massage table. It didn't look like much fun to me. Ron seemed to feel the need to prove himself by fucking Eva, and she seemed to humor him without experiencing much pleasure herself. I was surprised and somewhat appalled to learn that she had never had an orgasm by masturbating. One time when I massaged her and included yoni massage, she reported that it was the first time she's had an orgasm by manual stimulation.

Another time she came to me by herself, the only time I've seen her without Ron. I gave her a good thorough back massage, then turned her over and oiled her up. It immediately became clear that she was looking forward to genital massage — the merest brush of her public hair or her thighs brought sighs. I played with her a little bit, then asked if she'd ever used a vibrator. She said no, so I brought out my Hitachi wand and gave her a little introduction, then let her handle the vibrator while I massaged her, eventually slipping one then two fingers into her vagina. She went crazy with this, swimming on the table and moaning and bearing down with the Hitachi wand, having what looked for all the world like Annie Sprinkle's five-minute orgasm. She finally stopped after two climaxes, sweaty and flushed. I never saw her look like that after her husband fucked her on the massage table. This felt like my first experience of lesbian sex. I made sure she left with the address of Eve's Garden, a women's sex-toy shop in my neighborhood.

Eileen is another woman I've worked with extensively who came to me for several massages before shyly bringing up her interest in sexual healing. The story came out that she had been sexually molested by family members, and for many years simply shut down her sexual body. Now at 40 she wanted to reclaim it, but she couldn't let herself surrender to orgasms, and she was somewhat embarrassed that her primary turn-on was anal pleasure. Here's a note I have from our 19th session together: "She said she wanted to understand why her butt was so erotic, and I invited her to discover that understanding not by analysis and cognition but through experience. We hit on the notion of an intensity dial which she could turn up or down at will, by signaling me if she wanted more, or less, or to stop. We explored, starting with a back massage then moving into butt massage. She loves everything to do with having her butt touched. I slowly started stroking her pussy, which was sopping wet. I kept checking in with her about where we were on the intensity scale, and this was 8.5, which is as high as she'd ever gotten without scaring herself. (She has a fear of disappearing into Never-Never-Land, which my witnessing helps prevent.) I turned her over, oiled her up, and stroked her breasts. She'd brought a hand-held vibrator she's been experimenting with, and we tried adding that. I coached her about going slowly into intensity. I massaged her butt with one hand and her breasts with the other while she rubbed herself with the vibrator and added clitoral stimulation with her hand. This got quite intense, and eventually she needed to stop and rest. She said her skin felt like it was going to pop. I asked her where she was on the intensity scale, and she said she'd gotten to 12 out of 10. She felt like she was losing control, but it wasn't a bad thing, it was like shooting the rapids with a life preserver, the life preserver in this case being me. Since she'd never had the experience before, she didn't know that this is what an orgasm feels like."

All the clients I'm describing are people who did not and probably would not seek out clinical sex therapy, nor were they simply looking to get off. They mostly found me through the avenue of bodywork, and we developed a personal relationship that created a safe container for both of us to experiment with sacred intimate work.

For me, sacred intimate work is a constant dance between the sex-worker side of me, concentrating on healing through pleasure, and the psychotherapist, processing emotional issues. And all this takes place within the context of my own grounded spiritual practice, a consecrated ritual space, and my own sense of purpose, to wake people up to the joy of life in a body. I want to live in a world that honors and supports sexual freedom, erotic abundance, and healing through pleasure.

*

The phone rings. His name is Jim. He saw my ad. Maybe it was the one online that says, "TOUCH HEALS: Expert bodywork to nourish the soul." Maybe it was the one in the gay bar rag that says, "BODY & SOUL WORK: Expert touch and loving presence in a safe, conscious environment." Maybe it was the slightly racier ad in the national gay magazine that says, "SACRED EROTIC INTIMATE: Superior sensual massage by Portuguese man-of-love." No matter where he got my number, I give him my spiel. First I say, "I'm a certified massage therapist. What I offer is a good thorough full-body massage that also includes erotic touch. I work on a table." Sometimes I'll pause there and ask, "Does that sound like what you're looking for?" If someone's put off by the notion of erotic touch or (much more common) simply dialing for dick, that gives him an opportunity to say, "No, thanks" and move on.

If the answer is "Yes," then I continue. "The massage I do is a Swedish/Esalen-style massage with some acupressure and conscious breathing, and the erotic work is intended to raise and circulate erotic energy around your body so it's a full-body experience." I say how much it costs, where I'm located, and the hours I'm available. For most people, that's enough. If anyone still feels the need to ask "Is there a release?" I say, "It's your choice" — my subtle way of planting the notion that erotic touch doesn't have to lead to ejaculation. Often I get the question, "What do you look like?" I'm mellower about that than ever. I say, "I'm 5'8', 145 pounds. I'm half-Portuguese so I'm dark and hairy. I work out at a gym. I'm in good shape." Occasionally someone wants to know my age, and I've gotten braver about telling the truth, despite the times when the immediate response was "(Click)." [MFF: Of course the internet eventually made it possible to create a website containing all this information with photos, resources, blog posts, and links to my writing about the work that I do, so I don't have to repeat it over the phone endlessly.]

People are wacky. Some of the things they say on the phone make me laugh: *Do you get involved in the massage? Can you wear high-top sneakers? Do you give a release with the mouth? Do you spank? Are you ripped? What's your butt like? You're hung, or what? You like suckin' dick? Are you interested in a private photo session? Are you circumcised?*

Do you give an enema? Is it possible to, uh, suck you? Do you show erotic movies? Can you dominate a big man? By now I've learned that almost any questions beyond the basic what-where-when-how-much are a tip-off: this person is not going to book a session with me.

The good news is that people who do show up almost always want exactly what I offer. I've gotten much clearer about working with new clients, too. When they come in, we always sit down for a preliminary chat. I collect whatever information I need to know about their physical injuries or states of mind. Then I elaborate further about how the session will proceed. I reiterate that it's a full-body massage that incorporates erotic touch. "It lasts about an hour and 15 minutes. I spend the first 40 to 45 minutes working on your back, your neck, shoulders, legs, feet, to relax you out, paying special attention to the parts that call out for special attention. I start incorporating erotic touch as we go along."

I try to make sure that I'm making steady eye contact when I'm saying all this. I try to speak in a slow, pleasant voice and to breathe. I have to fight the temptation to race through this speech. "If you want to ejaculate at some point, you're welcome to. If you don't want to, that's fine with me. When I do erotic massage, my intention is to raise and circulate erotic energy around your body so it's a full-body experience, not just a genital experience. You can use this time as an opportunity to relax and feel good. You can make it a kind of meditation for yourself, to remember all of who you are. One thing it's not is an invitation to touch me back or interact with me sexually."

I can tell that sometimes this speech makes people nervous. Their eyes get wide or they freeze up when I look them in the face and talk about ejaculation. Sometimes people are visibly disappointed when I say they can't touch me. "We won't have sex?" a young Frenchman spluttered. "That's what I want!" I had no problem at all suspending the session right there — no hard feelings. Sometimes new clients look annoyed or afraid or impatient that I'm talking too much. In my drive for clarity, I know I risk sounding a bit cold or clinical, removing some of the mystery that makes an erotic encounter so alluring. But every time I've lost my nerve and not spelled out each of those points up front, I've regretted it later.

The payoff is that by the time someone gets on my table now, they're primed for the experience of receiving intimate touch without having to reciprocate. And they're more likely to leave visibly shaken and irrevocably transformed. "I never had anything like that before," said the Southern gentleman, looking dazed as he pulled up the suspenders on his Armani suit. "It's a public service, what you do," said the skier with dreamy blue eyes. "You are a magician ... You are an artist ... I feel like I'm stoned ... This is everything a massage should be ... Every person who's running for office should have one of your massages." Let me brag: I've lost track of the number of times I've heard, "That was the best massage I've ever had."

The hardest part of making the transition from interactive sex work to strictly erotic massage was announcing my new guidelines to old clients. I forced myself to say on the phone, "I've changed the way that I'm working. I'm happy to give you an excellent erotic massage, but I'm keeping my clothes on these days, and I'm not interacting sexually with my clients." Most of them were polite about it but never came back. I felt hurt for a while, then I got over it. Other people took their place. I saw the same number of clients every week and made the same amount of money.

Al called me from time to time, trying to wheedle

me into giving him the kind of session he likes. I'm sympathetic to his needs. I know he wants a kind of tender intimate experience you don't get when you buy a hustler, but I also know he's not happy unless he has sex, so I turn him down. Once I stopped getting naked, Eugene stopped coming to see me. I knew he'd gotten a tremendous amount of self-discovery from being with me, and I felt like he'd graduated and moved on. The same was true of Lester, my S/M client. I'd never gotten naked with him to begin with, but our work seemed to run its course, and he stopped calling. Meanwhile, Gerald remained a steady customer and even talked his lover Dwight into coming for sessions with me once in a while.

A good number of my clients are men who are coming out in late in life or men attempting to reawaken their erotic bodies after periods of numbness, addiction, or bad relationships. A huge number of men who shut down sexually because of AIDS have found butt-massage to be the key to a new, delicious sense of erotic wholeness. And I see plenty of busy, stressed-out New Yorkers who are looking for good touch and don't want to ignore or deny their sexuality to get it. Whoever they are, I touch them, I love them, I pray over their bodies, I stick my fingers up their butts and jerk them off, I cover them with a warm towel and remind them (and myself) to breathe and to feel.

Seeing the top of the mountain and getting there are two different experiences. Keep your eye on the goal but look at all the steps in between. You can't take them all at once. How can I convey or elicit that image with clients? How do I do it now? How do I show it? How do I speak it? How do I find the way to some real or imaginary temple of healing from the narrow, coded language of the massage trade? This takes me right back to chapter one, doesn't it?

It all comes down to everything packed into the conversation when a client asks, "Is there a release?" How do I want that conversation to go? What do I want to offer and what self-knowledge around sexuality do I want to empower my clients to recognize?

Those are the questions that face me as, at the end of a long journey, I arrive at the place where I'm ready to begin. I don't know how long I will stay on this path. Chances are, I won't always be doing this work. But I hope somebody will.

THE END

APPENDIX

Joseph Kramer
*Portrait of a
Sexual Healer*

In the April 21, 1992, issue of the Village Voice, I published a long article with the headline "Sexual Healing: Joe Kramer Sings the Body Electric." The article reported on my experience participating in Body Electric workshops and included some quotes from a long interview I did with Kramer in April of 1991. What follows is the complete transcript of that interview. Edited only in order to be comprehensible, the conversation goes into much greater detail about Kramer's background, his workshops, his vision of the vocation he calls "sacred intimate," Andrew Ramer's notion of the "consciousness scout," and his own understanding of the erotic consciousness scout and its function in society, among other topics.

I don't know anything about you or your background. The two-day workshop was a powerful experience for me, and as anyone discovers travelling around the country, there's a whole network now of people who've taken your workshop and are spreading the gospel. It's clearly having a transformative effect ...
Oh, look what you have here —is this in my honor? [He picks up a paperback copy of Walt Whitman's *Leaves of Grass* sitting on the windowsill, opens it, and reads from the first thing he sees.] "City of orgies! O Manhattan!" Perfect!
So I'd like to know your personal history and the story of how you got into doing this and how your work has evolved.
I'd also like to put out visions of the future.
Great.
So what do you want, the past, present, or future?
Go back to the beginning. Tell me where you're from.
I'll try to be as succinct and as powerful as possible. I grew up in St. Louis in a very religious family.
What religion?
Roman Catholic. My parents went to Mass every single

day, still probably do. I went to Catholic schools all the way through university. What Kinsey said in his studies in the '40s was only 10% of boys masturbate before puberty. What I've found as a sex researcher · is that a high percentage of those boys show up in my classes, and it's an indication of greater sexual power or energy after puberty. In some Polynesian cultures and other cultures, up to 90% masturbate before puberty. What that statistic says to me is how repressive our society is and how it clamps down on children's sexuality, a boy's sexuality. Even though I had this very repressive, guilt-ridden, mortal-sin mentality thrown at me in Catholic schools, that this was horrible, I loved to masturbate.

I think the Catholic church helped me there because it was a mortal sin to masturbate. So I figured, if it's a mortal sin, maybe even after coming I would just keep stroking, so it would only be one mortal sin. So I learned multiple orgasms. I didn't want to go in to the priest in confession and say I masturbated six times yesterday or 25 times last week. Just out of guilt and embarrassment, I would just keep on masturbating clear on through. Yeah, to keep the tally down. But I found that it was just like waking up more and more. So that was a positive benefit from this repressive environment.

The other thing that the repressiveness of Catholicism did was it brought God and sex together in my mind. God cared every time I had sex. It was a matter of life and death. And mostly, for me, it was eternal damnation in hell because I was enjoying this. It made sex not just some paltry thing. God of heaven and earth was concerned about me touching my little penis from the time I was five on. Later on, once I got rid of the guilt, I realized that the God space, the religious space, in me was still intimately tied up with sex. This was part of what spirituality meant to me. So unwittingly the Catholic church helped me out there.

Do you have siblings?
Yes, I have two brothers and three sisters.
Where are you?
I'm the oldest. They are all married and have kids. As Karen Finley would say, I'm the black sheep of the family. I went to a Jesuit school, an all-boys high school. And what the Jesuits taught me was male bonding. They were masters of male bonding. The Jesuits are a homosexual order that, instead of expressing sexuality, has learned a way of turning it around. In a Jesuit school, there's always a high percentage of gay kids, because you're going to an intellectual, all-boys school. But through the bonding they create amazing things. Great sports teams from intellectual kids. My school, when I was there, was twice the state basketball champ, the football champ, the soccer champ and all this. It wasn't that we had better talent than all the other schools. It's because the Jesuits knew about male bonding, the synergy of bringing people together.
What did they know about that?
They set up an environment. It's hard to describe. I've tried to take this apart and think of it. Part of it was making the homophobia very low, so touching was okay, when I was growing up. With gay liberation, it's kind of broken up normal male bonding. The high school kids today are more aware of it. They're either out or hostile. But when I was in school, there wasn't even a hint of homosexuality. I went four years of high school without having a homosexual experience, which is amazing, because I was so fed by the male intimacy. There was tremendous male intimacy. I think the Jesuits taught about that. They taught me to love myself and to love boys. Until I was 14, I really felt weird with my orientation, loving male bodies, boy bodies, my own body. I didn't once I went to St. Louis University High School. Then I went to St. Louis University. What that

homosexual/homoerotic high school experience did was it made me want to be a Jesuit. "I want to live in this environment where there are no other options. I want to teach boys, give my life to God." It all fit together.
Was this high school training boys for the priesthood?
No, no, no. It's like Xavier High School in the village, Regis High School, Fordham High School — those are the three Jesuit high schools in New York. The Jesuits run a network of high schools all over the country. That used to be the major source of vocations for people who joined the Jesuits. Boys coming from these homosexual, all-male environments of men who taught boys. There were no women faculty on the staff whatsoever, no women cheerleaders, no girls from other schools coming in. I wanted to stay in this. This was 1965, four years before Stonewall. The only other option I knew about homosexuals was there were homosexuals in prison. I read about homosexual rape. "Omigod, if I could just get into prison." But I was too good a boy to do anything bad. "Can they send me to prison without committing a crime?" So I joined the Jesuits. And I was a Jesuit for 11 years. I went back and taught at that high school.
What does being a Jesuit mean?
Joining a religious order. Training toward being a priest. It's a long training, 12 or 13 years. I left the Jesuits a year before I would have been ordained a priest.
So you went to college with that thought?
Yes, all my college was as a Jesuit. I also taught high school and ran all sorts of social programs.
When you're a Jesuit in training, are you called something, or do you use your own name?
In the first few years, we spoke Latin. It was still in the pre-Vatican II days.
During the Mass?
Oh, in the halls. Those were the rules. You spoke Latin.

So you were called Frater, the Latin word for brother. Frater Kramer. Later in high school the students referred to me as Mr. Kramer, although I wore a cassock. I wore a dress, open in the front. People were always looking: "what's under them?" We wore regular clothes with a cassock over them.

It was fun. It was fun. But as I went on ... my body tells me when I've gone too far. And I wasn't listening to my body. This was all an intellectual trip. I studied mathematics, philosophy, theology, all this on a spiritual trip, and for my body this was a celibate path. I was really good at it. I realized that the transmutation of eroticism is what empowers a lot of people, especially young Jesuits or young anything. But if it's transmutational without stoking the fires at all, after a while the fires dwindle, the coals burn out, and there is nothing.

So it got to that point. I went to Berkeley in 1972 to study theology as a Jesuit. There were nine other schools in Berkeley, including the Graduate Theological Union. The University of California at Berkeley is part of this. I took some courses at UC, some at other schools. When I went to Berkeley, I went to Sproul Plaza. Even when I was in high school, the free speech movement was important to me. I watched it on television. Because I knew I was not speaking the truth in my life. I couldn't speak the truth. I looked at my parents, I looked around, and I knew this was the place for free speech. I went and sat in Sproul Plaza for hours every day. It was the freest place. You'd see professors walk by and students and wheelchair people and street people and entertainers and always preachers and political people and the Hare Krishnas, Sun Myung Moon. And everybody got along. And I saw, "There is celebration of diversity here." In New York I think there's toleration of diversity, but in Berkeley there was celebration of diversity. Everybody recognized that this is what made this such a wonderful place. And I realized I was diverse, and I was not celebrating my diversity. I was fitting into a Jesuit mold, the Catholic mold, and I'd never been who I was.

So 1972 was my coming out in Sproul Plaza. 1 am diverse, too. I am a gay man. I want to say this. It didn't fit in with the Jesuit thing, because if you're celibate you don't have to say it. In fact, they have power over you if you're guilty about it. So most of the Jesuits are guilty, and that way they have power, as any organization does. But as soon as I started saying it, I felt liberated and out. Other Jesuits at that time were coming to the same awareness. So two years I studied theology there. It was Catholic theology, so I had to take very focused classes. Eventually it became clear living in Berkeley that I did not want to be a Jesuit. It wasn't for me. It took another year of discernment and looking at this. But I moved to New York, leaving the Jesuits, but with a kind of buffer. The idea was that if I still felt called to go back, I'd go back within six months or a year. But in January 1976 I moved to New York, for the Bicentennial year. That was my leaving the Jesuits.

One thing that happened with the Jesuits was that Vatican II had just happened. Pope John XXIII's whole thing was "Open the windows of the Catholic church." The emphasis was on love, rather than the old tradition of ... whatever, order, law. There was a lot of emphasis in that training on being in your heart, being really open. So following my heart is what I eventually did.

When I moved to New York, I moved from a monastic tradition, the seminary life, to New York City in '76.

You poor thing!

What I moved to was a sex monastery. Everybody was having sex. And when I went into sex, I wanted to drink life to the lees. I wandered around. I very quickly met a lover, who was my lover for four years, the whole time I was here. But we had an open relationship. Everybody I knew was having sex, everywhere. On the piers. Larry Kramer's book *Faggots* starts out with "There are 150 places I can go to have sex within a mile of here," something like that. That's what New York was like. Later, when I studied Reich, I realized it was like Reichian therapy. I was vibrating out all the dead spots in myself. And I felt everybody else was. It wasn't compulsive, addictive acting out. It was vibrating out and really being free. With my open-heart orientation, every time I met someone, it was like, oh, I'm right there with them, looking them in the eyes. And I thought everybody was doing this. I think there were just several thousand core people who were the real generators, then there were like 20,000 hangers-on from Fire Island all the way through to Manhattan.

Not to mention the out of towners.

Yeah. But this is where I learned tantra. Because it wasn't about cumming, it was about being in the erotic vibration. New York was this erotic vibration. I remember in '77, when one of the radio stations went disco, all the blacks, all the Puerto Ricans, and all the gays were listening to the same station. It had the highest jump in the ratings any radio station had ever experienced. The whole city played the same music for the next year or two. It was this erotic music. Now we chuckle at disco, but that was the sex music.

It still has vibrations, doesn't it?

Mmm. 12 West and everything. When *Saturday Night Fever* came out, I went and saw it and I thought it was the silliest thing ever. It was a nice movie, but I thought, "How heterosexual!" The idea, with that movie, is you wait 'til Saturday night to get into your sexual space. Well, forget it. Everybody I knew was in it all the time.

So this was what I'd always wanted. I met some of the greatest people. For the last 10 years I've been meeting people who I had sex with in New York and made such powerful connections with that I meet them again and again and again. Sometimes I'll meet people who I don't exactly recognize but I feel, "God, I've already connected with this person intimately. Maybe it was dark..." It may have been five minutes or five hours or five days. But I made amazing amounts of connections. It was open-hearted, fun, innocent. It was enlightening. Everyone I knew then was getting younger and healthier. Sex was clearing out all the shit in their lives. Everybody realized we were doing something new that hadn't been done before. I felt that consciousness all around me. It was everywhere — in the grocery store, anywhere on the subway. People just looked at each other. New York is always one level on top of another, but this one level was a vibration everywhere. Fire Island was the epitome of it for beauty. You'd go to the Pines or the Grove; I did for one summer. That was extraordinary.

What I learned during that was that I didn't want to cum, that I just wanted to be in this vibration, and cumming was the end. For me, it wasn't about getting off. It was about being in this state. There were peaks, certainly, when I wanted to come, but that's what hooked me into Tantra and Taoism. So, at the same time, I had to have a job in town. What did I know? Roman Catholicism. What did I know? Theology, Jesuits. Here I'm in New York. So I looked around for a job, and the job I got was teaching religion at the Convent of the Sacred Heart on Fifth Avenue, which is the utmost elite Catholic girls' school in all of Manhattan. It's where Caroline Kennedy went and all the wealthy kids. There were six girls in one class and 12 girls in another class. It's on 91st and Fifth Avenue in an old mansion. So by day I was teaching girls Roman Catholic theology, and by night I'd be in the basement of the Anvil or the Mineshaft. Actually, it was Man's Country and the piers and 12 West. Two days before the Everhard [the Everard Baths, informally known as the Everhard] burned down, I was there. And I remember going to a school picnic with all the girls in the spring, May or June, and the principal of the school said, "Did you see in the paper what happened last night?" I said no. He said, "The Everhard Baths, this homosexual place, it was so sad, five or eight people were killed." I was among all these girls, and I felt, "Yikes! My people!"

Were you openly gay at work?

I was not openly gay at work. But I was openly pro-homosexual in all my classes. So anytime there was anything homosexual, I brought it up. We were talking about Willa Cather. I said, "Why did she write such strong portraits of women? Because she was a lesbian. *My Antonia* is a beautiful thing, and it comes from her sexual preference." I was also on the board of directors of Dignity. Dignity used to meet in a Lutheran church. I said, why? I knew some of the Jesuits in the city. I asked an acquaintance on 15th Street, "Why can't Dignity meet here?" That helped Dignity move. They were just kicked out by the cardinal two years ago.

This was around the time the gay rights bill was coming up. I was giving talks around the city for the gay rights bill. Andy Humm was a biggie in Dignity, and he's political, so I was doing pro-gay rights stuff. But in the Catholic Church I would say, "I'm head of the theology department at Convent of the Sacred Heart" and go from there. Well, this grated on Cardinal Cook. He sent word out to the school. I was called in by the headmistress, and she said, "I've never gotten a letter from a cardinal about anybody like you." I said, "Forget it. This is the truth, what do you want me to say? Is this the middle ages?" Anyway, I got fired. I got fired because I went to a party with my lover, and somebody said, "What are you doing?" I said, "I teach at Convent of the Sacred Heart," and it got back to the school. I was open everywhere about it, so eventually it was going to happen. They fired me. I wanted to fight it. There was no gay rights bill. Even when the gay rights bill was passed, Catholic schools were exempt. They can still fire people.

When I was fired, it was February '78? '79? I had a contract, they paid out my contract for the rest of the year. And since they fired me, I knew that I could get unemployment in June. I had another semester to go to finish my theology degree. So I decided to go back to school, finish by June, look for a job, and be on unemployment. I went back to Berkeley to finish my theology degree. This time, I wanted to finish it in sex and spirituality.

What had you started in?
Oh, just whatever. I was interested in counseling all along. When I went back, I called it "counseling sexual minorities." That flew for a while. They're a liberal school. But since there wasn't a lot about gay studies or anything, I worked at the University of California in their gay counseling program. They have a great program there, and I counseled students as my internship for this theology degree. So two days a week I saw students in my office. It was coming out counseling. Eighteen-year-olds, 20-year-olds. I'd done the same thing in Jesuit schools, counseling boys, but here it was counseling gay kids about being normal and helping. It was wonderful. And I led groups.

You'd done that before you left Berkeley?
I'd done it as a Jesuit in Jesuit high schools, guidance counseling. But never gay counseling. This was out. I was doing it. So I got my degree, and I was focusing on sexuality and spirituality, how these two come together. My idea was that I was going to counsel, because that's what my internship was. But after counseling a lot, I

thought, "What every one of these boys needs" — there were women counseling the girls — Joseph Campbell said this once: "People don't need to know the meaning of life. They need to have the experience of it." These kids didn't need to know. They needed to have the experience of intimacy. So I realized counseling is not what I want to do. Right then I thought, "I'm going to massage school." I told the head of the counseling department that I wanted to do a massage weekend. I said there'd be no sex. But they're gay kids, all 18 to 22. They would just look at each other, and their social skills were -aagh! They were all raised straight. I said, "I want to do a massage weekend with these kids."

He said, "Absolutely not. This is a counseling department. You cannot do this." So I quit the counseling department and started to do massage groups.

You were working in the department after you got your degree?
I worked in the department as an intern before I got my degree and I stayed in the department, still as an intern. I was not paid — in fact, nobody in this program was paid, except for one staff person. Most people were accruing hours toward a clinical psychologist degree or whatever. I stayed in the program because I just liked doing it. I was very close to the director of the program. It was what I wanted to do with my life.

So if you did want to get some additional degree, you'd be racking up hours for that?
California has a degree called M.F.C.C. [Marriage and Family Counseling Certification]. It's a counseling degree. You needed 3000 hours. That's what I was doing. I thought I'd get this massage license. Finally, I just let it go. I wanted to do massage.

After a year?
I may have started the personal massage degree while I was doing all this counseling. I had about a year at UC.

I worked there as a math advisor. I got another job for two more years while I started my massage business and practice. I had a full-time job and then a part-time job with UC 'til 1983.

In the math department, it didn't bother them that you were running a massage business.
Right, no conflict. In fact, my boss was intrigued with what I did. He loved it. I didn't think he even knew I was gay. He came in one day and said, "What do you think of Harvey Milk?" This was a straight man. This is what I found Berkeley was like. People bending over backwards to be conscious. It was wonderful.

So then I decided to go into massage. What I was getting at was: What is my heart's desire? Maybe this is the same as What is my purpose in life, or What is my mission. And my desire was to celebrate men, in quality ways. And not so much verbally but with touch. So I wanted to find wonderful ways to touch men. For four years I had done wonderful things in New York. I think all sex is massage. It's body parts against body parts, rubbing and interacting. So I wanted to find wonderful ways to do that.

Had you encountered that in any kind of structured way?
I'd taken a couple of classes early on. I'd gotten my first massage in Berkeley when I was still a Jesuit. The first massage I had just woke my body up. This man gave me a massage, and it was a wonderful ritual way of making love to me. I said, "I want to do this. I want to know shiatsu. I want to know acupressure. I want to know every way I can to make love to men." This was my life's desire. I'm a man who loves men.

Did you ever go to Esalen?
No. Only late at night to sit in their spa, not for a class. Some of my exploration was fumbling. I wanted really precise instruction. I wanted to know what happened

beyond the skin, beneath the skin. I wanted to know about energy and breathing. I studied rebirthing —this was 1981 —for a whole year. So when people breathed, I found I had full-body orgasms. My rebirthing teacher was a wonderful lesbian. She right away said, "Hook this up with sex." So I would masturbate and breathe and move the energy around. So this was another level of learning about sexuality.

Is rebirthing all about breathing?

Yes. It's conscious breathing. Certain breathing patterns raise the energy. When one breathes fully, a lot of energy comes into the body, and you have power to take all kinds of wonderful action. If you're about pleasure, you have more power to put behind pleasure. And when you prolong your genital stimulation, sex, not a quick two- or five-minute thing, there's erotic energy coming at it. So you can have an orgasm from breath energy and an orgasm from erotic energy, and when the two orgasms come together, there's a synergy that causes a leap in consciousness if you choose to take it. It's a breakthrough of ego. The ego dissolves. That's the core of tantric teaching and Taoist teaching. The synergy of yin and yang come together, and something happens.

I gave a talk at Columbia University when I was here last year. Darrell Yates Rist invited me to give a talk. It was Tobias Schneebaum and myself and Annie Sprinkle. It was called "Sexual Radicals." I said what I just told you, and this man came up afterwards who was a Buddhist who said, "You should not have told these people that secret. You will burn in hell." I didn't even know Buddhists had a hell. He was really adamant that this was one of the great secrets of tantra, that the breath is the coming together of opposites, this alchemical thing.

Anyway, I got into breathing. It wasn't so much therapeutic as ritualistic. Men would come in and disrobe and they'd come into another consciousness,

and they would get on my massage table. Usually we'd stretch and breathe together. I didn't look at my massage table as a massage table, like therapy, but this place of celebration, almost like an altar, a high elevated place.
Of course you did. You're a Jesuit.
Right. I would hope that this came from another life, more pagan, among the grove of trees or in the great cave or in the kiva or something. They're on the table, and I anoint them with oil and make them shudder with delight in their own being and work out kinks. But I hated it when people came in and said, "I have lower back pain." I didn't want to be a fix-it. I wanted to go the other way, be a celebrant.

I found celebrating didn't mean the American Massage Therapy Association's way of celebrating, which meant no genital touching. So about 1983, '84, I started doing erotic massage. Some erotic massage is "I give you a massage and then a hand job," but this was from what I learned in New York. To celebrate was to take somebody to this erotic place, where the whole body was in this state. It didn't have anything to do with cumming. The Taoists call the cock the erotic generator, the generator of ching-chi or erotic energy. I studied Taoism a lot. So my goal in celebrating men is to charge them with as much ching-chi as possible. That's what everybody I knew in New York was doing and having a good time at it. Great results. And I became a massage monk. I did this 10 hours a day, 12 hours a day.
One on one?
All one on one. I did one class a week, Monday nights. I remember during the Haight Ashbury days, somebody wrote a book called Monday Night Class, and I kind of liked the idea, so I did a Monday night class every week for a year.
Was it people massaging each other?
Yes. It was massage class. Ways to touch. Not erotic.

None of it was erotic in that era. It was face massage, back massage, breathing and all this. One thing about that Monday night class was I knew I wanted to open a massage school. So I was practicing teaching all the different aspects I wanted to teach as a unified course.
Where were you giving these classes?
In my home in Berkeley. There was a fireplace and all this. At the same time I was giving talks on sex, on tantra and Taoism. This is '83, '84, so AIDS was already upon us. I wasn't giving the talks because of AIDS, but what I was putting out, what I knew about sex, was that you could have the best time in the world nonstop without ejaculating, so the exchange of bodily fluids — which was the big term in those days — was not a factor. I remember right at that time, the very first safe sex thing came out. Michael Callen wrote "How to Have Sex in an Epidemic." I was in New York and I picked it up at Walt Whitman Books on Christopher Street.
Oscar Wilde.
Oscar Wilde.
Walt Whitman is ... DC?
There used to be one in San Francisco. Anyway, his way was very basic, but it was the first safe sex thing, trying to get people to get their acts together. I remember people laughing and chuckling about safe sex in '83 and '84. There was a concern, but almost nobody had seen somebody die, so it wasn't that real.

This is a good part. I was giving these talks. And I gave this talk at University of California. It wasn't just students. It was the Gay People's Union, all these non-students and students. And somebody said, "This is a great lecture. When's the lab period?" I hadn't started my massage school, I was still teaching classes in my home, and I thought, A sex lab period! There were men and women there, and I said, "If any of you men are interested in a lab period, come up and give me your name and address afterwards and I'll consider doing a lab period."

It was the very first time I considered it. This was the forerunner of the class you've been in. About 25 men came up afterward, and I said, "Instead of names and addresses, how about tomorrow night at my house? How many people can come?" Twelve men said they could come. I said, "Good. I'm going to charge $10 for the night, and it's gonna be oil and it's gonna be nude." So all 12 men showed up, all Berkeley types, San Francisco types, and I was really nervous —what to do? And I thought, "Oh Joe, you had five hours of sex a day for four years in New York City — what do you mean, what are you going to do?"

When I moved to Berkeley, I was really going through withdrawal. So while I was finishing my degree at the graduate theological union, I had a part time job working 20 hours a week at the Steam Works.

Is that a bathhouse?

Yes, in Berkeley. So then I had total access to sex. Even when I wasn't working, because I was an employee, I could go there for free, so I would hang out there. That's where I learned that the Berkeley or California way of sex was very different from New York.

Tell me about that.

I had some experiences of conscious touching and conscious sex that just blew me away. One was with a very old man. Do you know Crazy Owl? It was like Crazy Owl, this old man. My type was energy, conscious touching, presence — it wasn't about any one look. Certainly there were parts that pleased me, but what I learned in New York was to go for the vibrancy and aliveness. There are beauties who have no energy and no aliveness, they're like statues.

So this guy had me stand there. He said, "Take some deep breaths." And he knelt down and he started sucking me. Then his fingers started doing different things. He

would hold them and vibrate them. Suddenly I started to recognize these feelings: he was doing was this whole energetic, acupuncture type stuff while he was sucking me. This went on for about an hour, and I said, "What is this?" He said, "I was just doing acupressure, pulling the erotic energy around through your body." Right after that I went and studied acupressure. I took four classes. Now in my school, it's a major part of all my trainings. A lot of men play with their tits. This is an acupressure point. But you can do this at any point on your body when you're in a high erotic state, pull the energy there. And this man taught me that.
At the Steam Works!
At the Steam Works. Oh, the Steam Works is a place of high erotic energy. It was called the Mayan Baths at this time. They had all this Mayan stuff. I remember I went there for the Harmonic Convergence a couple of years ago, because it was the Mayan place that I knew.
Does it still exist?
Oh, it's still there in Berkeley. It's the closest bathhouse to San Francisco, so it's packed, it's nonstop. I used to work for a minimum wage plus all I could eat. Now they have me come in for $100 an hour to give talks. So I've moved up in the world. They have a safe sex education program. It's a very hot place. But it's still a bathhouse, still restrictive. It's not my fun place to go. It's not a free, liberated place. I want to create my own spaces. I like the spaces that I create better.

Where was I? All these people came over for this very first sex class. They came over to my house for the lab period. There were 12 men there, and a boyfriend of mine, so there were 13 of us. We had just three hours. It was tribal. Everything was circle sex with breathing. Everything was structured that we did. Nobody came the whole evening. But four of the men at the end said this was the highest erotic experience of their lives.

This, surprisingly, did not make me feel good. It made me feel sad, because then I started to realize how paltry sex was in most people's lives. All that happened was they got out of their rut, and it was like Wow! So this is where I started to understand what shamanistic sex could be. Just pulling people out of wherever they are and playing in another realm. I said, this is what I want to do. It's so easy just to set up environments where people can play, just jump to another level.
So this was structured in terms of breathing, group massage ... ?
We had a fire going, genital touching, sometimes six people were kneeling in a circle and six people stood on the outside, and the kneeling ones touched their heart and genitals. Then the men in the middle would move to the next man.
Recreating your Steam Works experience?
Yeah, a little bit, but ritualizing it. What I'm really good at is creating rituals with groups of men. When I went to the Radical Faeries, I expected that I would be among people who were doing all this. I first met Mark Thompson at Pecos in 1980, it was a great gathering, the third national gathering of Radical Faeries. I found rituals, but I didn't find any erotic rituals. There was no consciousness of this. So I made my own. I've heard that because of what I'm doing, there's more sex rituals happening at faerie gatherings all around. But I was hoping that I didn't have to recreate the wheel. I wanted to find some group that's already doing this. There were no groups! I still feel that about where I'm going in the future. I'd like to find some sex monastery. Why do I have to start it?
Tell me about the process. Let's go a little deeper into that. Without there being a path or models of erotic ritual, how did you search in yourself for how to make them?

There are a couple of gifts that I know I have. One of my shamanistic, tribal names is Sacred Weaver. I'm a weaver. I have this ability to weave people and things together. The other is I have the gift of foresight. I can see things ten years in the future, where things are going, where things need to go. When AIDS came along, I saw exactly what's happening now. I was working at the Steam Works. The very first time I read about gay cancer, I stopped having unsafe sex at that moment. I could see exactly what was going to happen. I started developing alternatives that were no risk. I didn't even like the idea of low risk. So I kind of categorized sexuality in tribes: there's the anal penetration tribe, there's the oral tribe, and then there's the hand tribe. (You can belong to more than one tribe.) Well, this is the era for the hand tribe. Even if you're not in the hand tribe, you need to learn the rituals of the hand tribe, because it's about reaching ecstatic places without risk. The oral and anal tribes' rituals still involve degrees of risk.

Growing up Roman Catholic in the Midwest, I was taught that who I was was immoral, illegal, sick, psychologically. I cleaned all that out. Now I don't believe all that. All of sudden AIDS came in and tainted again this innocent space. This is my mentality: I don't want to ever have to say, "Did I give something to somebody, or did I get something from somebody?" This is too special, this interaction between men. One man who started the Body Electric School with me lives in New York now. He has AIDS, and he has a recurring dream. He sees man after man over him, fucking him, and he keeps saying, "Was it you? Was it you? Was it you?"

Right at the very beginning I thought, "God, I know enough about tainted love. I do not want my love of men to be tainted. AIDS is not going to be a part of this." As much as possible that's what I've developed —no-risk sex.

Did you find resistance from partners?
Oh, people were going, "How stupid." You'd have these beautiful, hot people who just had totally different belief systems. The faeries would go, "Just have unconditional love and don't worry." I remember the first faerie dying in the Bay Area. It just shocked this whole circle. The idea that faeries don't get AIDS. You know what? I didn't think they were wrong or right. I just knew that I didn't believe this. I thought, maybe they're right, but I'm not going to risk this. What I felt happened in the '70s is that gay men became my people. The people I grew up with were not my people. All of a sudden I found a community that became my father, my brother, my mother, my teachers, my sons. And like I committed myself to the Jesuits, I committed my life to this. This is my path. This is my purpose. This is what I want to be about. I want to celebrate. This is where Whitman comes in —the Dear Love of Comrades. That's what I call everything I do. That is my motivation, to celebrate the dear love of comrades. And the major celebration was that we be in our bodies electric. That we just sing our bodies. Whitman's two images, his mystical images, became mine. The healing image is body electric, the other is celebrate the dear love of comrades. Period. That's all I want to do with my life. I dedicate myself to that.

Is there a moment when that epiphany happened?
I remember in college in St. Louis reading *Leaves of Grass*. I started reading it aloud, and I got high. I'd never smoked marijuana before that, and later when I smoked marijuana I remembered I'd had this feeling reading *Leaves of Grass*. But I didn't even know Walt Whitman was gay when I started reading *Leaves of Grass*. I just got into this state. Then a few years later, in the early '80s, when I started thinking about starting my school, I wanted to know what to call it. I thought of naming it after the 56th hexagram of the I Ching, which is Fire

on the Mountain. Sexuality taken to the mountain. But something happened in 1983 in Berkeley that made Body Electric come to me. I can't believe I'm even saying this ... what I felt then was that Walt Whitman's energy was there. That he loved men, and I had the exact same feelings he did. I felt the spirit of Walt Whitman was there. I felt compelled to call it Body Electric. I have a lot of connection with Walt Whitman, and I feel there is a part of him alive in me.

Stage directors often describe that feeling, of doing a play by Shakespeare or Moliere and feeling the playwright in the room with them.

Well, I felt this. Then when AIDS came along, it reminded me that Whitman said at one point, in "The Wound Dresser," that the turning point of his life as a poet was the Civil War and spending three years taking care, holding and loving and writing letters for boys, soldiers. I was a masseur, and I was taking care of people, in a sense celebrating them. They weren't dying then, but some of the people I celebrated started to get sick. In 1984, when AIDS really hit, I started the first AIDS hospice massage team in the United States, for Hospice San Francisco. I called all the masseurs that I knew, got them together. That team is still going. There's only one person from that original team still on the hospice massage team, but it's influenced Elisabeth Kubler-Ross and the American Massage Therapy Association.

I feel right now there's two aspects to what I do. I run a massage school where one of the main themes is touching people with life-threatening illness. We gay men have lived so much in our bodies; it's very different from our grandmothers dying or our parents dying, who don't need to be touched as much as they die. Maybe they need it, but they don't expect it. This is a branch of what I do. I run a massage school where that's an emphasis.

The other thing is celebrating the dear love of comrades. So part of it is taking care of people as they die, and the other part is just celebrating it. All the classes that I teach came from that. All the men and women and teachers who come around and teach with me come from those two visions — being with people in the physical as they are dying, and celebrating the dear love of comrades.

Most of the rituals I've done, it's as if I'm remembering things that have already been done. I feel like we're doing something that has happened in Babylonian or Egyptian or Guatemalan culture. My experience in New York opened me up to interact with men in very high energetic environments. I became part of a web, a very open and sensing energy. So if Jung is right and there are archetypal energy fields, I'm real clear where the energy fields are coming from.

The men's movement, Robert Moore especially and Robert Bly and all these people, talk about energy fields and archetypes: the warrior, the lover, and the king, etc. They say that awareness of these archetypes will help us live out our life. Well, I think there are other archetypes prevalent today. One that I vibrate with is ritual leader. I pull all the ritual leader energy I can feel, and just let it express itself.

There's another archetype that I've tied into, and that's consciousness scout. It's the same energy field that Karen Finley calls Black Sheep. She says, "Their contribution is never recognized 'til the next generation." Well, it's naming what a lot of my life has been and what I've seen a lot of other people's life has been, as artists or outsiders. Black Sheep is the way the culture names it, from inside the culture. Consciousness scout is naming it from the outside.

I've always been interested in consciousness scouts. Even in the movies with the wagon trains. I wasn't interested in the wagon trains so much but those guys who rode out. And often they looked up and there were three Indians up there on the ridge, who were the scouts from the Indian tribe. Like *Dances With Wolves* — here's this soldier, who goes to the very outskirts, then the Native Americans from the tribe come, and it's scouts meeting scouts. I thought, "This is my movie!"

So this is a time for all the consciousness scouts to really activate. Right this minute [in the middle of the Persian Gulf War], we need someone who's a consciousness scout who knows how to turn off 600 oil wells, because the regular people say it's going to take 5 years, 10 years. I think it's going to happen. It's going to take a lot of work, but somebody who's really an Einstein will figure out, click, all of a sudden, how to put those fires out.

I think erotic consciousness scouts are three hills out. Here's the big sludge, in the middle, and the consciousness scouts invite people outward. Erotically we're in a big constriction time.

When you said there were a lot around in the '70s, who do you mean?
I think there were hundreds and thousands of people who were exploring the outer realms of what it meant to be erotic. A lot of gay liberation then was exploring the realms of what our bodies could do and what that could affect in us. There was a lot of exploration with drugs along this line — acid was big, speed and poppers and alcohol. It was exploring. I think some of it was compulsive, but a lot of it was really exploring what's possible.

Once the exploring is done, you get into addictive behavior. But at the beginning it was consciousness scouts. Now I feel all the consciousness scouts hook up. Annie Sprinkle is my best friend. She's the only woman that I've had sex with in the last 15 years. She says, "Let's move in together." I've spent time with her in Europe.

The only reason I don't stay with her is she has two cats, and it's me or them when I stay there. But she's a consciousness scout. She's right on the edge. Heart and genitals. Betty Dodson. Michael Callen, I think. Michael Callen told me two weeks ago, "I'm sick to death of these walk-quietly-into-the-light workshops. Yours gets down. Thank you." And during one erotic massage, I played his version of "Where the Boys Are." He says, "I've never heard it so good."

He did the workshop in LA?
Yeah. In fact, here's his thing about sex. He did this two-day workshop on Thursday and Friday. Then we did a Saturday and Sunday, but he was leaving on Sunday with the Flirtations for a tour. He said, "Can I come back just for one day on Saturday, because this is charging me up for this tour. This is bringing in erotic energy so I can sing like I've never sung before." That's understanding erotic energy.

I don't know if you know Michael Goodwin, who makes videos. You know what he does? He does art while he jerks off. I've seen him do this. So he knows how to transmute the erotic energy right into these amazing drawings. They're very graphic. These are transmuters of erotic energy to other media. I think people like Picasso and Georgia O'Keefe were like this.

Some writers probably write with one hand on their typewriter and one hand on their magic wand. Anyway, right now I need to listen to erotic consciousness scouts because there's no consciousness around sex. Safe sex education is scurvy for the soul. I was in New Zealand two weeks ago and did my classes, and the two main safe sex educators in the country came and took my class. Afterwards they decided this is one of the major directions they're going to go for education in all of New Zealand. We're going back there for ten more workshops in the next year, in little towns.

Do they have enough of a gay population to do it?
The classes we had there were full. They're also more liberated sexually. It's Polynesia. There's no one like Jesse Helms around. Only 6% of the population goes to church. That's a fact. They were the hottest classes I've ever taught. Here's a whole country's AIDS education program deciding this is the direction.

Looking at the future, the other archetype I'm most interested in is what I call sacred intimate.

I was going to ask you about that. This has just emerged in the literature.
It comes from what was called the sacred prostitute. And the sacred prostitute is the greatest challenge of all to this culture. It weaves together spirituality and sexuality. It was a great challenge to the Jews. But Andrew Ramer pointed out to me that in the Old Testament, the Jerusalem Bible, when they talk about male sacred temple prostitutes, the translation was "the holy ones." Even the Jewish interpretation of it was, "These are the people you have sex with to have sex with God." In New York in the '70s there were times when I had sex, and I had sex with God. Everything became white light, and it was clear that that's why I did it. If it was about paltriness, why continue with this? Why commit your whole life to this? But it was about a connection with wholeness, with the divine, with god/goddess, whatever names you want to say.

I've learned something in the last few years. And I have a special place, because I've done 100 weekend workshops and six-day workshops, all over the country, all over Germany, in Amsterdam, in New Zealand, where the risk-takers, the pioneers show up who know they're going to take their clothes off and have tribal sexuality. I look around at all these risk-takers, and what I see is that some men are so gifted sexually they glow in a special way. They shine. It comes out not just in their cock but their heart, their cock, their eyes, everything. Just by being around them other people shudder. Sometimes they're old, sometimes they're fat, sometimes they're ugly, and sometimes they're *Blueboy* centerfolds, or *In Touch*. It doesn't matter what they look like, it's an energy. What I see is they belong to the sacred intimate. I don't like the word "prostitute," because it's an ugly word that we as a culture have put on that phenomenon to denigrate it. In Starhawk's book, *Truth or Dare*, she says, "As long as we use the word prostitute, we hold some arrogance or superiority over that vocation." So I see all kinds of gay men who are sacred intimates. When they're intimate with you, a transformation takes place. You feel your wholeness. There are plenty of prostitutes around, so you can go and get off with a prostitute. And you might feel a craving to do it the next day and the next day. This is about being around someone who you're transformed by. You either model him, like Mitch Walker's idea of the double, where you see that energy and you can bring it into yourself. Or maybe there's an energy that comes from higher places through this person into you. Or you have the experience of being with an unconditional lover, just for a while, that changes you and you learn what unconditional love can be.

This is what's important: these are the teachers, but there's no place for them to teach. So what happens to a lot of them is they end up in Love and Sex Addicts Anonymous and Sexual Compulsives. I've gone to these meetings, and I went to a national convention in Oakland last year, and I think half the people there are sacred intimates. These are people who've been given special gifts. If you believe in lifetime after lifetime, they've brought this gift into this lifetime. And this sick, dysfunctional society has no place for them. So when they feel a desire to act this out, to be in that space, it ends up being in a bookstore tricking, or paltry sex. So I've been thinking about how to activate this profession.

I committed myself in 1988 to teaching erotic massage; I committed myself to it for three years. People say, "How can you do this every weekend?" I love it. But — three years. I want to get as much of it done as possible. So in three years I've done 100 workshops, teaching this approach to erotic spirituality. I've trained three master teachers. One's from LA, John Pasqualetti. He's a Tantric of the highest order. Erik [aka Chester] Mainard, from Madison, Wisconsin, is the person who's been teaching Taoist erotic massage the longest besides me. He's been teaching it at faerie gatherings and everywhere for the last six years all through the Midwest. The other is Matthew Simmons, who's been assisting me for the last couple of years.

So I've trained these teachers. I've made a video that explains everything that I know about Taoist erotic massage. I'm leaving that, and what I'm going to do now is focus on activating the archetype, the vocation of the sacred· intimate. Because we need sexual healers. We need those people who are healers to be there and stand there. Annie Sprinkle is doing this with Prostitutes of New York, PONY. She's putting this out among women. And we're going to work together. But the first year, I want to bring together as many people as possible in whom this archetype is activated. I have some ideas to develop a specific training so that their gifts could be used in this culture.

There's all kinds of sacred intimates. By the way, where sacred intimate is most activated in the gay culture right now is as midwives to the dying. This is one of those sacred intimate roles. People were brought to the temple, and as they died they were there with the divine, with the god/ goddess person. I think lots of people who sit with people while they're dying or do hospice work have moments where all of a sudden they recognize that they are living out a very old profession, midwife to the dying. This erotic energy is about the leaving of that energy, too, from the body and going on.

My next two years will be devoted to training and activating and being a cheerleader of this archetype. The men's movement is centered around archetypal imagery and activating those images. It started with *He*, the Robert Johnson book. And Mark Thompson and Mitch Walker are coming out with their version of Gilgamesh, which will be the gay equivalent of that.

Yes, I've been waiting to see what the gay archetypes are, what the gay input will be to that mythology. Ritual leader is one that hasn't been talked about much. I don't think even Bly mentions it. The priest function isn't quite the same as the magician in Robert Moore's language.

But it overlaps. It's a shaman tradition, ritual leader. Erotic shaman is similar to sacred intimate. The shaman is the mediator between the two worlds.

I guess it's related to the berdache tradition.

Exactly. The chief would take a second wife, being the berdache, because he wanted to connect to the great medicine. Sex being the great medicine.

The main role of the sacred intimate is to clear out one's body totally of toxins and just to bring in light and wholeness and holiness and God, and by seeing that, other people are transformed. It's a very personal path. In the old days it was done in the temple, so there were many people together. And there were teachers. They taught each other, and they had teachers. That's what I call right now a sex monastery. But I really am interested in temples, where people come together and do this. Clear themselves out.

For the last three years, I've noticed I put all my energy into being a ritual leader and let go of some of the bringing the light into myself. And it was fine. It was a trade-off that I wanted to do. But now I'm starting a different path and a different myth and letting go of that. The erotic massage is going to continue and grow and take all kinds of forms. We're teaching teachers and safe-sex educators.

Some sacred intimate stuff as it's reached the culture: Leonard Cohen's song "Suzanne" is a song about a sacred intimate. "Suzanne takes you down to her place by the river. .. " And just when you think nothing's happening, she gets you on her wavelength, and barn! Pasolini's movie *Teorema* is about a sacred intimate. This boy shows up, has sex with the whole family, leaves and they're all transformed, crazy, whatever. Their whole lives are changed by his interaction with them.

Erotic consciousness scouts — I think of Henry Miller. The movie *Henry and June* is worth seeing for one scene about erotic energy. Anaïs Nin gets into this state at a party at a nightclub. She's on the dance floor, and she clicks into this erotic state where she's just there. It's not a rough erotic state, it's like honey. She's totally turned on, and she looks around the room, at the men and the women. The camera makes a 360-degree turn, and all the people recognize that state. She weaves everybody together because she's in that state and she's exuding it. I've never seen it on film before. I've felt it and known it but I've never seen in so clearly on film as there. It made the whole movie worth it. I have to say I don't like a lot about Henry Miller. I read all of Henry Miller when I was young because he was the most erotic writer. I liked John Rechy, because it was like, sex, that's all there is.

I used to stand up in the library jerking off reading Genet. That was the only erotic writing I could get my hands on.

I was too young when I read Genet. I was 22 or 23. I

heard *Our Lady of the Flowers* was his masturbation fantasy, so I read it and tried to get into it but I couldn't. Do you recommend anything in particular?
I did the same thing. I was only reading it for pornography when I was 13. I distinctly remembering crouching in the aisle of the Aurora Public Library in Denver. My face would get hot reading. I've tried sometimes to go back and find these passages that were so loaded with eroticism for me, and it's hard because your erotic sense is so different when you're an adult from when you were 13 or 14. For some reason those boys in jail sniffing each other's farts someone totally turned me on.
Here's a transformation point in my life. The Jesuits sent me to Regis College, in Denver, and I worked at Little Sisters of the Poor, an old folks' home. There was another guy who worked there, kind of a hippie type. This was 1968. I remember going to a concert in the college gym. I'd never been to a real rock concert. It cost $3, and I went in, and it blew me away. It was Jimi Hendrix. This guy says, "Do you want to smoke some grass? Come over to my place and smoke some grass." I'd never smoked grass. I'd been in the Jesuits three years, and I'd never masturbated. I loved masturbating, the world's most ardent fan. So here I was, 17 to 19 or 20, not having masturbating.
You just gave it up?
Well, I joined the Jesuits, and you made a promise of celibacy, you're not going to have sex, you're not going to masturbate. So when I entered the Jesuits ... I was going to enter on a Tuesday, and I remember deciding to spend the whole weekend beforehand jerking off, because this was going to be the last time in my life I was going to have sex. Then on Monday, like a good Catholic boy, I went to confession and confessed that I masturbated 25 times or something, and that was

the end. I joined the Jesuits. And for three years, no masturbation. There was craving, but no masturbation.

Then in Denver, I go to this guy's house. I didn't realize he was gay. I didn't realize 'til years later. He put on Donovan albums and got out some grass, and he says, "I'm going to take a bath, if you want to take a bath with me, it's a big bathtub." I went, ugh, no. He sat in the bathtub and we smoked, and then I went out and started trying to feel what the grass was doing. And Donovan's playing, "Mellow Yellow" and all this. I didn't know what I could feel. And he kept saying, "Are you sure you don't want to come in? Take off your clothes, come into the tub." I didn't see this as a come-on, I just saw it as a threat. I wanted to, but I didn't want to. I was fearful. I didn't understand what was going on.

So I figured I'd better go back to Regis College, to the dorm. I went back to my room, and my body was going, "Whoa!" Something was going on with my body. I started touching myself all over, and all of a sudden my hands were on my cock, jerking off wildly. This went on for hours! I played with myself, and I said, "I know masturbation is supposed to be morally wrong, but this is not morally wrong. This is God, this is the best thing that could happen."

That was my Denver experience. Since then, never has more than a few months gone by, even though I was in the Jesuits, without masturbation. I'd try not to, but I'd fail. Self-erotic massage was happening. But Denver was a breakthrough. My first drug experience just turned on my sexuality.

Did drugs play a role in your New York experience?
Acid. I was the type of person who had to read every book on acid and read Timothy Leary's books. I don't remember whether I read Stanislav Grof at that time, but I read everything I could on acid, a very intellectual approach. In four years I took about 20 acid trips. I've

never seen drugs as something you do and go out to a party. I've always seen it as a real private thing. But I do remember one time ... I was still Catholic at the time. I took acid, I was in my apartment, and I go, "I want to go to Man's Country." It was like 4:30. So I'm walking over to Man's Country, which is on 15th Street, and the next block was St. Francis Xavier. I'd been a Jesuit. It was getting close to Mass time. So I decided I was going to go to Mass. Here I am on acid, this is the only time I've ever done this, I'm kneeling in the church, there's like 20 people in this big cavernous church, I'm kind of toward the back. I was in this amazing place. When the priest held up the host and said "This is my body," I saw lights coming out of it and all that. So at communion time I went up, and I thought, "Can I even walk? Will they know I'm on acid?" I was just exploring. I took communion, and the priest looked at me. He was probably cruising me, but I thought he looked right through me. I wasn't paranoid, but I took communion, and it was wonderful coming into me. I left church after Mass and went right across the street into Man's Country to take other men into my mouth and into my body in other ways. I felt no cognitive dissonance. I felt these two meshed together perfectly. My spirituality. But more and more I let go of Christian spirituality.

I didn't know what was going on on acid. This was the first time I'd ever gone out of my own meditation on my own body. So I was having sex with this man, thinking "This is really interesting having sex on acid." I thought, "I'm really doing fine, this is okay." And the man I was having sex with said, "It's okay, I know where you're at, I know what you're doing right now." I said, "How can you know?" He said, "I know this is your first time having sex." And I go, "What!?!" I thought, "Hmm, maybe I'm not doing as well as I thought .... " That made me realize this is not something you should go out into the city with.

I had this view in the '60s that drugs were a window on a way of being. Every drug has taught me different things, but the drug that I found that taught me a lot was poppers. It taught me to go from a stress mode to a relaxation mode.

That's funny. I don't think of poppers as relaxing.

It puts the autonomic nervous system in massage mode. A lot of men will lose their erections because they're too relaxed to have an erection. What always interested me was those men, maybe 10%, who got harder on poppers — they were the ones who, in the parasympathetic mode, which is the heart mode, the relax, the lover mode, could have an erection. The men who sniffed poppers and lost their erections were often the men who only had sex in a sympathetic mode, stress mode, fight or flight. Tension. There's a toxicity to poppers, though. Early on, it was supposedly the root of AIDS. So for years I laid off. Maybe once every couple of years. Recently I've tried it, before it became illegal. Just last month, poppers became illegal nationally.

I didn't know that.

They're gone forever. But I learned a lot. Sometimes when I'm with someone having sex, I'll say, "Let's imagine taking poppers. Breathe in, now shift" -which I think is the goal of any drug, to learn how to do whatever that shift is, without the drug. Certainly it's easier sometimes with the drug. It's easier to walk with crutches. But if you can throw the crutches away and walk, then do it.

Tell me about starting the school. How did that happen?

After teaching Monday Night Class for a year, I clearly saw I wanted to start a center, a commune, a group. I wasn't sure what form it was going to take. I knew it had to do with the ritual touching of men. Women have come to Body Electric over the years, I have to say, but it's the only massage school probably in the country that has been predominantly men. Although I'm an excellent masseur with women, my passion is that I'm a man who loves men. So men show up knowing that they're especially welcome.

So in this year of teaching Monday Night Class, I became very skilled. About 20 men in the course of this year said, "You've turned us on to massage so much that I want to do this as a profession," and they'd go off to massage school. And I go, "This is crazy, because a lot of these people I'd like to hang out with more." Then it became clear that the form of what I wanted to do was not just to teach massage but to have a school. This was when the Walt Whitman influence came — Body Electric, Body Electric, Body Electric. I also knew that breathwork was important, rebirthing, so I started the Body Electric School of Massage and Rebirthing.

In those days there was no consciousness of rebirthing. Hardly anybody knew what rebirthing was. Today it's, like, ho-hum. When I teach class, even in New Zealand, two-thirds of the men in the class have done rebirthing, breath work. So I started out, AIDS was coming along, so one of the first things I did was provide touch. I gave 50% discount on tuition to any people who were volunteers in AIDS agencies. There were only three agencies in the Bay Area — Hospice San Francisco, Shanti was just starting, and the East Bay Pacific Center. So I knew all the people, and a lot of people got training in massage. It just started growing. I was still doing a lot of massage and then teaching at the massage school two evenings a week and some weekends. Everything was located in Oakland, where Body Electric is now.

Were you still working out of your house?
No, as I opened the school in January-February of 1984,

I separated where I slept and lived from where I did work. So all my work was done at the school. It was a very powerful space. I wanted a space on Telegraph Ave, because Telegraph Ave is a street that comes right out of Sproul Plaza, and I felt that was the place where I got an insight about celebrating my diversity and freedom of speech. So I wanted to extend free speech to ecstatic touch. That was my contribution from my kinesthetic perspective.

I started this school, and right from the beginning people came. The main reason is that all the other massage schools — and there were 25 or 30 of them in the Bay Area; it's the massage capital of the world — had, I thought, a great deal of homophobia. This is 1984, you'd think there'd be a gay consciousness, but in schools where I was there were fears. I went to six different massage schools to take different classes, and I noticed that two-thirds of the men were gay, and nobody came out to each other or to the classes. I thought, "This is the dark ages." About half the women were lesbians. Then I realized this is a profession of gay men and lesbians. And they're all getting trained in straight massage schools. So I said, "This is a school dedicated to a homophobia-free environment." Everybody flocked. It was an instant success; we could come and be among ourselves. Gay men and lesbians are further away from each other than people think. This was a real weaving together. Many lesbians have been abused by men, and here were gay men who were touching them. They were nude together in classes and breathing together. It's amazing how many gay men and lesbians have been abused. I would say 50% of the people who come to my school have been physically or sexually abused, and all of them have had psychological/spiritual abuse.

What I understood in the first year was that the whole psychotherapy tradition of coming out was one-dimensional. Coming out of the closet meant that we had physical constrictions that we were holding. We held our energy, we screened our movements and our bodies. If you went to a straight massage school to learn to relax, you still didn't learn, you were still in the closet. All of a sudden, this was a free space where gay men and lesbians could come out in their bodies, their energy, in their breathing, and let go of it all. There's very few spaces —there's psychotherapeutic spaces, but not physical spaces. The homophobia-free environment meant that people could come out physically and heal themselves physically.

I started doing intensives because I was doing three weeks in a row, all day every day, men and women. Incredible transformations took place. A third to a half of the people who came through my school said, "This was the most important, transformative week of my life." A lot of people looked at becoming masseurs as downwardly mobile —manual labor. That's one way the culture looks at it. In Japan, it's a trade that's accepted on a professional level; it's part of the healer motif. Here I found that doctors, Ph.Ds would show up and take massage training. All these people were tying into their shamanistic traditions or sacred intimate tradition.

Right from the beginning I started to educate people, and the way that I did it is I said, "No matter if you ever do erotic massage, masseurs are waking up the body erotically, so you are sexual healers." This is a theme to men and women, gay and straight, who are in my school. So I've been training sacred intimates right from the beginning. A lot of Body Electric graduates aren't doing genital massage but are very aware and not fearful of the erotic. They're aware that's a major energy force. It's not just like the elbow or some other place. It's a major place to be honored and respected and awakened.

As the school got going, it took up a lot of my time. I toned down doing individual sessions. My practice was one-third women, one-third gay men who didn't have AIDS, and one-third were people with AIDS. The women came to me, gay and straight, because I was gay and dealt with sexuality. Just by touching they felt they would get a male energetic environment, but they didn't want a straight man putting energy on them. I wasn't doing genital massage, but they just wanted that environment. I see this with a lot of people I educate. A lot of women need healing work with men, but there's always the fear that we're going to cross a boundary. With gay men, that boundary is already clearly set, so you can work deeply without crossing that boundary, because there's not the natural inclination to cross it. I still think boundaries can be broken in that situation, but it is a very safe situation for women.

One thing that happened during my individual sessions was more and more people with AIDS were coming. The major thing I saw early on in the epidemic was men terrorized. Not just in fear, not just in depression — those were states that all kinds of human beings had. I never saw so many people in terror in all my life. Terror just shuts down everything. It immobilizes someone. Psychotherapy takes a long time to deal with terror. But breathwork and massage and touching and caressing is like spring thawing out the ice.

Working with terror, I found that I had not dealt with my own terror about death. So for two years I became an expert in relieving terror or breaking up terror in others, and it accumulated in me. I'd not dealt with the fact that I was mortal. So I made it my commitment to do that. And the way to do that is to go into sexuality. Because from the tantric perspective, the way someone dies is the way someone has sex. That became very interesting to me.

First I want to say, I had let go of doing individual sessions, because I found it took me three or four days to clear. It wasn't that I took on their terror -my own terror was activated. I didn't find somebody who could heal me or clear it out the way I was doing with somebody else. I became immobilized a lot. I decided I had to stop doing this until I could deal with death. This was about three years ago. It became a commitment to deal with death — to practice dying, to do visualizations about death. The Big Draw, that we teach in the class, is the Tantric way of dying. I read *The Tibetan Book of the Dead*. I noticed in America there's the same attitude of denial toward sex and death — they're not a main part of our life. These core things — erotic life force energy and the passage beyond this — are just not important. But both are coming back now, and AIDS brings the two together. Sex and death. AIDS and Woody Allen.

That consciousness scout Woody Allen.

It's the American rugged individualist way to go off by yourself and deal with this or meditate and find spiritual enlightenment. But I feel now that terror is best dealt with in a communal context. It's not about hermits. So part of my interest in sacred intimates and being midwives to the dying is to be clear in myself on what this is. That's part of my path now.

When I bring it up to a lot of people dealing with AIDS or a life-threatening illness, I notice it's not talked about a lot. All of a sudden someone's naming a major thing that might happen at three in the morning — they wake up petrified, immobilized with terror. A lot of people do this — you don't have to have a life-threatening illness. People have anxiety attacks and they're just terrified. It's an existential angst moment. But that's what I'm interested in dealing with. I feel that the activating of god energy, life force energy, sexual creative energy in myself and around me as a sacred intimate — I want to do that.

Tell me about how you created the Healing the Body Erotic two-day workshop.

I was teaching erotic massage and prolonging orgasm for a couple of years, ever since that first night when I did a lab period. I started doing lots of evening things, but people didn't want to come to the lectures anymore. They wanted the lab period. So I taught classes that all involved breathing and non-ejaculation. Men sometimes ejaculated, but the idea was: if you don't ejaculate, if you commit yourself to the energy, then instead of a quick going from A to B, what happens is that you reach a high erotic state, and the breathing was to circulate that energy. Conscious breathing keeps people from going off into fantasy. It keeps them right in the moment. I had learned that state well in New York, in Chelsea, in the Village, in the piers, on Fire Island, and now I was finding ways that I could recreate the state in a classroom for long periods of time.

So then I got a call from Buck Rhoades. He has a foundation for gay spirituality in Albuquerque, called the New Mexico Foundation for Human Enrichment. They put on the Gay and Lesbian spirituality conference every year now. He called me and said, "I've heard of you, and we have a group of 25 men who for 10 years have been meeting and gathering and doing spiritual work. We do massage, we do hot tubbing, a lot of spiritual investigation. Where there is a block is sex with friends." This is 1987, we're in the middle of the AIDS era. He says, "We would like to cross through that threshold. Can you come to New Mexico and do a weekend with us on sex with friends?" I don't know what he wanted or if he thought it would be a discussion weekend or what, but I said, "Let me think about it." And it just came to me. Everything I was doing wasn't about lover sex, it wasn't about casual anonymous sex — it was about male bonding sexuality. I call it tribal tantra now. I called him back and said, "I can do it. How about the weekend after the march on Washington?" I wanted to use the energy from the March on Washington to go down there.

The March on Washington was incredible. It was the most open-hearted gathering of gay men and lesbians. It was all heart. I didn't listen to one word of the speeches. Did you march with the faeries?
No, I didn't.
I marched with the faeries, and a chant came up there. It was "Purple hands of healing." Have you heard that chant?
Sure. "Faggot god, faerie god/My love, come to me."
Here it was! Purple hands of healing! It was this empowering chant. As the faeries went down the street, all kinds of people joined in. It was incredible. It was the first time I ever saw ACT UP. There was this dark, angry mass with arms coming out of it. It kind of scared me. I guess I'm scared by anger. Then came the faeries, tra-la tra-la, frolicking … Anyway, I took that purple hands of healing energy with me to New Mexico.

That was the first time I did this two-day workshop. I knew we had to breathe, to come together. I knew we had to take each other's clothes off. We had to honor and touch from the heart, and touch genitals, and play, and exorcise all the dead places in the genital area. So we did erotic massage. We had some massage tables, but some people on the floor. We did it at this place called The Place of Peace in Albuquerque. It's Buck Rhoades' wonderful home. Twenty-five men were there.

I'd been in Pecos to the faerie gathering in 1980. This was 7 years later, and all I knew about the area was that it felt to me energetically like I was coming to the Tibet of the United States. I said to the group, "I am honored. I am coming to the Tibet of the United States."

Then at the end of the workshop, one man said, "Well, if this is the Tibet, the Dalai Lama has just shown up." I'm embarrassed ... actually, I'm not embarrassed, I was proud of that. Because I was teaching tantra. We activated something that was just wild.

So I've gone back every year and done a reunion class with that group. And I've gone to the Gay & Lesbian Spirituality conference. They had 120 people at this Gay & Lesbian Spirituality conference a couple of summers ago. I went to the first big one at the Lama Foundation. I didn't want to teach. I wanted just to take. There was nothing on erotic spirituality. People talked about spiritual paths of lovers, but nothing about sex as part of the spiritual path of lovers. That's where I got the idea that I am an erotic consciousness scout. This person is a drummer, this person is a meditator, this person does Tai Chi. All their gifts are different. This is my gift.

There aren't that many erotic consciousness scouts out there teaching in the major league. There weren't any there at Lama. I got angry that I had to do it. I taught a class I wasn't scheduled to teach. Matthew led an erotic ritual where men marched into the woods and we did this "soloving" ritual. "Soloving" is my word for what used to be called masturbation — solo and loving coming together.

Anyway, after that first two-day workshop, I came back and decided to teach this two-day form, because it was very powerful. The form constantly changed, because I'm an artist. Different people taught with me. Matthew has taught with me recently, and these other teachers who work with me now have all contributed, and it's changed over the years. It's gotten more focused and powerful, with the breathing and erotic energy. **It's evolved pretty fast then into one of the central things of the Body Electric School.**
Here's what happened. In '88, about four months into

this, I said, "I'm going to do this for three years. This is my commitment." At the end of '88, I said, "I don't have the energy to run a massage school." So for a year I let go of the massage school. As soon as I let go of it, Amsterdam, Australia, Berlin, Paris, people started saying, "We want you to come here and teach this." I put all my energy into this, and it just expanded.

About eight months ago, because I knew this was coming to an end, I decided to bring back those massage trainings. When I did that, they were packed with men who'd taken the two days. They said, "You really taught us well how to touch and honor men's genitals, the genital area. I want to be able to do that head to toe, back to front, with Eastern approaches and Western approaches." The majority of people who've come to the school, from all over the country and New Zealand and Germany, could go to another massage school, but they want a massage school that has this energy.

The massage trainings are California state-approved trainings, so there's no erotic massage in them. And they're men and women, gay and straight, but the majority are people who've been through this two-day class, who are actually sacred intimates, who want to celebrate the dear love of comrades in the physical.

So it's a three-week intensive training, and they get their certificate?
Yes. California only requires 100 hours. I cut that down to two weeks now. I just offer the minimum. My feeling is that then people can train in all kinds of other modalities.

I'm coming to understand how massage is related to neurolinguistic programming. The majority of people contact the outside world through visuals; a lesser amount contact the outside world through hearing, the audio. Even a smaller amount, maybe 10%, contact the world kinesthetically, through feeling states. This is an anti-touch culture, and if you're a kinesthetic, you're out of luck. You're dysfunctional by the time you reach our age. The mantra of grade schools is "Keep your hands to yourself." We get all these messages not to touch. So a lot of people show up at massage schools who've been frustrated all their lives. In whatever else they do, they're kinesthetic, and all of a sudden they're given training and permission to celebrate the world of touch. And they get paid for it! That's one reason massage has come so quickly into the culture, because there are people predisposed to it.

Tell me about your theoretical training and study in these things. You mentioned studying Reich.

I studied mathematics, philosophy, psychology, a lot of systematic things, how everything fits together. I see myself as a sex researcher. I belong to the Quad-S: Society for the Scientific Study of Sex. But I'm not in universities using rats. I'm really researching and exploring a lot of things, keeping journals and notebooks. The philosophy of sex and the theories behind it are very important to me. Why is this happening? There are some dead ends, like: why are people homosexual, why are people heterosexual? There are loops you can get into, but I'm interested in some of the arguments. Sociobiology and stuff. But mainly my philosophizing and thinking comes from the data that's so evident: "Here's what I see." The sacred intimate idea came from seeing this gift and seeing it frustrated. Not many people are creative enough to activate it in healthy ways.

Let me go into one theoretical area that I'm really looking at: addiction. I think core to healing codependency is learning to make love to yourself ceremonially. First of all, I think John Bradshaw's the most radical cultural prophet today that's having the widest effect — especially as far as we gay people

APPENDIX 355

go. [Bradshaw is the author of the best-selling pop-psychology book *Healing The Shame That Binds You*.] Because the conservative right and the fundamentalist Christians say "Homosexuals and pornography are the problem and they're destroying the family." He's got it: the family has created the perverts, the addictions. It's in the family. Family is where all the abuse and the sexual stuff takes place. He's speaking eloquently on public television and in his books to middle-class and working-class people. That's radical. That's having an influence. Not homosexuals.

The major thing that's come out of all this addiction stuff is that the underlying addiction is addiction to codependence — it means I need something outside myself to be me. And maybe that's true. But if it's not, it means that if I make love to myself, I know that right here I am enough.

I think we Westerners learn an addictive way of having sex. Boys especially, because we learn right away that "I'm not enough." I need an image outside myself, or I need a memory, or I need a video. Codependence right away! We're hooked into it.

Kinsey said 95% of men masturbate while having fantasies. Codependence. We learn that early on. That's the American way. This is not the tantric or Taoist or Native American or Sufi way. The Cherokee word for masturbation translated means "heart pleasuring." So masturbation means to open up your heart to all your relations. But we've got these fantasies.

My underlying supposition is if we can make love to our selves and we are enough, it's cutting the bonds of codependence. A lot of 12-step programs say "100 meetings in 100 days." Or "60 meetings in 60 days and you get over the hump." I say 60 hours of soloving in 60 days. If you can make love to yourself every day, it's cutting those bonds of codependence, because it's saying

"I am enough." It's not jerking off, it's not addiction to the sedation of ejaculation. It's making love, it celebrates, it's bringing that energy up. This is enough. This is life force. I don't need alcohol, cocaine, television, romance, whatever the addictions or compulsions are. I can have them, but I don't need them, because I know who I am and I love who I am and I'm satisfied.

We are creatures of ritual. I think most addictions are rituals of loving. I'm going to drink this, it feels so good, this margarita — it's a ritual. Grass was always a ritual. Cocaine has become one. Pretty soon the ritual of loving becomes like that. We love ourselves so much we have to numb ourselves out. We have to go away. Part of sacred intimate training is soloving every day — a session of making love with yourself to be clear in your body.

I have to say I have been doing this only erratically, and I can feel the lack in my body. But part of my commitment is to really look at substances that I use, moods that I use, and to make love to myself every day.

Is this your last cup of coffee?
There's all kinds of other things I'm aware of that control me more than coffee. Rather than saying "I'm not going to drink coffee," I'm going to make love to myself and be centered in my self.

Now, why will this not work? Because — this is where Reich and others come in — I have in my body emotional records from 3, 4, 5. All the abuse, all the self-abuse, all the horrors of my life, and I can't just go "Here I am, making love to myself!" So there are levels of soloving, of raising this energy, that are about emotional clearing.

This is where Wilhelm Reich comes in. All kinds of people do Reichian therapy, and in a sex-negative culture they don't even tie it into sex. He said, "Orgasm is the healing state. And if you can have a full-bodied orgasm, toe to fingertips, not just genital, you've cleared out everything." So I feel soloving, making love to yourself, is a healing path to clear out your emotional records.

Those people who believe in past lives, that you bring emotional records from other lives, it's a clearing of the physical. It's a vibration. It's a self-love vibration. And one's attention isn't out with Jeff Stryker or Joey Stefano's butt but it's with oneself. And it's not about getting off quickly because you can't stand the vibration. It's about being in that vibration and vibrating it out. What I foresee is a temple for sacred intimates, a place where you can stay in that vibration for a long time.

There are certain people —Gary Wright [at the time, coordinator of the New York Jacks, a j/o-only sex club] is an example. He's a mystic in this. Gary went to Paris, and he went to the chateau where the Paris Jacks have an annual gathering. He came back and told me he had a wonderful time, three days of jerking off, masturbating, whatever words he uses. My question is always, "How many times did you cum?" He said, "Oh, let me think —I didn't cum." He went to be in that state! Now that's a high place, a healing state, a clear state. Gary's one of the clearest people I know. Ten years he's been doing that stuff. I call him a flesh mystic. He's vibrated out. And he's so clear with his massage clients now. He's so successful, people come because he's a sacred intimate. He loves his work, he honors his clients, and he himself is clear.

Theoretically, the important thing is ceremonies of self-loving. Instead of going to 12-step programs and not having sex, have sex! What if one in ten times that we jerked off, we actually made love to ourselves? You don't have to make love to yourself every time, but just half the time, bring that intention to it, whether it's five minutes or five hours. So part of my training for sacred intimates is we learn to give ourselves full-body massages. I've taught hundreds, thousands of people to touch each other. Now learn to touch yourself and wake up. Just as that man in the baths put his mouth on my cock and moved the energy all around, I see raising the erotic energy and pulling it around the body and waking up the whole body. To heal codependence. I don't need anybody else, as long as I can make love to myself. Then I'm ready, from that loving place, to be with other people who are loving themselves, to share. It's an alternative to "I'm looking for someone to turn me on," which is the ultimate codependency. "He doesn't turn me on, she does, he does, she does, he does."

The idea of a sex temple is fascinating.
Can this work in San Francisco? I'm going to try it. There are three gay supervisors. In the middle of the AIDS epidemic, we should be able to legally touch each other's genitals in therapeutic and healing and ceremonial situations and set up a sex temple where people come even for a week to have this kind of experience. If it can't, the place where it can be done is Amsterdam. I'm already looking at setting this up there.

What's the legal obstacle?
The legal obstacle is if there's a monastery, and this is somebody's profession, and people give any money to this temple, then it's prostitution in this society. When people went to the temple, they contributed to the god or goddess, and that was the upkeep of this whole temple. I'm really into value for value, in body work and healing. Anybody who gives value gets value. That's why it's illegal in this country. If you get sexual gifts, you're not supposed to give back. It's only within committed relationships. In Amsterdam you can have a sex temple where people contribute to the temple.

But this is the thing: how can people dedicate their whole lives to this? You have to be independently wealthy if you are a sacred intimate. Or your right livelihood has to come somehow. That's been the problem: "I work as an office boy or a computer programmer, but my gift is healing with people sexually." I'm not clear on this. The form hasn't come to me. But there's no place in the United States where it's going to be accepted. Amsterdam is one place where it could be. Or where there's some independent source of income so money doesn't have to be involved at all. Which would be fine.

The idea is people would go to the sex temple and … what?

Every sacred intimate is different. The temple is just a place for a gathering of people who share this vocation. One of my goals is to put this image out as strongly as possible, so that it will be activated in people.

For example, what's happening right now is soldiers are coming back from the war. One of the roles of the sacred intimate in other times was to have sex with the soldiers. You vibrate the war out of them so they can come back to this country. I feel the war coming back into this country. I just saw in the Atlanta airport all these boys getting off the plane in their fatigues and I felt bad. They have war in them. I'm sure there are many gay men who'd volunteer to have sex with them.

You could set up a booth right in the airport.

This is what used to happen. At least it's part of the mythology, and it makes sense to me on an energetic level, even if there's no historic precedent. During the Vietnam War, there were people thinking about the sacred prostitute, that there should be women who love the horrors of war out of the men as they come back.

There are all these different functions, like midwives to the dying. Someone who sits all day with someone who's dying, the society's not going to have any trouble with; they're reimbursed for that. But if there's any kind of sexual touch … And I think the sacred intimate role in the past has been sometimes just to talk.

Maybe there wasn't sex. Sometimes they just washed the person, and the person was so transformed it was enough. Sometimes they fed the person. They went away feeling, "I'm full, I'm whole." Sometimes they just touched them; massage was enough. But sometimes they had sexual contact. In all those traditions, these were people who lived in the temple, and money was given to the temple. Value given for value. Or a cow was given. Whatever.

So one of my commitments is not just to activate sacred intimates but to acknowledge this culturally and present it as a valid profession, just as a computer programmer is. A sexual healer is a valid profession. It's the prejudice of the society that doesn't allow that.

This is a little different from, though parallel to, COYOTE or those other organizations that say prostitution is valid. I agree with that, too. Prostitution is a valid profession. But this is sacred healer. I'm not sure what form this will take. Part of the way that I work is you put out an idea, and it comes back. One way is a sex monastery where people come together just to heighten this energy.

I had an interesting experience when I came back from LA after interviewing Madonna ["The X-Rated Interview," for The Advocate in 1991], which was a stressful experience in various ways. I was kind of depressed and tense and angry and down. I went to a movie, felt really terrible, and I decided to go to the Jacks. And two hours at the Jacks, being naked in a room with men, it was a particularly special night. It was one big group scene. Something Dionysian happened. I walked out of there and I felt totally myself, as opposed to whatever I felt when I went in. It was an amazing experience. I miss that. I want to be in that place tonight. I want to have some place to go.

I have all kinds of unformed ideas, but I see two men working together as healers who get into that energy, without touching each other, and build it up. They're in that state and stay in that state, and other men one at a time come in and see what it's like to be in that state. And the healers invite that man to get into that state himself.
Two Flutes Playing.
Well, that's where it came from. Andrew Ramer. I got from Andrew the idea that two people in such a state invite other people in and teach techniques and all this. A lot of sacred intimate work that would be legal is soloving, where you never touch the person but you help them make love to themselves, showing it and modelling it, mirror work.

I'm offering a whole training program. But I'd like to go further. I don't expect validation. I just expect celebration of diversity and to allow someone to do what they are.
Do you know anything about these places in Thailand?
I've talked to everybody that I can who's visited.
But you've not been there.
No. There they have, I think, the prostitution model with a consciousness of sexual healing that is getting weaker all the time. People who embody the joy of sex, being in the physical with an open heart, men and women, boys and girls. Al Goldstein, who does *Screw* magazine, did a column in *Penthouse Forum* just about a year ago and said, "Everybody talks about Thailand, Thailand, Thailand. So I finally went there. First thing I want to say is everybody reading this must go there immediately. It's the most healing place in the world for sex, the most transformative. You cannot believe the consciousness. I love pussy, and I fucked pussy for two weeks straight. Pussy, pussy, pussy, and they were the most beautiful women in the world. They loved me, they cared for me, they caressed me." Here's this guy, Mr. Sex, and he says,

"Here is utopia." But he was talking about it in different terms, which I found really interesting.

One more thing he said was, "I had this experience where these women put me on the table and they had this mixture of all kinds of soap suds and they start massaging my cock and all around the front of my body and I got into a state where my whole body was like a penis. It was an amazing state. Then I went and had another week of fucking." And I realized — his thing is to fuck. He experienced this most amazing state, which was what I'm teaching, Taoist erotic massage, but it was like, "Good, that's interesting, but fucking is the real thing."

So I talk to all the men I can who go to Thailand. I would like to go because of the consciousness of the boys and men. But it's waning more and more. AIDS has caused so much fear there now. Even in the last five years it's changed drastically. But it's like New Orleans, there's a different consciousness about slow living. I found this in Amsterdam, too. It's different from the United States, much freer, in terms of types of bodies and so on.

In Thailand, isn't there a whole town devoted to the god of sexuality? The polytheistic idea that there is a god who governs sexuality, and you must pay homage to that god because it's part of human life, and it's in a whole cosmic context. I've heard this, but none of the people I've spoken to who've come back have spoken of it. I've quizzed them. That may be the historical motivation, but the tourists don't seem to get it.

The reading list you distribute in your workshops has a bunch of books by Rajneesh.

He's one of the greatest popularizers of tantra in the whole Western world.

Is that how you encountered tantra?

No. I encountered tantra not from any one teacher but from thousands of teachers who are men in New York City. I learned tantra by doing it. I learned the names and things later.

There are about 20 major tantra teachers in the U.S. now. Most of them know each other or know of each other. I'd say two-thirds of them are influenced directly or indirectly by Rajneesh. When I was in Europe, I'd say one-fourth of the men who took my classes had been sannyasins, followers of Rajneesh. For one thing, he put out so much information in books to teachers, so several thousand people had received in-depth training, not a weekend workshop but months, in Poona and in Oregon. It was the largest tantra school for a while. Rajneesh was a popularizer. Whatever the machine guns and the Rolls Royces, he popularized tantra. The books on my reading list are two thin little books that are easy to read that give a lot of information. In my workshop there's not a lot of giving of traditional information.

I'm impressed with Rajneesh. He's been a major teacher of mine through books. I've read everything I could about tantra and Taoism. There's a lot coming out right now. Margo Anand is a new teacher on the scene. She's a sannyasin from Germany who's now teaching in the U.S. Jowalla is a major tantra teacher in the U.S. Annie Sprinkle's been greatly influenced by Rajneesh through other traditions. I don't think anybody who does tantra has not been influenced by him, just as the Maharishi exported TM, his gift to the world.

It's fascinating to me that you put him on your reading list, because he's someone who's been sort of discredited because of the publicity.

It depends on your view of gurus or teachers. You look at what the teaching is rather than the publicity. I know a lot of people who consider him their guru. They're plugged into him. I'm not plugged into him. He's been an information giver to me, and those books resonate with me.

It's one of the problems of our culture that anybody who seems to be a guru, whether they say so or not, is automatically a bad thing. Have you noticed that in the media? It's a way of putting someone down. It's like saying you're a villain, a con artist. Guru equals con artist.

One of the reasons I have allowed myself to be 30 pounds overweight and drink coffee and alcohol and all this is to make sure that I don't have to deal with the guru stuff. I am a teacher. I have some information. I'm a ritual leader. Take from this what you will. You're in charge of your own process. I do have some things to offer. But nobody mistakes me for a guru. Nobody. People show up and say, "You look so ordinary. You look so dumpy. I was expecting somebody who looks enlightened." I hear this all the time.

What's the difference between teacher, ritual leader, and guru?

I think a guru is someone who says, "I have reached a level of enlightenment in my body, and I am living this, and you can learn by looking at me and plugging into me because this is in my being." A guru is supposedly self-realized. A teacher isn't. I am struggling. I am on my path. Gurus have already gotten there. Rajneesh was there. Yogananda supposedly realized it.

So I'm influenced by the work of Wilhelm Reich, Rajneesh, Chinese medical system of energy movement and sexuality, Mantak Chia, Mitch Walker, Walt Whitman. But other than those traditions, almost all my training has been one on one with men, when I was honoring men on the massage table, on my altar, I wanted to take them to the highest place they could possibly get. Then when I started working with groups, I wanted the whole group to go to the highest place it could as a group. Carlos Castaneda would call it looking at the assemblage point of someone and raising it to the pleasure place.

The two-day class is a version of that that's just about pleasure. The Big Draw, the erotic massage, the synergy of the whole room is me kinesthetically doing that, rather than doing what some healers do — sensing the pain and working on the pain, the lower back or the psychic pain. That's another form of healing. I'm using my skills as a kinesthetic empath to create areas where people are in their highest vibration. Not many people have been in a tribal situation where they've been that high. I just wish there were more places — like every street corner.

The New York Jacks now meets in a bar where anybody can go in, so there's a mixture of Jacks members and anybody who wants to come in off the street. You can always tell which is which, because the Jacks immediately get naked, and the others often stay fully dressed for a while, sit at the bar, watching, getting comfortable, thinking it's a one-on-one scene. But when there are enough Jacks people there, something gets going, and they inevitably join in. It becomes something else. On nights when there aren't enough Jacks members, then it's mostly defined by people who will maybe take off their shirt and want to go off in a corner with someone.

I pride myself on having the gift of foresight. But I was totally wrong about something. Five years ago, I thought there'd be 100 jerkoff groups in Manhattan by now and 100 in San Francisco. I thought there'd be amazing clubs everywhere. It hasn't happened.

What I didn't figure in was the amount of sex that's addictive, compulsive, and paltry. I think for huge amounts of people, jerking off is five minutes. Kinsey said the average length of heterosexual intercourse was two to four minutes; now Masters and Johnson say four to six minutes. This is not enough time to get into any state, not without a lot of foreplay. This is heterosexual.

Well, for the majority of gay men, jerking off means ten minutes or under, and it's functional. To get from A to B and release. One of the advantages of pornography, of video, is that a lot of gay men prolong sexplay because they watch the videos. There's more of a charge built up.

This is where I as a teacher come in. A lot of people are opposed to teachers, but people don't have any social skills. **Also a lot of the leaders, the consciousness scouts, died. The people who had the social skills to make it happen went away.**

This is not the time to be an erotic consciousness scout. They're not honored at all. My brochures were sent to the Gay Community Center in LA, and they were taken away as inappropriate to be in the center. I thought, "This is erotophobia." In one of my old brochures, I quoted somebody from the Center for Disease Control talking about safe-sex education who said, "We're using fear, because the more fear the better." That's what we're in — we're in a state of fear.

My next move is all about soloving, for everybody, gay, straight. Imagine if a 13- or 14-year-old boy were given videos and instruction to be free. You learn to make love to yourself and be free, celebrate that energy. Once you do that, it's like learning to breathe. You're free. Nobody else can take that away from you. You are yourself, and you can celebrate yourself. This goes beyond gay, straight, man or woman. I think it does speak to the male wound. It softens the aggressiveness. One of the reasons I think we're so aggressive as males is sexual frustration. We don't get in that state enough.

Have you had contact with the men's work, the men's spirituality stuff?

I've read and listened to some of Bly's stuff and I get *Wingspan*. We have gay drumming circles at Body Electric now, and get-in-touch-with-your-poweranimal. But the issues are not my issues, so I've not been attracted. I read an article about drumming that said, "We got so liberated in the woods that we stripped down to our boxer shorts." I thought, "That characterizes the liberation of the men's movement. I'm sorry."

A friend of mine went to see Robert Bly last week in LA, and he said, "A lot of straight men are just discovering that there's such a thing as issues." Friendship with men is not my issue. I have that. That's what it's about for a lot of them: I don't have any mirrors, any close friends. So that's not my issue. Raising sons isn't my issue. In *A Gathering of Men*, though, Robert Bly says, "If you have not hugged a young man in the last month and told him you love him and how wonderful he is, you are perpetrating the same state you're in right now." He's saying radical things for transformation, for change. But I'm not attracted.

For example, his whole image of wild men is eviscerated. He's missing the erotic component. The comfort with sex with women and with male bonding sex. Wild men feel comfortable dancing around the fire erect, in the presence of their brothers. So even developing his major image, the wild man, he's still buying into the homophobia. Even his major image, wild man.

You know. what someone said to me? "Don't criticize Robert Bly, add to it. Supplement. He's doing his gift, do yours." So I'm an adjunct. We're walking parallel paths, and people can take nourishment from both. That's my perspective. If I found it nourishing, I would follow that path more. I like Robert Moore's work. I've just read the synopsis of his books in Wingspan, I haven't read the book, but I'm going to look at it more, because I do feel empowered by archetype, and I want to look at that. My warrior is strong, but I want to see what he says about lover. I think it's important.

A thing that Bly said that really makes sense to me is that almost all the men who show up there are over

35. He says, "Until men are 35, they don't know their life isn't working." I started looking at my workshops, and almost everybody is about 30 or 35. "It's not working for me sexually, so I've go to look around for something that's going to kick-start my sexuality." He gave me a real insight there.
When were you 35?
Eight years ago.
Was that when you started the school?
Yes. That's right when I started the school. Thank you, Robert Bly.
Do you know anything about Justin Sterling?
Yes. He once advertised himself, about 1985 or so, as teaching "Beyond Tantra." I thought, "People will put anything in their ads. I consider tantra a coming together with the universe. So what is beyond tantra?" I called him up and asked him that. I was actually quite hostile. He said, "Well, you know, most people don't know what tantra is. They think it's just having sex slowly. So I'm using this to say that I'm teaching more than what most people say."

What he is doing, though, in his "Men, Sex, and Power" workshop is creating a male initiation rite. He'll have 100 or 400 men, and they come for all weekend. It's almost like est or boot camp. You stay up late. There's a part of it where everybody takes off their clothes. There's a certain liberation involved in 400 men with their clothes off. There's usually only about five gay men. He's really good at a group that size. My limit is 30 or 40 for my rituals. He's good at leading this whole group through this initiation into honoring being a man, as opposed to "We're the war-mongers, we're the polluters, we're the abuser." It's a rite of passage. He's done a version of this since 1984, seven years, eight years. A lot of gay men who've come to my thing have been empowered by going through initiation. I've changed a lot. There's

some initiation stuff now. Did you go through adolescent initiation when you did my two-day?
I think so.
Oh yeah, it was the very first time. Whenever I teach a new class, I get all kinds of new rituals. In June I did my first intensive. There's some wonderful initiation processes now, and I got it from Robert Bly and Justin Sterling's emphasizing that men are uninitiated. We've never walked through the threshold and said, "I now am in this space." Puberty, sexual initiation, is about saying, "I now feel myself and others in a new way. Sexuality gives me a feeling state." For most people, it's a quick feeling state. In a sex-negative culture, we only want to have it for a little bit. We're not taught at that time that this is a hormonal leap where you now will feel the world, yourself, everything, in a new way. We're taught that you get hair, you ejaculate or whatever. But it's more than that. It's really about new ways of feeling.

I've only heard good things about Justin Sterling, aside from my own little thing about tantra. And only good things about Michael Meade and Robert Bly. I've watched for homophobia in Justin Sterling. I see no homophobia. I see a celebration of heterosexuality. And in Robert Bly, there's just blind spots. In *Iron John*, he says, "This is mainly for straight men, gay men may get something out of it." In his workshop, if somebody challenges him, he says, "I'm a straight man, we're talking to straight men, there's a difference." But that's been important to me. I don't find this to be a homophobic movement.
Bly once said something in an interview, he criticized John Ashbery, saying that in his poems there were no women, and I took that to be a homophobic remark.
For me, Bly has an androgyny that's like a Tiresias. He could be a gay man or a straight man, but he's reached this age where there's both female and male energy.

He says, at the very beginning of *Iron John*, "Most of the language in this book speaks to heterosexual men but does not exclude homosexual men. The mythology as I see it does not make a big distinction between homosexual and heterosexual men." I agree with you that there are things that are left out. But I have the same attitude that the idea is to add on to it, to look for parts that he skips over, or look at masculine mythology and see where things are different between gay and straight men.

Here's something that's come to me — the latest insight about my tribe. When I was in New York, everybody I knew had sex. They taught me tantra. I used to think gay men were sexual men, erotic men. What I found is there are some straight men who are very erotic and who are not homophobic and who are into male bonding sex, and they're coming to my classes. In Amsterdam half the class were straight and half were gay. They had a wonderful time. Male bonding sex, liberated men. Afterwards nobody was upset. It was refreshing.

So what I've come to is maybe my tribe right now is not gay men. It is sexual consciousness scouts. I'm really interested in those people who honor sexuality. There are some gay men who are not erotic. When Stonewall first happened, it was the far-out edge. Now we have people who are totally within the culture: gay Republicans who have nothing in common with the Radical Faeries or a drag queen. This comes up all the time: why can't those people assimilate? I'm not talking just about assimilationists but the people whose sexuality is like their brother's and sister's exactly. They just happen to be same-sexual. Whereas there can be heterosexuals whose sexuality is totally different from their tribe.

The image of consciousness scout is from Andrew Ramer. The biggest mass of society has settler mentality. The people live in the center of town, and the awareness moves very slowly. Then there are people who go out one hill or two hills or three hills or ten hills. They go way out on the edge and come back. When the really far out erotic consciousness scouts bring back information, the whole town screams, "Aagh, save the kids!" They don't want to have anything to do with it. It frightens the horses. But what I find now is I identify as an erotic consciousness scout; that's my tribe. I also belong to the tribe of men who love men, but some of those men are horrified by erotic consciousness scouts.

I used to think that almost all gay men were consciousness scouts. They overlapped. But you don't have to go out ten hills to be a gay man anymore. You can be right in the middle of town. That's what Rob Eichberg and The Experience is about: assimilationism. It's about being safe within the town. But I really want to get all the people who are sitting out on the hills by their fire together and build a monastery out there, or a temple, ten hills out and get that crowd together. A lot of them are coming together. There's a lot of networking. Annie Sprinkle is way out there. She did all this porn, and that gave her the wisdom to explore further and further and further out.

Almost everybody I know who's an erotic consciousness scout is not about a better ejaculation or higher erotic pleasure. It's about the pleasure of weaving together every level of our being, especially the heart and genitals. It doesn't mean romantic love or couple love. It's something about the erotic energy as wholeness.

So right now I see my tribe, the people who most feed me, are erotic consciousness scouts. My path for the next two years are sacred intimates, people exploring the limits of what the erotic can bring into our bodies. I would hope that in six months, in a year, in two years, when you see me you'll see a different person.

Because my commitment is to do a different thing with my energy. Not just to put it out but to pull it in.

Annie Sprinkle's major movement, when she's in sexual bliss, is pulling energy in to her bosom, to her breasts. (She does have bosoms, too!). She's teaching me this. I always was uneasy with that.

Why were you uneasy? Because men are only supposed to be giving it out?

I don't know. But I know something new is beginning for me. I want to teach soloving, sacred intimate, advanced tantra. I want to teach longer trainings. I have scheduled six classes in the next year and a half during the summer, including six days of anal massage.

Last year was the first time you did the weeklong intensive?

Six days. Yes. That was what I called a maithuna ritual. It's a five-day tantric ritual. Classically a couple comes together to a pleasure garden to spend five days to raise the erotic energy. There's bathing and eating and lots of sex without ejaculation on the man's part to go higher and higher 'til at the end of the five days there's stillness on the outside and vibrant communion. We did this with 50 men. For five days our commitment was with breathing and erotic massage and all these rituals to raise the energy to the highest height we could. One of the things we did was take that whole energy and cast it as a healing energy over anybody healing from AIDS. Another intention was for each of us to take into our own bodies any of that energy we needed, the group energy. The rest was just left as an erotic weave in which we are connected. About one third of those people quit their jobs last year. They decided, "I don't want to do what I've been doing," and they moved into other realms. They weren't all 35 either, but many were around that age.

I'm doing it three times this summer because there are 150 men who want to do it. There's people

coming from all over the world this time, so it's like a weave of men from all over the world coming together in that pleasure garden. One other area that I want to learn is anal massage. Anal massage is where our fears and our security issues collect, and it's the place of kundalini activation. We have all kinds of trauma from potty training on. A lot of gay men have trauma from what is considered ecstatic anal sex - "It'll only hurt for a while, then it'll feel good." The idea is to spend six days clearing out all that trauma and waking up the prostate and especially the anal sphincter and connecting the heart-cock energy with that.
Is anal eroticism something that's new for you?
I teach it in some other classes. A technique I use a lot is called flooding — intense focus on something, rather than mete it out a little at a time, like psychotherapy once a week. Somebody can play with themselves for half an hour, but what about 25 hours of erotic massage in six days? Then having modeled what's possible from somebody else, it releases the chains. It allows a neurological imprint. Quick flashes of experience may be an interesting thing, but there's not a neurological imprint. I may be somewhat Skinnerian here. The more, the deeper.

Rajneesh said, and I've found this to be true, that if somebody is in a prolonged orgasmic state for three hours, they're cured — he uses the word cured — of normal sex forever. Why would you ever want to do a quickie? Once you get to these ecstatic states and you're there for a while, not just a flash, if you have the choice that's where you want to go. It's finding the technology to get back there and stay there for as long as you want.

So anal sex is a particular technology. You need to know the breathing, the letting go, the trust level that you need, the cleansing, so any hygienic issues that you or your partner have are out of the way, and the ability

simply to be present with the pleasure. Most people in anal situations go off into some other place. These are areas I'm exploring, so that's why I want to teach them.
Both the week-long and the sacred intimate training sound very appealing.
This is what I learned from Robert Bly and Robert Moore. When you name archetypes and people understand them, it frees them to structure the dynamic. Since I've been putting this out the image of the sacred intimate in my classes, people come up to me and say, "You spoke to me." One 28-year-old boy said, "I'm in AA, I've been a drunk for five years. I've been blotting out my sexual gift. Before that I was a prostitute for a while. I didn't know why I was doing this. When you talked about sexual healer, that's me. Since I was a little boy, people around me, I've been special in that energy. And I don't know how to use it. Alcohol was blotting it out. Now I'm going to Sex and Love Addicts Anonymous because I think it's an addiction." He says, "This is the first time I've heard anything like this, and it all clicks." So as soon as people see it and recognize it, they're free to activate it in themselves.

In Robert Johnson's *He*, he says a boy has his first grail experience in his teen years. I think it's post-puberty where finally the sexuality flashes through his body. The rest of his life he's searching for that grail experience. Johnson doesn't interpret it as sexual, but I interpret that whole myth from a kinesthetic point of view. He's searching for the wholeness of sexuality. Not a sexual orgasm, but finally where sexuality hits every level of his being. Robert Johnson says it doesn't happen until someone reaches mid-40s or middle age or beyond that, in their 50s. I think it's when sexuality seems to settle a little bit. The expectations of the young man, the ragged sexuality, finally integrates, and he comes to the grail castle, and he has the second grail experience.

What is Quad-S? What is the Institute for the Advanced Study of Human Sexuality?

In San Francisco, there's a professional school that gives a Ph.D. and Master's degrees in sexuality. There's no hands-on stuff. There's some touch, but it's mostly sex counseling. Wardell Pomeroy used to be the dean; he was a co-signer of the Kinsey reports. It's prestigious. I've given talks there and taught my Eastern approaches to sex. But Pomeroy is a scientist, and he thinks this is bullshit. When I gave my first talk in 1987, I heard the student body was just ecstatic. Several people wanted to do their Ph.Ds on tantra, and he said, "No, no, this is a school. Scientific research! Forget spirituality!" But people go there to get information.

I did teach a class at UCLA on this, in the public health department, for a limit of 20 students. I thought there'd be a lot of gay students. Well, there were ten men and ten women, and only two were gay. I invited the boys to take my two-day class for free. Not one of them came, not even the gay ones. The highest compliment was this sorority girl who was always furiously taking notes. My main perspective is male sexuality, and she's taking furious notes every day. We became friends, and she said, "I want to tell you why I'm taking these notes. Every night at dinner after your class, all the girls want to know the latest techniques. So I give a ten minute talk summarizing what I learned in class today." I thought, "Yay!"

Note: In October of 1992, Joseph Kramer sold the Body Electric School to his longtime associate Collin Brown. There have been several subsequent owners, and in recent years the school has become a not-for-profit entity. Body Electric faculty members continue to teach Celebrating the Body Erotic in cities around the country. See bodyelectric.org for further information.

In 1992, Kramer created EroSpirit Research Institute

and the New School of Erotic Touch to support his somatic sex education work. That work involved creating or co-creating over 100 hours of sex education videos with master somatic educators (Chester Mainard, Barbara Carrellas, Joe Miron, Jaiya, and Annie Sprinkle). In 2003, he completed a Ph.D. in Human Sexuality at the Institute for Advanced Study of Human Sexuality in San Francisco. With the intention of evolving the profession of sacred intimacy into the legal realm, he collaborated with author and sex therapist Jack Morin, to establish the profession of Sexological Bodywork, which involved touching genitals for educational purposes. Sexological Bodyworkers wear clothes in private sessions and the touching is one way—practitioner to client. The state of California approved both the Sexological Bodywork training and the profession. Since 2003, Kramer has had a hand in founding six international schools offering Sexological Bodywork certification trainings. He continues to train sex educators, sex workers, and sacred intimates. All of the educational materials and videos he developed for the profession of Sexological Bodywork are available online (YogaofSex.com) to anyone who wishes to explore cutting edge somatic sex education for their personal or professional use.

Acknowledgements

Multiple paths converged in the creation of this book. I first heard about the Body Electric School from Gary Wright, then-coordinator for the New York Jacks, whom I met thanks to Billy Toth. I first took the "Celebrating the Body Erotic" (CBE) workshop in July 1990; over the next two years, I took the workshop again as a participant and assisted Joseph Kramer at two more workshops. In June of 1991, I attended "Dear Love of Comrades," a Body Electric intensive at Wildwood, a retreat center an hour north of San Francisco, along with AA Bronson, whom I'd met and befriended at my first CBE. At "Dear Love," I met several people who became important friends, teachers, and colleagues: Collin Brown, Jim Curtan, Keith Hennessy, and Erik (aka Chester) Mainard. In September of that year, I returned to Wildwood for the first-ever "Sacred Intimate Training," where I met other people who would become essential collaborators over the years: John Ballew, Harry Faddis, Mark Fleming, Sebastian Schwerdtfeger, and Ken Symington.

Amy Virshup, an editor at the *Village Voice*, assigned and edited my feature story about Kramer, which was published in April 1992. I had been writing about theater, music, books, and film for the *Voice* for a dozen years, but this was the first time I published anything explicitly about sex. Writing the word "cock" repeatedly was both exhilarating and nerve-wracking. The following September I did Year 2 of "Sacred Intimate Training," an 18-day marathon whose intensity took us all by surprise. I would go back for another round of training in 1994. In the interim I hung out my shingle and began my practice as an erotic masseur and sacred intimate in New York City. Gary Wright gave me invaluable professional coaching as a veteran bodyworker, and my old friend Clinton Anderson volunteered to provide supervision, helping me navigate the emotional and psychological aspects of a new and edgy healing practice.

Taking notes on sessions with clients became an essential part of developing my sacred intimate skills, and over the next few years a narrative started to emerge from these notes. The early work of writing this book grew out of a year-long string of weekly meetings with my friend David Lida. We were a two-man writing group, working on our books, reading each other's drafts, and giving comments over lunch, often at the Violet Café on the NYU Campus. David's patience and the thoroughness of his feedback substantially contributed to how the book improved draft after draft. Residencies at two prestigious artists' colonies — Yaddo and the MacDowell Colony — allowed me to complete a first draft. Many friends read and gave valuable feedback on early drafts: the late great Eric Rofes, Michael Cohen, Keith Hennessy, Mark Thompson, Steve Karakashian, Sarah Schulman, Kevin Bentley, and Stephen Holden. Novelist and college writing professor David Guy, with whom I had struck up a literary correspondence without our ever meeting, went way out of his way to offer cogent, deep, honest, and personal notes that amounted to a graduate seminar on writing. Literary agent Mitchell Waters at Curtis Brown Ltd. agreed to

Acknowledgements

represent the book, but we were never able to find a mainstream publisher who took an interest.

Meanwhile, sections of the book took on a life of their own. In particular, "The Nether Eye Opens" (Chapter 32) has been published several times as a free-standing piece, first in *Hard at Work* (Zipper Books, 1998), edited by David Laurents. It was selected by Travers Scott for *Best Gay Erotica 2000* (Cleis Press, 1999). Richard Labonte chose to include it in *Best of the Best Gay Erotica* (Cleis Press, 2000), and Kerwin Kay reprinted it in *Male Lust: Pleasure, Power, and Transformation* (Harrington Park Press, 2000). Chapters 14, 15, and 16 were published under the title "Daddy Lover God" in *Overload* (Zipper Books, 2000) and reprinted in *The Mammoth Book of New Gay Erotica* (Carroll & Graf, 2007), edited by Lawrence Schimel. Chapters 29 and 30 were published in a slightly different form as "Eugene" in *Afterwords: Real Sex from Gay Men's Diaries* (Alyson Publications, 2001), edited by Kevin Bentley, who also included Chapter 35 ("Geisha in the Pigpen") in the anthology *Boyfriends From Hell* (Green Candy Press, 2003). Some sections from Part 2 (The Daddy Variations) became part of an art book that I created with artist and illustrator Harvey Redding. I hold much gratitude to the editors who published these excerpts; they helped me build confidence, clarity, and stamina for shaping the text.

The same can be said for the people who invited me to give public readings of this material at venues in New York City and San Francisco: Ishmael Houston-Jones, C. Bard Cole, and Keith Hennessy, among others.

There are friends who are so deeply woven into my life that their support and care have contributed directly to my well-being and indirectly to this writing: Laurie Anderson, John Ballew, Glenn Berger, Misha Berson, Michael Bronski, Paul Browde, David Carrino,

Michael Cohen, Craig Cullinane, Liam Cunningham, Paul Dennett, Tom Dennison, Kai Ehrhardt, Jeff Guss and James Lawer, Marta Helliesen, Robert James, Jonathan Lerner, Michael Mele and Andy Holtzman, Joe Martin, Jay Michaelson and Paul Dakin, Linda Mironti, Dave Nimmons and George Russell, Paul Pinkman, Eli Andrew Ramer, Jallen Rix, Stanley Rutherford and Giuliano Nieri, Allen Siewert, Steve Schwartzberg, Stephen Soba, Melissa Stewart, Ben Seaman, Billy Toth, John Ward, Michael Whitson, and Winston Wilde.

This at-long-last published edition owes much to the team of artists who helped create my previous book, *The Paradox of Porn*: the cover designer and book-making wizard Chip Kidd and the meticulous, ever-friendly, surpassingly patient page designer Todd Cooper. Two people were especially instrumental in getting this book across the finish line. My dear friend David Zinn, always a source of bright light and nourishment for my soul, delivered extremely detailed and helpful line-editing on the final draft. And besides being an excellent professional copy editor, close reader, and first-rate stickler, my husband Andrew Willett has made every day of our life together a joy with his quick laughter, his kindness, his tech savvy, and his love.

About the Author

Don Shewey is a writer, therapist, and pleasure activist in New York City. As a journalist and critic, he has published three books about theater and written hundreds of articles for the *New York Times, the Village Voice, Esquire, Rolling Stone,* and other publications. He has chronicled his psycho-sexual-spiritual adventures in essays that have been included in numerous anthologies, including *The Politics of Manhood, Best of the Best Gay Erotica, The Queerest Art: Essays on Gay and Lesbian Theater, and Men Like Us: the GMHC Guide to Gay Men's Sexual, Physical, and Emotional Well-Being.* His most recent book is *The Paradox of Porn: Notes on Gay Male Sexual Culture.* He is a New York state-licensed psychotherapist whose private practice specializes in sex and intimacy coaching (bodyandsoulwork.com). In 2018 he completed training at California Institute for Integral Studies in psychedelics-assisted psychotherapy. His work as a teacher and community health activist revolves around healing through pleasure, adult sex education, and grounded daily spiritual practice. He is active on social media and maintains two blogs, Another Eye Opens (cultural commentary) and Food for the Joy Body (smart thinking about sex, intimacy, and life in a body). An archive of his writing is available online at donshewey.com.

www.ingramcontent.com/pod-product-compliance
Lightning Source LLC
Chambersburg PA
CBHW071949070526
44583CB00015B/1120